19TH EDITION • 1996-97

W9-BWZ-818

GRANTS

AND

AWARDS

AVAILABLE

TO

AMERICAN

WRITERS

A PUBLICATION OF PEN AMERICAN CENTER

Grants and Awards Available to American Writers
19th Edition 1996–97
© 1996 PEN American Center
Printed in the United States of America
ISBN: 0-934638-14-4

A publication of
PEN American Center
568 Broadway
New York, NY 10012-3225

Cover: Susan Mitchell

First printing: June 1996

CONTENTS

A Note on Using This Book

Because the term *writer* covers many categories, we felt that we should break it down into the following seven:

Fiction	Ⓕ
Poetry	Ⓟ
Drama	Ⓓ
Journalism	Ⓙ
General Nonfiction	Ⓝ
Children's Literature	Ⓒ
Translation	Ⓣ

Most prizes which apply to more than two of these categories will be designated by the symbol Ⓜ. These symbols are located in the left-hand margin of each page next to the award description.

Residences for writers are designated by the symbol Ⓡ.

Awards for which one may not directly apply on his own behalf are designated in the text of each entry as "By Internal Nomination Only" and by the symbol [IN].

The appendix provides a guide to state commissions and agencies on writers-in-residence, poets-in-the-schools, and arts and humanities. It also lists provincial Canadian arts councils. Three indexes list organizations, awards, and categories. The category index uses the above symbols to identify each category.

Deadlines given are, for the most part, confirmed for 1996 and 1997. Writers should always reconfirm deadlines before submitting applications.

EDITOR'S NOTE

This is the nineteenth edition of PEN's comprehensive list of grants and awards available to American writers for use in the United States and abroad. Additional listings of grants and awards available to Canadian writers are included. (In these entries, all dollar amounts are given in Canadian dollars.) Programs in foreign countries which are available to American writers are alphabetized under the name of that country or, if the scope of the prize encompasses more than one country, under INTERNATIONAL. To our knowledge, *Grants and Awards* is the most complete listing that combines domestic and foreign grants for a wide range of American writers. First published in 1969, *Grants and Awards* is updated every two years by PEN American Center, the association of literary writers, in order to provide a low-cost, one-volume directory that is accessible to writers of all income brackets, at work in all genres. PEN assumes no responsibility for the conduct of those organizations listed, and invites readers to report on their experiences with any of those included.

This edition's principal researcher, Victoria Vinton, has listed primarily grants and awards which offer a cash stipend of $500 or more, or publication of a manuscript, or production of a dramatic or performance work. In a few cases, an award is included because, although its stipend is less than $500, we believe it confers a special distinction in the field it honors. Some of the prizes offered by established literary magazines are given only to the authors of works that have appeared in that publication during the past year or season; therefore, no deadline is listed. Also, we have included a select number of grants that are not exclusively for writers, but whose purposes are so broadly defined that writers are among the larger pool of eligible applicants. Some of these are research grants or fellowships sponsored by foundations or academic institutions; the main criterion we have used in deciding to include them is whether the research grant is likely to allow its recipient to produce writing of a literary, rather than a purely technical, nature.

The revisions in this edition are based on replies to a survey conducted in the latter half of 1995, supplemented by information gained from the latest references in the field and responses from readers. A total of 182 new awards from 115 organizations are included in this edition; 52 discontinued programs have been dropped from the last edition.

To assist readers in easily spotting those awards that may be of specific use to them, we have coded most entries according to the area of writing involved. The category Writers' Residences—coded by the symbol R—refers primarily to retreats, colonies, or other residences where writers may work undisturbed, and which are won by competitive application. Not coded as such are "teacher-in-residence" or "playwright-in-residence" positions that involve academic responsibilities or oblige the writer to lead workshops, lectures, or readings.

The symbol IN refers to those prizes or fellowships for which one may not directly apply; recipients are selected by jury or appointed panel. As a courtesy to the organizations sponsoring these awards, who cannot answer the numerous inquiries they receive, the words *By Internal Nomination Only* appear at the end of the description of the award, and the usual information on deadlines, restrictions, and to whom one applies, does not appear in the listing. We want to stress that no applications for these awards are accepted or even considered. Furthermore, please note that several large and well-known foundations are not listed in *Grants and Awards* at their own request, because they do not solicit nominations and wish to discourage pointless applications. (See "A Note on Using This Book" for a detailed description of the codes used within.)

Many organizations have elaborate application forms and very specific guidelines, which our listings summarize and condense. PEN suggests that as a matter of course prospective applicants write to the sponsor of a grant or award before sending books, manuscripts, or other material. Because deadline dates are often subject to change, we suggest applicants reconfirm upcoming deadlines. Include a self-addressed, stamped envelope (SASE); it is always a standard courtesy. Some awards are not given annually, or not at all in 1996 or 1997, but the foundation or association is active and will administer prizes in the future. Wherever we have been informed that a reading fee is required, we have noted it.

This edition of *Grants and Awards* remains current until mid-1998, when the twentieth edition will be published. However, no directory of this nature can be definitive. Additional reference sources include the annual editions of *Study Abroad* and the Theater Communications Group's *Dramatists Sourcebook* (one of several directories designed specifically for playwrights and other scriptwriters). Monthly or bimonthly writers' magazines such as *Poets and Writers Magazine, The Writer*, and *Writers Digest* are full of up-to-the-minute information. Especially useful are the newsletters and occasional publications of the American Society of Journalists and Authors, the Authors League, the Dramatists Guild, and Editorial Freelancers Association. The *AWP Newsletter*, published by Associated Writing Programs, is particularly helpful in obtaining information on writers' residences, by summer or by academic year, and on writers' conferences. The Modern Language Association publishes four lists annually, entitled the *MLA-ADE Job Information List*. Some of the positions are of definite interest to writers.

For our readers residing in—or passing through—the New York metropolitan area, the library of The Foundation Center (79 Fifth Avenue, New York, NY 10003) makes available to grant-hunters extensive, reliable, up-to-date, and well-organized information on foundations offering grants, awards, and fellowships. Write to the center to obtain locations on its regional offices.

Each state government has a state council or commission on the arts, usually located in the state capital. These agencies often sponsor grants, fellowships, or short-term residences, such as the poets-in-the-schools programs, for which writers may apply. Accordingly, these state-agency–sponsored programs are available only to residents of that state and pertain specifically to arts and cultural matters of that region. Some of the more notable ones are listed in *Grants and Awards*. The appendix lists the addresses of all state arts councils in the United States, Puerto Rico, and the U.S. Virgin Islands, as well as those of Canadian provincial councils.

For writers interested in writing abroad or researching a subject which necessitates foreign travel, the cultural attaché of the country concerned—usually at the embassy in Washington, D.C., or in New York City—can often be a source of information on periods of advanced study, research, and international literary awards.

As we go to press, we realize that burgeoning sources of information may be available to writers on the Internet and the World Wide Web. In fact, some of the organizations included in this edition accept inquiries and send application forms via fax, have e-mail addresses, and soon, perhaps, will even offer Web sites. Rather than be selective and incomplete now, we have decided to broach the area of electronic reference sources and the information superhighway with listings in future editions of *Grants and Awards*.

PEN American Center wishes to thank the many foundations, universities, publishers, professional organizations, and foreign and American government agencies that furnished the information for this publication. Additional listings, suggestions for the improvement of subsequent editions, and feedback on the sponsoring organizations currently included, would be greatly appreciated. Correspondence should be addressed to: PEN American Center, 568 Broadway, New York, NY 10012-3225; fax: 212-334-2181; e-mail: pen@echonyc.com

John Morrone
January 1996

GRANTS AND AWARDS

The Academy of American Poets
584 Broadway, Suite 1208
New York, NY 10012

(P) The *American Poets Fund*, established by Peter I. B. Lavan, assists poets of demonstrated ability who are in a state of financial need of an immediate and urgent nature. Grants from this fund may not be used to promote or otherwise to improve or enhance the literary talent or reputation of the recipient, but are intended solely to relieve the recipient of burdens of financial distress.

Available to: U.S. citizens
Apply to: Applications are not accepted; Academy Chancellors, Fellows, and prizewinners may bring the circumstances of qualifying poets to the attention of the American Poets Fund committee by sending a letter of nomination to the Executive Director of the Academy, including specific data concerning the nominee's current financial situation.

[IN] The *Fellowship of The Academy of American Poets* is awarded in recognition of "distinguished poetic achievement." One fellowship of $20,000 is awarded annually. *By Internal Nomination Only.*

(P) (T) The *Harold Morton Landon Translation Award* is given for a published translation of poetry into English from any language. Such a translation may be a book-length poem, a collection of poems, or a verse-drama translated into verse. One prize of $1,000 is awarded annually. No anthologies or collaborations are accepted.

Available to: U.S. citizens
Deadline: Manuscripts are accepted from January 1 to December 31
Apply to: Above address; nominations by publishers only

(P) The *James Laughlin Award* is given annually for a poet's second book of poetry. The Academy awards a cash prize of $5,000 directly to the poet and contracts to purchase 3,000 copies of the winning book for distribution to its members. Only manuscripts already under contract with publishers are considered for the *Laughlin Award*.

Available to: American poets who have already published one volume of poems in a standard edition
Deadline: Entries accepted from January 1 to April 30
Apply to: Nomination by publishers only; publishers should obtain required entry blank from the Academy before submitting manuscripts

[IN] The *Peter I. B. Lavan Younger Poet Award*, of $1,000, is given annually to three poets, age forty years or younger, who have published at least one full-length collection of poetry. *By Internal Nomination Only.*

(P) The *Lenore Marshall Poetry Prize,* of $10,000, is given annually for the most outstanding book of poems published in the United States during the calendar year. Books must be published in a standard edition (40 pages or more in length, or 500 or more copies); self-published books are not eligible. To enter the contest, publishers should send four copies of the book to the Academy. The prize is administered in conjunction with the *Nation* magazine.

Available to: No restrictions
Deadline: June 1
Apply to: Lenore Marshall Poetry Prize, above address

(P)
(T) The *Raiziss/de Palchi Translation Award,* consisting of a $5,000 book prize and a $20,000 fellowship, is given biennially for the translation of modern or contemporary Italian poetry. The book prize is awarded for a published translation into English of a significant work of modern or contemporary Italian poetry by a living translator. The fellowship is awarded to a U.S. citizen engaged in a translation into English of modern or contemporary Italian poetry; the fellowship stipend may be used to enable the winning translator to travel, study, and otherwise advance a significant work-in-progress. No applications are accepted for the book prize. For the fellowship applications, send an SASE for complete guidelines and the required entry form.

Available to: U. S. citizens
Deadline: Fellowship applications accepted from September 1 to November 1, 1997
Apply to: Raiziss/de Palchi Translation Award, above address

[IN] The *Tanning Prize,* endowed by the painter Dorothea Tanning, annually awards $100,000 in recognition of outstanding and proven mastery in the art of poetry. *By Internal Nomination Only.*

The *Walt Whitman Award* is given annually for a manuscript (fifty to one hundred pages) of original poetry in English by a poet who has never had a book of poems published in a standard edition. The winning poet is awarded a cash prize of $1,000 by the Academy and publication by a distinguished publisher. The Academy purchases 3,000 copies of the book for distribution to its members. An entry form and entry fee are required. Send an SASE in late August to the Academy for complete guidelines.

Available to: U.S. citizens
Deadline: Manuscripts are accepted from September 15 to November 15
Apply to: Above address

The Academy of Motion Picture Arts and Sciences
Nicholl Fellowships
8949 Wilshire Boulevard
Beverly Hills, CA 90211

(D) Up to five *Don and Gee Nicholl Screenwriting Fellowships,* of $25,000 each are available each year for original, full-length feature scripts of 100 to 130 pages with the understanding that the recipients will complete a new feature screenplay during the fellowship year. Entries must originally have been written in English and must display exceptional craft and engaging storytelling. Writers must not have sold, optioned, or earned money for writing a feature screenplay or teleplay. Send a business-sized SASE for further information. There is a $30 entry fee.

Available to: Writers in English
Deadline: May 1
Apply to: Nicholl Fellowships, above address

The Actors' Fund of America
1501 Broadway, Suite 518
New York, NY 10036

4727 Wilshire Boulevard, Suite 310
Los Angeles, CA 90010

203 North Wabash, Suite 1308
Chicago, IL 60601

The Actors' Fund offers emergency financial assistance for basic living expenses and ongoing financial assistance for people living on fixed incomes due to older age or disability, when a disparity exists between income and basic living needs. Professionals and their dependents who earn their living in the areas of legitimate theater, film, radio, television, music, dance, circus, and variety may be eligible for assistance. Individuals applying for financial aid must have worked for the past five years in the American entertainment industry, earning at least $3,500 per year for three of those years, or must have worked for the past ten years in the industry, earning at least $2,000 per year (exceptions are made on a per case basis). Financial assistance is also available to those over sixty-five whose career earnings have come from the American entertainment industry.

Available to: Entertainment industry employees, as described above
Deadline: None
Apply to: Any Actors' Fund office, above addresses

Actors' Playhouse at the Miracle Theatre
280 Miracle Mile
Coral Gables, FL 33134

Ⓓ The *National Children's Theatre Festival* offers a $1,200 prize for a musical and an $800 prize for a play plus production, travel, and housing to attend and participate in the festival. All submissions must be unpublished and original. Plays must be for young people ages 12 to 17, 45 to 60 minutes long, with a cast limit of six (actors may play multiple roles), and minimal sets suitable for touring. Musicals should be for young people ages 5 to 12, 45 to 60 minutes long, with a cast limit of eight, and a maximum of two major or four simple sets. Work dealing with social issues, including multiculturalism in today's society, is preferred. There is a $10 entry fee. Write for guidelines and entry form.

Available to: No restrictions
Deadline: December 1
Apply to: National Children's Theatre Festival, above address

Actors Theatre of Louisville
316-320 West Main Street
Louisville, KY 40202

Ⓓ *The National Ten-Minute Play Contest* awards $1,000 to the best ten-minute play submitted to the competition. The winning play may be considered for production by Actors Theatre of Louisville. Plays submitted must not have had a previous Equity production. There is a limit of two scripts per author, and each manuscript must be typed and fastened. The author's name and address must appear on the title page, and a self-addressed, stamped, manuscript-sized envelope must be included. Each play should be no more than ten pages.

Available to: U.S. citizens and residents
Deadline: December 1
Apply to: The National Ten-Minute Play Contest, above address

The Adamant Program
PO Box 73
Adamant, VT 05640-0073

Ⓡ The Adamant Program is a cultural retreat for artists, writers, poets, playwrights, ceramicists, and composers located in the Green Mountains of Vermont near Montpelier. Participants work in separate, simply furnished studios with optimum freedom and privacy in a noncompetitive environment for eight weeks beginning in early September. The fee for the program is $25 a day; a limited number of partial or full grants are available for participants who demonstrate clear financial need for support.

Available to: No restrictions
Deadline: June 1
Apply to: Patricia Hutchinson, Assistant Resident Manager, above address

Agricultural History Society
Center for Agricultural History
618 Ross Hall
Iowa State University
Ames, IA 50011

Ⓝ Three awards are given annually to writers: the *Theodore Saloutos Award* of $500 for the best book published in the field of agricultural history in America; the *Vernon Carstensen Award* of $100 for the best article published by a scholar in the quarterly journal *Agricultural History*; and the *Everett Edwards Award* of $100 for the best article in agricultural history submitted by a graduate student.

Available to: No restrictions
Deadline: Inquire
Apply to: R. Douglas Hurt, Editor, *Agricultural History*, above address

Alabama State Council on the Arts
One Dexter Avenue
Montgomery, AL 36130

Ⓜ Fellowships in fiction, poetry, nonfiction, and playwriting of $5,000 to $10,000 are available to writers who have been residents of Alabama for at least two years.

Available to: Alabama residents
Deadline: May 1
Apply to: Becky Mullen, Literature Program Manager, above address

Alaska State Council on the Arts
411 West Fourth Avenue, Suite 1E
Anchorage, AK 99501-2343

Ⓜ *Career Opportunity Grants,* of up to $1,000, are awarded to cover travel costs and additional expenses for individual writers to take advantage of impending, concrete opportunities that will significantly advance their work or careers.

Available to: Alaska residents
Deadline: Thirty days prior to travel/opportunity
Apply to: Above address

Edward F. Albee Foundation
14 Harrison Street
New York, NY 10013

Ⓡ The Albee Foundation offers one-month residences to writers and visual artists from June through September at its center in Montauk, Long Island. Admission is based "on talent and need." Residents are given housing, but they must provide their own meals. Write for guidelines.

Available to: No restrictions
Deadline: April 1 (no applications accepted prior to January 1)
Apply to: Above address

alicejamesbooks
University of Maine at Farmington
98 Main Street
Farmington, ME 04938

Ⓟ The *Beatrice Hawley Award* annually offers publication for a book of poetry by alicejamesbooks without the work commitment usually required at this cooperative press. The winner will receive one hundred copies of the book. There is a $15 reading fee. Send an SASE for complete guidelines before submitting manuscript.

Available to: No restrictions
Deadline: January 15
Apply to: Beatrice Hawley Award, above address

Alleyway Theatre
1 Curtain Up Alley
Buffalo, NY 14202-1911

(D) The *Maxim Mazumdar New Play Competition* annually offers $400, production with royalty, and travel and housing expenses to attend rehearsals for an unproduced full-length play with a cast limit of ten and a simple set. A $100 prize and production at Alleyway's annual One-Act Festival is also offered for a one-act with a cast limit of six. Work with an unconventional setting that explores the boundaries of theatricality is preferred. There is a $5 entry fee per playwright; only one submission is allowed in each category. Send an SASE for return of script.

Available to: No restrictions
Deadline: September 1
Apply to: Maxim Mazumdar New Play Competition, above address

American-Scandinavian Foundation
725 Park Avenue
New York, NY 10021

To encourage study and research and to increase understanding between the United States and Denmark, Finland, Iceland, Norway, and Sweden, the foundation administers fellowships and grants to enable well-qualified university graduates to undertake projects of study or research in those countries. Approximately twenty-five awards, ranging from $3,000 to $15,000, are given annually.

Available to: U.S. citizens and permanent residents
Deadline: November 1 for completed applications (for the following academic year)
Apply to: Exchange Division, above address

(T) The *ASF Translation Prize* is offered annually by the foundation for the best English translation of poetry, fiction, drama, or literary prose written by a Scandinavian author born after 1800. The award includes $2,000, publication in an issue of the *Scandinavian Review,* and a commemorative bronze medallion. The *Inger Sjöberg Award* of $500 is given to the runner-up. For complete rules and instructions, write to the foundation.

Available to: No restrictions
Deadline: June 1
Apply to: Translation Prize, above address

American Academy of Arts and Letters
633 West 155th Street
New York, NY 10032

Awards and honors are conferred for work of distinction with the purpose of furthering literature and the fine arts and stimulating and encouraging the arts in the United States. Academy members are not eligible unless otherwise noted. *Applications are not accepted for any of the following awards. By Internal Nomination Only.*

[IN] The *Arts and Letters Awards of the Academy* are awarded "to honor and encourage distinguished artists, composers, and writers who are not members of the Academy." Eight awards of $7,500 each in literature are given annually.

[IN] The *Award of Merit Medal of the American Academy of Arts and Letters* consists of a medal and a cash prize given annually to an outstanding person in America, not a member of the Academy, representing one of the following arts: the novel, poetry, painting, the short story, sculpture, or drama.

[IN] The *Witter Bynner Award for Poetry*, of $2,500, is given annually to a young poet.

[IN] The *Gold Medals of the American Academy of Arts and Letters* are given each year for distinguished achievement in two categories of the arts: belles lettres and criticism, and painting; biography and music; fiction and sculpture; history and architecture (including landscape architecture); poetry and music; and drama and graphic art.

[IN] The *Howells Medal of the American Academy of Arts and Letters* is given once every five years in recognition of the most distinguished work of American fiction published during that period.

[IN] The *Sue Kaufman Prize for First Fiction*, of $2,500, is given annually for the best published first novel or collection of short stories of the preceding year.

[IN] The *Rome Fellowship in Literature* is given for a year's residence at the American Academy in Rome. This award is given annually and is subsidized by the American Academy in Rome and the Academy of Arts and Letters. The recipients are selected by the American Academy of Arts and Letters.

[IN] The *Richard and Hilda Rosenthal Foundation Award* is granted for an American work of fiction published during the preceding twelve months which, though not a commercial success, is a considerable literary achievement. One award of $5,000 is given annually.

[IN] The *Mildred and Harold Strauss Livings* provide writers of English prose literature with an annual stipend to cover their living expenses so that they can devote their time exclusively to writing. The most recent Livings, each amounting to $50,000 annually, were awarded in 1993 to two writers for a period of five years. Recipients must resign positions of paid employment before receiving the Livings. They will be given again in 1998.

[IN] The *Harold D. Vursell Memorial Award*, of $5,000, was established in 1978 to single out recent writing in book form that merits recognition for the quality of its prose style. It may be given for a work of fiction, biography, history, criticism, belles lettres, a memoir, journal, or a work of translation, provided it is rendered in distinguished and exceptional English prose.

[IN] The *Morton Dauwen Zabel Prize*, of $5,000, is given every year to an American poet, writer of fiction, or critic, in rotation.

The American Academy in Rome
7 East 60th Street
New York, NY 10022-1001

The *AAR Rome Prize Competition* offers up to twenty-five fellowships with stipends of $5,800 to $17,800 for individuals of exceptional promise or achievement in architecture, landscape architecture, conservation and preservation, design, literature, musical composition, visual arts, archaeology, classical studies, history of art, modern Italian studies, and postclassical humanistic studies. Fellows receive free housing, a study or studio, and full access to library and other facilities. Applicants should be U.S. citizens who possess a bachelor's or master's degree, depending on the field of application. Some fellowships are open to postdoctoral candidates. Please note: Unlike the Rome Prize fellowships in other disciplines, there is no formal application process for the Rome Prize in literature. Nominations for the literature award are made only by members of the American Academy of Arts and Letters (see listing above).

Available to: See above restrictions
Deadline: November 15
Apply to: Fellowships Department, above address

6

American Antiquarian Society
185 Salisbury Street
Worcester, MA 01609

The *AAS-American Society for Eighteenth-Century Studies Fellowships* of $950 per month promote research in any area of American eighteenth-century studies. The award is jointly funded by the American Society for Eighteenth-Century Studies and AAS. Degree candidates are not eligible. ASECS membership is required upon taking up an award, but not for applying.

The *AAS-National Endowment for the Humanities Fellowships* provide at least two long-term fellowships, tenable for six to twelve months. The maximum available stipend is $30,000. NEH fellows must study full time and may not accept teaching assignments or undertake any other major activities during the tenure of the award.

The *Stephen Botein Fellowship*, which supports research in the history of the book in American culture, is funded by the income of an endowment established at AAS in memory of Stephen Botein by his family and friends. The stipend is $950 per month.

The *Kate B. and Hall J. Peterson Fellowships* award stipends of $950 per month for periods of one to three months to individuals who are engaged in scholarly research and writing in any field of American history and culture through 1876.

Available to: No restrictions
Deadline: January 15
Apply to: Above address

Ⓜ At least three *Visiting Fellowships for Historical Research by Creative and Performing Artists and Writers* will be awarded for four- to eight-week residences at the society. The stipend is $1,200 per four-week period, plus an allowance for travel expenses. (There are no funds available for housing, but housing is available in the society's Goddard-Daniels House. Room rentals range from $275 to $495 per week.) The society seeks fellows whose goals are to produce works dealing with pretwentieth century American history that are intended for the general public rather than for the academic or educational communities. Research and study carried out under these fellowships may focus on virtually any subject within the general area of American history and culture before 1877. The end products of research developed under these fellowships may include (but are not limited to): historical novels; nonfiction works of history designed for general audiences of adults or children; plays or screenplays; magazine or newspaper articles. Write for additional information and guidelines.

Available to: No restrictions
Deadline: October; inquire for exact date
Apply to: John B. Hench, Director of Research and Publication, Room 301, above address

American Association for the Advancement of Science
1333 H Street, NW
Washington, DC 20005

Ⓝ The *AAAS Prize for Behavioral Science Research* is given for a "meritorious essay in socio-psychological inquiry that uses the kind of methodology proven fruitful in the natural sciences and that extends the understanding of the psychological, social, and cultural behavior of human beings." Entries must have appeared in peer-reviewed journals since January 1 of the preceding year. One prize of $2,500 is awarded annually. Award criteria are currently being reevaluated. Contact AAAS before applying.

Available to: No restrictions
Deadline: July 1
Apply to: Catherine Campos, AAAS Prize for Behavioral Science Research, above address

(J)
(N) The *AAAS Science Journalism Awards* are given "for outstanding journalism on the sciences and their engineering and technological applications (excluding medicine), in newspapers, general-circulation magazines, radio, and television." Entries are judged on the basis of their initiative, originality, scientific accuracy, clarity of interpretation, and value in promoting a better understanding of science by the public. There are five awards of $2,500 each: for writing in newspapers with a daily circulation of more than 100,000; for writing in newspapers with a circulation of less than 100,000; for writing in general-circulation magazines; for writing for radio; and for writing for television. An entry must have been published in a newspaper or magazine or aired in the United States during the contest year, which runs from July 1 through June 30 of the following year.

Available to: Those who have published or aired in the United States
Deadline: August 1
Apply to: Office of Communications, AAAS Science Journalism Awards, above address

American Chemical Society
1155 16th Street, NW
Washington, DC 20036

(J)
(N) The *James T. Grady–James H. Stack Award for Interpreting Chemistry for the Public* is given to recognize and encourage outstanding reporting directly to the American public that increases the public's knowledge and understanding of chemistry, chemical engineering, and related fields. This information must have been disseminated through the press, radio, television, films, the lecture platform, or books or pamphlets for the lay public. One award, which consists of $3,000 and a gold medal, is given annually. Recipients must be nominated by a colleague for a career accomplishment.

Available to: No restrictions
Deadline: February 1
Apply to: James T. Grady–James H. Stack Award, above address

American Council of Learned Societies
228 East 45th Street
New York, NY 10017

The council offers various types of grants for which writers may at times qualify, when doing research in preparation for a book.

Fellowships are given for holders of the doctorate or its equivalent tenable in the United States or abroad for research in the humanities. Stipends of not more than $20,000 are offered annually for a period of six to twelve consecutive months.

Available to: U.S. citizens and permanent residents
Deadline: September 30
Apply to: Office of Fellowships, above address

American Fiction
Moorhead State University
PO Box 229
Moorhead, MN 56563

(F) The *American Fiction Contest* annually offers a first prize of $1,000, a second prize of $500, and a third prize of $250 to unpublished fiction manuscripts under 10,000 words. All finalists (approximately twenty to twenty-five) will be published in *American Fiction*. Write for guidelines before submitting manuscript; entries accepted only after February 1. Entry fee of $7.50 for each story submitted is required.

Available to: No restrictions
Deadline: Inquire
Apply to: Alan Davis, Editor, above address

American Historical Association
400 A Street, SE
Washington, DC 20003

As of 1996 the cash stipends for the following awards will vary from year to year. In 1994 stipends ranged from $500 to $1,000. For exact amounts for specific awards, please query the American Historical Association.

Ⓝ The *Herbert Baxter Adams Prize* is awarded for an author's first book on ancient, early, or modern European history.

Available to: No restrictions
Deadline: May 15
Apply to: Above address

Ⓝ The *George Louis Beer Prize* is awarded annually in recognition of outstanding historical writing on European international history since 1895.

Available to: U.S. citizens
Deadline: May 15
Apply to: Above address

Ⓝ The *Albert J. Beveridge Award* is awarded annually for the best book, in English, on the history of the Americas (the United States, Canada, or Latin America).

Available to: U.S. residents
Deadline: May 15
Apply to: Above address

Ⓝ The *Paul Birdsall Prize* is awarded biennially for a major work on the subject of European military history and strategic history since 1870.

Available to: U.S. or Canadian citizens
Deadline: Inquire
Apply to: Above address

Ⓝ The *James Henry Breasted Prize* is offered annually for the best book in any field of history prior to 1000 A.D.

Available to: No restrictions
Deadline: May 15
Apply to: Above address

Ⓝ The *Albert B. Corey Prize in Canadian-American Relations* is awarded for the best book on the history of Canadian-American relations or on the history of both countries. One award is available every two years. The prize is awarded jointly by the Canadian Historical Association and the American Historical Association.

Available to: U.S. and Canadian residents
Deadline: May 15
Apply to: Above address

Ⓝ The *Premio del Rey Prize* is awarded biennially for the best book, in English, in the field of Hispanic history and culture (in Spain and other Hispanic countries) prior to 1516.

Available to: No restrictions
Deadline: Inquire
Apply to: Above address

Ⓝ The *John H. Dunning Prize* is awarded biennially for a book of any subject relating to U.S. history.

Available to: No restrictions
Deadline: May 15
Apply to: Above address

Ⓝ The *John K. Fairbank Prize in East Asian History* is awarded annually for an outstanding book on the history of China proper, Vietnam, Chinese Central Asia, Mongolia, Korea, or Japan since 1800.

> Available to: No restrictions
> Deadline: May 15
> Apply to: Above address

Ⓝ The *Herbert Feis Award* is awarded annually for the best book, article, or policy paper by an independent scholar or public historian. It is funded by a grant from the Rockefeller Foundation.

> Available to: U.S. residents
> Deadline: May 15
> Apply to: Above address

Ⓝ The *Morris O. Forkosch Prize* is given biennially for the best work published in the field of modern British, British Imperial, and British Commonwealth history written by a U.S. citizen.

> Available to: U.S. citizens
> Deadline: May 15
> Apply to: Above address

Ⓝ The *Leo Gershoy Award* is awarded annually to the author of the most outstanding work, in English, on any aspect of the field of seventeenth- and eighteenth-century European history.

> Available to: No restrictions
> Deadline: May 15
> Apply to: Above address

Ⓝ The *Clarence H. Haring Prize* is awarded every five years to the Latin American who has published the most outstanding book in Latin American history during the preceding five years.

> Available to: Latin American historians
> Deadline: May 15
> Apply to: Above address

Ⓝ The *J. Franklin Jameson Prize*, a quinquennial award for outstanding achievement in the editing of historical sources, will next be granted in 2000.

> Available to: U.S. residents
> Deadline: May 15
> Apply to: Above address

Ⓝ The *Joan Kelly Memorial Prize in Women's History* is offered annually for the best work in women's history and/or feminist theory.

> Available to: No restrictions
> Deadline: May 15
> Apply to: Above address

Ⓝ The *Waldo G. Leland Prize*, offered for the most outstanding reference tool in the field of history, is awarded quinquennially. The next award is in 1996.

> Available to: U.S. residents
> Deadline: May 15
> Apply to: Above address

Ⓝ The *Littleton-Griswold Prize* is offered annually for the best book on any subject in the history of American law and society.

> Available to: No restrictions

Deadline: May 15
Apply to: Above address

(N) The *Helen and Howard R. Marraro Prize* is given for the best work on any epoch of Italian history, Italian cultural history or on Italian-American relations.

Available to: U.S. and Canadian resident citizens
Deadline: May 15
Apply to: Above address

(N) The *James Harvey Robinson Prize*, awarded biennially, is offered for the teaching aid that has made the most outstanding contribution to the teaching of history in any field. The next award is in 1996.

Available to: U.S. residents
Deadline: May 15
Apply to: Above address

American Institute of Indian Studies
University of Chicago
1130 East 59th Street
Chicago, IL 60637

The American Institute of Indian Studies annually offers Senior (postdoctoral) Research Fellowships, Senior Scholarly Development Fellowships, Junior (dissertation) Fellowships, and Senior Performing Arts Fellowships for research in India. Award funds are made available in foreign currency only. Requirements vary; query the institute before applying. (Also available is a limited extensive language program in India; contact the institute for further information and deadline.)

Available to: U.S. citizens at the doctoral or postdoctoral level and foreign nationals enrolled at the doctoral level or teaching full-time (postdoctoral) at American colleges or universities. U.S. and Indian government employees are ineligible for AIIS grants.
Deadline: July 1
Apply to: Above address

American Institute of Physics
Public Information Division
One Physics Ellipse
College Park, MD 20740

(M) The *Writing Awards in Physics and Astronomy* are given to stimulate and recognize distinguished writing that improves public understanding of physics and astronomy. Entries must be articles, booklets, or books written in English. Material from professional scientific, technical, and trade publications is not eligible. Three prizes of $3,000 are awarded annually in journalism, science writing, and children's literature.

Available to: U.S., Canadian, and Mexican residents
Deadlines: Journalists: February 6; Scientists: May 19; Children's Books/Articles: July 24
Apply to: Above address

American Jewish Archives
3101 Clifton Avenue
Cincinnati, OH 45220

Six fellowships for active research or writing at the American Jewish Archives are offered to doctoral and/or postdoctoral candidates in American Jewish Studies. Stipends of $2,000 are awarded for postdoctoral fellows; doctoral fellows (with all but the dissertation requirements completed) receive $1,000. Write for further information and application guidelines.

Available to: No restrictions
Deadline: April 1
Apply to: Administrative Director, above address

American Library Association
50 East Huron Street
Chicago, IL 60611

The *Eli M. Oboler Memorial Award* biennially offers $1,500 and a certificate of recognition for the best published work on the subject of intellectual freedom. Books may be nominated if published in the two-year period prior to the year in which the award is granted (the 1996 award will be given to a book published in 1994 or 1995).

Available to: No restrictions
Deadline: Mid-December; inquire for exact date
Apply to: Eli M. Oboler Memorial Award, c/o Anne L. Penway, IRFT Staff Liaison, above address

American Musicological Society
201 South 34th Street
Philadelphia, PA 19104-6313

Ⓝ The *Alfred Einstein Award* is given annually to the author of the article on a musicological subject deemed by a committee of scholars to be the most significant published in a periodical during the preceding calendar year. The award consists of $400 and a certificate signed by the president of the society.

Available to: U.S. and Canadian citizens or permanent residents in the early stages of their careers
Deadline: June 1
Apply to: Consult the AMS directory for name and address of current year's committee chairperson

Ⓝ The *Otto Kinkeldey Award* is given each year for the work of musicological scholarship deemed by a committee of scholars to be the most distinguished of those published during the previous year in any language and in any country. The award consists of a prize of $400 and a certificate signed by the president of the society.

Available to: U.S. and Canadian citizens and permanent residents
Deadline: None
Apply to: Consult the AMS directory for name and address of current year's committee chairperson

The American Poetry Review
1721 Walnut Street
Philadelphia, PA 19103

Ⓟ The *Jessica Nobel Maxwell Memorial Prize*, of $2,000, is given annually for the best poems appearing in the *American Poetry Review* by a younger poet.

Available to: Poets whose work has appeared in *American Poetry Review*
Deadline: Ongoing
Apply to: Submit manuscripts for publication to above address; include SASE

Ⓟ The *Jerome J. Shestack Poetry Prizes* are given annually for the three best groups of poems appearing in *American Poetry Review* each year. The prizes carry cash awards of $1,000, $500, and $250.

Available to: Poets whose work has appeared in *American Poetry Review*
Deadline: Ongoing
Apply to: Above address; include an SASE

American Political Science Association
1527 New Hampshire Avenue, NW
Washington, DC 20036

Ⓙ *APSA-MCI Communications Fellowships,* of $28,000 plus a small travel allowance, are available to journalists with a B.A., a minimum of two years' full-time experience in newspaper, magazine, radio, or television, and a demonstrated professional interest in telecommunications. Preference is given to those applicants who have not had extensive Washington experience. The fellowship year consists of a three-week orientation period, followed by full-time assignments as legislative aides in the House of Representatives and the Senate, combined with a seminar program with leading congressional, governmental, and academic figures.

> Available to: No restrictions
> Deadline: December 1
> Apply to: APSA-MCI Communications Fellowships, above address

Ⓙ *Congressional Fellowships,* of $28,000 plus travel allowance, are available to journalists for a program including a three-week orientation period, nine months working as a full-time aide to members of the House and the Senate, weekly seminar meetings with leading congressional, governmental, and academic figures, and opportunities for research. Preference is given to applicants without extensive experience in Washington.

> Available to: Professional journalists with a B.A. and between two and ten years of experience in newspaper, magazine, radio, or television work
> Deadline: December 1; write for additional details
> Apply to: Director, Congressional Fellowship Program, above address

Ⓝ The *Woodrow Wilson Award* is given for the best book of the year published on politics, government, and international relations. One award of $5,000 is available annually. Nominations are made by publishers.

> Available to: U.S. citizens
> Deadline: February 1
> Apply to: Above address

American Psychiatric Association
Division of Public Affairs/Media Awards
1400 K Street, NW
Washington, DC 20005

The *Robert T. Morse Writers Award,* of $1,000, is given annually to popular news writers or groups of writers who have covered the mental illness field over an extended period of time or who have written a major article or series of articles which are intended for the general public and that address pertinent mental illness issues and explore the role of psychiatry in these issues. For the next award, articles must have been published between August 1, 1995, and July 31, 1996.

> Available to: No restrictions
> Deadline: July 31, 1996; inquire for 1997
> Apply to: Gus Cervini, Media Coordinator, above address

American Short Fiction
University of Texas at Austin
PAR 108
Austin, TX 78712-1164

Ⓕ The *American Short Fiction Prizes for Fiction Competition* offers a $1,000 first prize plus publication in *American Short Fiction.* A $500 second prize and a $200 third prize are also offered with possible publication. Manuscripts must be 4,000 words or fewer and must be original, unpublished, and not submitted elsewhere. Multiple entries allowed, but each entry must include a $20 entry fee, which includes a one-year subscription to *ASF*. Send an SASE for an entry form.

Available to: No restrictions
Deadline: May 15, 1996; inquire for 1997
Apply to: ASF Contest, above address

The American Society of Church History
PO Box 8517
Red Bank, NJ 07701

Ⓝ The *Frank S. and Elizabeth D. Brewer Prize* offers $1,000 to assist an author in publishing a book-length manuscript on church history. The winning manuscript will be published in a manner acceptable to the society. If competing essays are of equal quality, preference is given to topics relating to the history of Congregationalism.

Available to: No restrictions
Deadline: November 1
Apply to: Henry W. Bowden, Secretary, The Frank S. and Elizabeth D. Brewer Prize, above address

American Society of Composers, Authors, and Publishers
One Lincoln Plaza
New York, NY 10023

Ⓙ
Ⓝ The *ASCAP-Deems Taylor Awards* are given in two categories: one for the best nonfiction book, and the other for the best nonfiction newspaper or magazine article about music and/or its creators—they may be biographical or critical, reportorial or historical (but not a textbook, how-to guide, or work of fiction). Books are awarded $500 and a plaque; articles $250 and a plaque.

Available to: Writers whose works have been published in the United States in English during the calendar year under review
Deadline: April 30
Apply to: ASCAP-Deems Taylor Awards, above address

American Society for Eighteenth-Century Studies
Computer Center 108
Utah State University
Logan, UT 84322-3730

Ⓝ The *James L. Clifford Prize*, of $500, is awarded annually for an outstanding article appearing in a journal, *Festschrift*, or other serial publication. The article must be an outstanding study of some aspect of eighteenth-century culture, interesting to any eighteenth-century specialist, regardless of discipline. The article may be nominated by any member of the society, by its author, or an editor of the publishing journal. Nominations must be accompanied by eight copies of the article.

Available to: Members of the society
Deadline: January 1
Apply to: Jeffrey Smitten, Executive Secretary, above address

Ⓝ The *Louis Gottschalk Prize*, of $1,000, is awarded annually for an outstanding historical or critical study on a subject of eighteenth-century interest. Books, which may be commentaries, critical studies, biographies, or critical editions, may be written in any modern language. Books that are primarily translations are not eligible. Books must be published between November 1 and October 31 of the award year.

Available to: Members of the society
Deadline: November 15
Apply to: Jeffrey Smitten, Executive Secretary, above address

The American Society of Journalists and Authors Charitable Trust
1501 Broadway, Suite 302
New York, NY 10036

The *Llewellyn Miller Fund* is open to professional free-lance writers in financial need who are sixty or older, disabled, or who are caught up in an extraordinary professional crisis. The award provides grants of up to $2,500. Proof of professional free-lance work must be supplied to the fund committee.

Available to: See above
Deadline: None
Apply to: ASJA office, above address

American Society of Magazine Editors
919 Third Avenue
New York, NY 10022

The *Magazine Internship Program*, a ten-week summer session during which students learn about magazines by working in the editorial offices of consumer magazines and business publications, is available to college students between their junior and senior year. Applicants must be journalism majors or liberal arts majors who have held responsible positions on the campus magazine, newspaper or yearbook and have had at least one summer job or internship in journalism. Interns will be temporary employees of the magazines to which they are assigned and will be paid a minimum stipend of $300 a week before deductions. The emphasis of the program is on editing, however at some magazines, there may also be reporting and writing opportunities, even a few bylines. Interns are responsible for their own travel, housing, food, and personal expenses; ASME will assist in making dormitory arrangements in New York and Washington, D.C. Applications are available through deans, department heads, or professors.

Available to: See above
Deadline: December 15
Apply to: Magazine Internship Program, above address

American Translators Association
Honors and Awards Committee
1800 Diagonal Road, Suite 220
Alexandria, VA 22314-2840

(T) The *ATA German Literary Translation Prize*, of $1,000, is awarded biennially for translations from the German into English that have been published in the United States by an American publisher, within the two years preceding the prize year, as a single volume or as part of a collection. Submit two copies of the book and ten pages of the German original.

Available to: No restrictions
Deadline: Inquire
Apply to: German Literary Translation Prize, above address

(T) The *Lewis Galantiere Prize* of $500 is awarded biennially for distinguished published literary works translated from any language other than German into English. Submit two copies of the book and ten pages of the original.

Available to: No restrictions
Deadline: Inquire
Apply to: Lewis Galantiere Prize, above address

The Amy Foundation
PO Box 16091
Lansing, MI 48901

(N) The *Amy Foundation Writing Awards* offer a $10,000 first prize, a $5,000 second prize, a $4,000 third prize, a $3,000 fourth prize, a $2,000 fifth prize, plus ten prizes of $1,000 each for "creative, skillful writing that presents in a sensitive, thought-provoking manner the biblical position on issues affecting the world today." Submitted articles must have been published in a secular, nonreligious publication during the preceding calendar year. Send an SASE for guidelines.

Available to: No restrictions; U.S. citizens preferred
Deadline: January 31
Apply to: Writing Awards, above address

Anamnesis Press
PO Box 581153
Salt Lake City, UT 84158-1153

(P) The annual *Anamnesis Poetry Chapbook Competition* offers a first prize of $500, second prize of $200, and chapbook publication and ten free author's copies to both winners. Poets may submit twenty to thirty poems for consideration. There is an entry fee of $10 per poet.

Available to: No restrictions
Deadline: Submissions accepted between January 1 and November 1; notification in December.
Apply to: Chapbook Competition, Anamnesis Press, above address

The Mary Anderson Center for the Arts
101 St. Francis Drive
Mount St. Francis, IN 47146

(R) Residences at the center, from one week to three months, are available for six writers and visual artists concurrently. Residents pay what they can afford. The suggested minimum fee is $25 per day and there is a possibility of funded residences. A private studio/ bedroom, communal kitchen and dining room and meals are provided.

Available to: No restrictions
Deadline: Inquire
Apply to: Sarah Roberson Yates, Executive Director, above address

Anhinga Press
PO Box 10595
Tallahassee, FL 32302

(P) The *Anhinga Prize for Poetry* is awarded annually for a book-length manuscript of original poetry in English. The winner receives $2,000 and publication of the manuscript by Anhinga Press. There is a $20 reading fee. Send an SASE for application instructions.

Available to: No restrictions
Deadline: Submissions accepted from January 1 to March 15
Apply to: Rick Campbell, above address

Archaeological Institute of America
656 Beacon Street, 4th Floor
Boston, MA 02215-2010

The *Anna C. and Oliver C. Colburn Fellowship,* of $11,000, is awarded biennially to an incoming Associate Member or Student Associate Member of the American School of Classical Studies at Athens. Candidates must apply concurrently to the American School for associate membership.

Available to: U.S. or Canadian citizens or permanent residents
Deadline: February 1, 1996; inquire for 1998
Apply to: Above address

The *Kenan T. Erim Award*, established by the American Friends of Aphrodisias, awards $4,000 annually to an American or international research and/or excavating scholar working on Aphrodisias material.

Available to: No restrictions
Deadline: November 15
Apply to: Above address

The *Olivia James Traveling Fellowships* are awarded for an academic year to students desiring to travel and study in Greece, the Aegean Islands, Sicily, Southern Italy, Asia Minor, or Mesopotamia. The classics, sculpture, architecture, archaeology, and history are the most suitable areas of study. The institute specifies that the word "student" should not be taken to mean that awards are restricted to persons registered in academic institutions. The institute will award $15,000 as a single fellowship.

Available to: U.S. citizens or permanent residents
Deadline: November 15
Apply to: Above address

The *Harriet Pomerance Fellowship* is awarded to enable a person to work on an individual project of a scholarly nature relating to Aegean Bronze Age archaeology. Preference will be given to candidates whose project requires travel to the Mediterranean. One fellowship carrying a stipend of $3,000 is available annually.

Available to: U.S. and Canadian residents
Deadline: November 15
Apply to: Above address

Arizona Commission on the Arts
417 West Roosevelt
Phoenix, AZ 85003

(M) Poetry, playwriting, and fiction grants, of no less than $5,000 and no more than $7,500, are available in certain years to Arizona residents of at least eighteen years of age.

Available to: Arizona residents, eighteen years and up, no students
Deadline: Inquire
Apply to: Tonda Gorton, Public Information Office, above address

Arizona Theatre Company
Box 1631
Tucson, AZ 85702

(D) The *National Hispanic Playwriting Contest* awards $1,000 and possible inclusion in ATCs *Genesis: New Play Reading Series* for a full-length play or adaptation by a playwright of Hispanic heritage residing in the United States, its territories, or Mexico. Plays may be written in English or in Spanish with an English translation. The contest is sponsored in association with Centro Cultural Mexicano de Phoenix. Write for guidelines.

Available to: See above
Deadline: November 1
Apply to: National Hispanic Playwriting Contest, above address

The Arrowhead Regional Arts Council
101 West Second Street, Suite 204
Duluth, MN 55802-2086

(M) The Arrowhead Regional Arts Council annually offers *Individual Artists Fellowships*, of $1,200, to writers in the seven-county Arrowhead Region of Minnesota. Write for further information.

Available to: Residents of the Arrowhead Region of Minnesota

Deadline: December 13, 1996; inquire for 1997
Apply to: Individual Artists Fellowships, above address

(M) *Career Development Grants* are also offered to Arrowhead Region writers. The grants are designed to provide financial support to developing and established regional artists wishing to take advantage of artist-generated or impending, concrete opportunities that will advance their work or careers. Applicants may request grants of up to $750. There are two deadlines per year.

Available to: Residents of the Arrowhead Region of Minnesota
Deadline: March 29 and August 27, 1996; March 28 and late August, 1997
Apply to: Career Development Grants, above address

Artist Trust
1402 Third Avenue, Suite 404
Seattle, WA 98101-2118

(M) Fellowships of $5,000 are available to Washington residents in literary and theater arts. Awards in literature are given in odd-numbered years; in theater (including playwriting) in even-numbered years.

Available to: Washington residents
Deadline: Spring/early summer
Apply to: Above address

Arts Foundation of Michigan
645 Griswold Street, Suite 2164
Detroit, MI 48226

(M) The Arts Foundation, in partnership with the Michigan Council for Arts and Cultural Affairs, offers grants to Michigan residents in fiction, nonfiction, poetry, playwriting, and screenwriting. Funding is not available to those enrolled in degree or certificate granting programs.

Available to: Michigan residents
Deadline: Inquire (usually in early May)
Apply to: Mark Packer, Program Director, above address

Arts International
Institute of International Education
809 United Nations Plaza
New York, NY 10017

The *Cintas Fellowship Program* offers up to twelve grants of $10,000 each in architecture, music, literature, and the visual arts for Cuban professional artists living outside of Cuba. Fellowships are awarded annually but may not be used for study programs.

Available to: Cuban citizens or lineage
Deadline: March 1
Apply to: Cintas Fellowship Program, above address

The Asian Cultural Council
1290 Avenue of the Americas, Room 3450
New York, NY 10104

(R) The Asian Cultural Council helps support residences in Japan for American artists interested in pursuing creative projects. Preference is given to performing and visual artists, though playwrights and writers will be considered. Duration is usually one to six months.

Available to: U.S. citizens

18

Deadline: February 1
Apply to: Ralph Samuelson, Director, above address

Associated Writing Programs Award Series in Poetry, Short Fiction,
the Novel, and Creative Non-Fiction
Tallwood House, MS-1E3
George Mason University
Fairfax, VA 22030

Ⓜ The *AWP Award Series* for poetry, short fiction, the novel, and creative nonfiction, are offered
by the AWP and university and independent presses that have combined their efforts
to publish a number of book-length manuscripts each year. No mixed genre manuscripts
can be accepted. Manuscripts are welcome from published as well as unpublished writers. The winning works will appear through prearranged agreements with four university presses; AWP acts as a literary agent to try to place finalists' manuscripts.
Authors will receive a standard royalty from books sold. A $2,000 honorarium is given
in each category every year. The judges will accept collections that are being considered
by other publishers provided the author includes a statement explaining to whom the
manuscript has been submitted and agrees to inform the AWP if his/her book is accepted
by another publisher. Manuscripts will be accepted with postmarks of January 1 through
February 28 only. There is a $15 nonmember, and $10 AWP member reading and handling fee. Send an SASE for guidelines.

Available to: No restrictions
Deadline: Submissions accepted from January 1 to February 28
Apply to: Appropriate series, above address

The Association of American Colleges and Universities
1818 R Street, NW
Washington, DC 20009

Ⓝ The *Frederic W. Ness Book Award*, of $1,000, is given for a book published in the preceding
year that is judged to have made the most significant contribution to studies in liberal
education. Histories of colleges and books by multiple authors are ineligible.

Available to: No restrictions
Deadline: August 15
Apply to: Frederic W. Ness Book Award, above address

Association for the Care of Children's Health
7910 Woodmont Avenue, Suite 300
Bethesda, MD 20814

Ⓒ The *Joan Fassler Memorial Book Award* offers $1,000 for a book that makes an "outstanding
contribution to children's literature dealing with hospitalization, disease, disabling conditions, death, and dying." To be considered for the award, a book must have been
published in the English language in the award year.

Available to: No restrictions
Deadline: December 31
Apply to: Joan Fassler Memorial Book Award, above address

Association of Jesuit Colleges and Universities
One Dupont Circle, Suite 405
Washington, DC 20036

Ⓝ The *National Jesuit Book Awards* are sponsored by Alpha Sigma Nu, the national Jesuit student
honor society. Three cash prizes, of $1,000 each, are given annually for the best hard-
cover or paperback book in three categories, which alternate on a three-year cycle. The
1996 award will be for the best book published in the preceding three years in the

sciences (social or physical); the 1997 award will be in the professional fields; and the 1998 award will be in the humanities.

Available to: Any faculty, administrator, staff, or student (religious or lay, full- or part-time) at one of the twenty-eight Jesuit colleges or universities in the United States
Deadline: March 1
Apply to: Application forms are available from any local ASN chapter; send books and applications to above address

Association for Library Services to Children
American Library Association
50 East Huron Street
Chicago, IL 60611

© The *John Newbery Medal* is awarded annually to the author of the most distinguished contribution to American literature for children published in the United States during the preceding year. Authors and publishers are invited to submit books to the medal committee for review during the ALA midwinter meeting. (No cash award is given; winners receive a medal. However, the high prestige of the Newbery Medal in the field of children's literature warrants its inclusion here.)

Available to: U.S. citizens or residents
Deadline: January; inquire for exact date
Apply to: John Newbery Medal, above address

Astraea National Lesbian Action Foundation
116 East 16th Street, 7th Floor
New York, NY 10003

The *Lesbian Writers' Fund Awards* offer several grants, of $10,000, each to emerging lesbian writers who have published at least once in a magazine, literary journal, or anthology. Write for guidelines and the required application form.

Available to: Lesbian writers
Deadline: Early March; inquire for exact date
Apply to: Lesbian Writers' Fund, above address

[IN] The *Sappho Award of Distinction* offers $5,000 to an established lesbian writer. There is no application process. *By Internal Nomination Only.*

Atlanta Bureau of Cultural Affairs
675 Ponce de Leon Avenue
Atlanta, GA 30308

Artist Project Grants are designed to support practicing, professional artists, including writers, residing in the city of Atlanta. Grants up to $3,000 are offered for projects by poets, fiction writers, creative nonfiction writers, and playwrights who demonstrate a consistent level of high-quality work.

Available to: Residents of Atlanta
Deadline: Inquire
Apply to: Sophia Lyman, Grants Administrator, above address

The *Mayor's Fellowships in the Arts* program annually awards $6,600 to a practicing professional artist who has been residing in the city of Atlanta for at least three consecutive years prior to the deadline. The awards rotate among several artistic disciplines. The 1996 awards will be for literary arts; 1997 will be for theatre arts, including playwriting. Write for guidelines and application.

Available to: Residents of Atlanta
Deadline: Mid-February; inquire for exact date and yearly discipline
Apply to: Sophia Lyman, Grants Administrator, above address

Austin Community College
Northridge Campus
11928 Stonehollow Drive
Austin, TX 78758

(P) The *Balcones Poetry Prize* awards $1,000 for the best book of poetry written in English during the year. The winning author will be invited to read at the Northridge Literary Festival, which takes place each April on ACC's Northridge Campus in Austin. Three copies of poetry books, forty-two pages or more, may be submitted by the author or publishers; books must be copyrighted in the calendar year under consideration. The prize, first awarded in 1995, is intended to be annual, but Austin Community College recommends querying prior to submission. There is a $15 entry fee.

Available to: No restrictions
Deadline: December 1
Apply to: John Herndon, Director, Balcones Poetry Prize, above address

Austin Writers' League
1501 West 5th Street
Austin, TX 78703

(M) The *Violet Crown Book Awards* honor outstanding books published by Austin Writers' League members. The awards offer a $1,000 cash stipend and trophy in each of three categories: fiction, nonfiction, and literary work (poetry, essays, and short stories). Books must have been published between September 1 and August 31 of the award year. A $10 entry fee is required. Entrants must be members of the Austin Writers' League; membership is $40 annually, and writers may join the League when submitting their entry.

Available to: Members of the Austin Writers' League
Deadline: August 31
Apply to: Violet Crown Book Awards, above address

AUSTRALIA
Arts Management Pty, Ltd.
180 Goulburn Street
Darlinghurst NSW 2011
Australia

(D)
(F) The *Miles Franklin Award,* of $25,000 (Australian), is offered annually for a published novel that best presents Australian life "in any of its phases." If no novel is judged of sufficient literary merit, the award may be made to the author of a radio or television play.

Available to: No restrictions
Deadline: January 31 for work published in the preceding year
Apply to: Above address

The Authors League Fund
330 West 42nd Street
New York, NY 10036

The fund makes interest-free loans to professional, published authors and produced playwrights in need of help because of illness, misfortune, or some other temporary emergency. The fund does not make grants.

Available to: No restrictions
Deadline: None
Apply to: Susan Drury, Administrator, above address

Authors in the Park
PO Box 85
Winter Park, FL 32790-0085

(F) The *Authors in the Park Short Story Contest* offers a $500 first prize, a $250 second prize, and a $125 third prize for unpublished short stories written in English. Send an SASE for guidelines prior to submitting a manuscript.

> Available to: No restrictions
> Deadline: March 31
> Apply to: Short Story Contest, above address

Baker's Plays
100 Chauncy Street
Boston, MA 02111

(D) The Baker's Plays *High School Playwriting Contest* offers a first prize of $500 and publication in Baker's Plays *Best Plays from the High School* series for a full-length or one-act play by a high school student. The winning play should be suitable for production on high school stages and preferably should be about "the high school experience." A second prize of $250 and a third prize of $100 are also awarded. Write for further information and guidelines.

> Available to: High school students
> Deadline: January 31
> Apply to: High School Playwriting Contest, above address

Bantam Doubleday Dell
Books for Young Readers
1540 Broadway
New York, NY 10036

(C) The *Marguerite de Angeli Prize* is awarded annually to encourage writing fiction for children that examines the diversity of the American experience, either contemporary or historical, in the spirit of the works of Marguerite de Angeli. Manuscripts must be between forty and ninety-six pages and be suitable for readers seven to ten years of age. The award consists of a $1,500 cash prize and a $3,500 advance against royalties when the winning manuscript is published by Doubleday Books for Young Readers.

> Available to: American or Canadian writers who have not previously published a novel
>   for middle-grade readers
> Deadline: Manuscripts must be postmarked between April 1 and June 30
> Apply to: Marguerite de Angeli Prize, above address

(C) The *Delacorte Press Prize for a First Young Adult Novel* offers a book contract for a hardcover and paperback edition, a $1,500 cash prize and $6,000 advance against royalties. Submissions should consist of a book-length manuscript (100 to 224 typed pages), with a contemporary setting, that will be suitable for ages twelve to eighteen. Write for complete submission guidelines.

> Available to: American and Canadian writers who have not previously published a
>   young adult novel
> Deadline: Manuscripts must be postmarked after Labor Day and before December 30
> Apply to: Delacorte Press Prize, above address

Barnard College
3009 Broadway
New York, NY 10027-6598

(P) The *Barnard New Women Poets Prize* offers an honorarium of $1,000 and publication by Beacon Press for a book-length manuscript of poems by a woman who has not yet published a book. Poets who have published chapbooks or similar works of fewer than 500 copies remain eligible. Write for submission details prior to sending a manuscript.

Available to: Women poets
Deadline: October 15
Apply to: Barnard New Women Poets Prize, above address

The Bellagio Study and Conference Center. *See* **The Rockefeller Foundation**

Berea College
CPO 2336
Berea, KY 40404

The *W. D. Weatherford Award* has been established for the writer whose published work "best illuminates the problems, personalities, and unique qualities of the Appalachian South." One award of $500 is given annually, and a special award of $200 is sometimes given.

Available to: No restrictions
Deadline: December 31 of publication year
Apply to: Above address

The Berkshire Conference of Women Historians
M.A. and Liberal Studies Program
Ramapo College
404 Ramapo Valley Road
Mahwah, NJ 07430

Ⓝ The *Publication Awards* offer a $1,000 prize for the best published book and a $300 prize for the best published article of historical scholarship in any field of history by an American or Canadian woman. Publishers are notified of the competition and asked to submit eligible works, but submissions by individual authors are also welcome.

Available to: Women historians of U.S. or Canadian citizenship
Deadline: January 15
Apply to: Sydney Weinberg, Secretary-Treasurer, above address

Bertelsmann USA
1540 Broadway, 33rd Floor
New York, NY 10036

Bertelsmann's *World of Expression Scholarship Program* offers a $10,000 first prize, a $7,500 second prize, a $5,000 third prize and fifty-five $1,000 fourth prizes to New York City high school seniors in two categories, musical and literary composition. In addition, a $1,000 grant will be awarded to the music and English teacher with the most student entries in each borough. Write for additional information and guidelines.

Available to: New York City high school seniors
Deadline: March 1
Apply to: World of Expression Scholarship Program, above address

Beverly Hills Theatre Guild Playwright Award Competition
2815 North Beachwood Drive
Los Angeles, CA 90068

Ⓓ The *Beverly Hills Theatre Guild Julie Harris Playwright Competition* awards an annual cash prize of $5,000 for the best play submitted by an American playwright. An additional $2,000 is available to help finance a showcase production if the award-winning play is presented in the Los Angeles area within one year of receiving the award. The second-place *Janet and Maxwell Salter Award* offers a prize of $2,000, and the third-place *Dr. Henry and Lilian Nesburn Award* offers $1,000. Entries must be original, full-length plays that have not been published, have never had an Equity or non-Equity production for which actors or authors were paid or admission was charged, and are not currently under option. Musicals, one-act plays, adaptations, translations, plays that have won any other competition, or plays that have entered previous Beverly Hills Theatre Guild Competitions are ineligible. Send a letter-sized SASE for rules and an application any time after July of the current competition.

Available to: U.S. citizens
Deadline: Submissions are accepted August 1 through November 1
Apply to: Above address

Birmingham-Southern College
Box 549003
Birmingham, AL 35254

(F)
(P)
The *Hackney Literary Awards* offer $2,000 in prizes for poetry and short stories and a $2,000 award for the novel. There is a $5 per poem or per short story reading fee and a $20 reading fee for novels. All submitted work must be original and unpublished. Send an SASE for guidelines.

Available to: No restrictions
Deadlines: December 31 for poetry and short stories; September 30 for novels
Apply to: Hackney Literary Awards, above address

The Black Warrior Review
University of Alabama
PO Box 2936
Tuscaloosa, AL 35486

(F)
(P)
The *Black Warrior Review* will award $500 to both a poet and a fiction writer whose work has been published in either the Fall or Spring issue of the *Black Warrior Review*. Only those authors whose manuscripts have appeared in these issues are eligible for the award. Winners will be selected by a prominent writer or critic; names of the recipients of the award and the award judge will be announced in the Fall issue of the *Review*.

Available to: Writers published in the *Black Warrior Review*
Deadlines: July 15 for Fall issue; January 15 for Spring issue
Apply to: The Editor, above address

The Susan Smith Blackburn Prize
3239 Avalon Place
Houston, TX 77019

(D)
This annual award is given to women playwrights for full-length, unproduced plays or plays that were produced within one year of the deadline. The award carries a first prize of $5,000 and a signed and numbered de Kooning print made especially for the prize; a second-place prize of $2,000; and $500 to each of the eight to ten other finalists. Plays will be received only from recognized sources, which include professional regional and off-Broadway theaters and other organizations regularly reading new works. Send an SASE to the above address for a listing of these "sources." Applications by individual playwrights or their agents are not accepted and will not be considered.

Available to: Women playwrights of any nationality writing in English
Deadline: September 20
Apply to: Susan Smith Blackburn Prize, above address

Blue Mountain Center
Blue Mountain Lake, NY 12812

(R)
The Blue Mountain Center offers fourteen four-week residences four times a year: mid-June through late October. The residences are open to writers and provide free room and board. Spouses must apply individually. Send a brief bio, work samples, reviews, and

a project description to apply. Specify preferred period of stay. There is a $20 application fee.

Available to: Established writers, particularly those whose work shows social and ecological concern
Deadline: February 1
Apply to: Admissions Committee, above address

(M) The *Richard J. Margolis Award*, of $1,000, is given annually to a poet, essayist, or journalist "whose work recalls Richard J. Margolis's warmth, humor, and concern for social issues." To nominate a writer, send three copies of at least two samples of the writer's work, published or unpublished, of no more than thirty pages, and a short biographical note.

Available to: No restrictions
Deadline: July 1
Apply to: Richard J. Margolis Award, 101 Arch Street, 9th Floor, Boston, MA 02110, Attention: Harry S. Margolis

Borderlands Theater
PO Box 2791
Tucson, AZ 85702

(D) The *Border Playwrights Project* offers three five- to ten-day residences for unproduced, full-length plays by playwrights whose work reflects the culturally diverse realities of the Border region, and the Border as metaphor. Latino, Native American, African American, and Asian playwrights are encouraged to apply. Winning scripts receive a public staged reading and playwrights receive an honorarium, travel, and lodging.

Available to: No restrictions
Deadline: Inquire
Apply to: Border Playwrights Project, above address

Robert Bosch Foundation
c/o CDS International
330 Seventh Avenue
New York, NY 10001

(J) The *Robert Bosch Foundation Fellowship Program* offers journalists and other young professionals the opportunity to participate in an intensive nine-month work and study program in Germany. Applicants must be U.S. citizens with a graduate degree or equivalent work experience; evidence of outstanding professional performance and/or academic achievement; and the ability to communicate well in German. Fellows receive round-trip transportation between their U.S. residence and Germany, a stipend of DM 3,500 per month for the duration of the program, tuition and fees for language course and group seminars, limited health and accident insurance, and financial support for an accompanying spouse. Write for additional information and application.

Available to: U.S. citizens
Deadline: October 15
Apply to: Fellowship Program, above address

The Boston Globe
PO Box 2378
Boston, MA 02107-2378

(C) The *Boston Globe-Horn Book Awards* are offered by the Boston Globe Newspaper Company and the Horn Book, Inc. The awards foster and reward excellence in text and illustration of children's books. There is no age limit, although reprints and textbooks are not considered. Three awards of $500 are offered: for fiction, nonfiction, and picture books. Publishers may submit up to ten books from each juvenile imprint divided into any of the three categories, and submissions must be sent directly to the judges (see below). Awards are made each autumn at the New England Library Association conference.

Available to: Authors of children's books published in the United States between June 1 and May 31 of the following year
Deadline: May 15
Apply to: For list of judges' names and addresses, write Boston Globe-Horn Book Awards, above address, or The Horn Book, Inc., 11 Beacon Street, Suite 1000, Boston, MA 02108

Ⓕ The *L. L. Winship/PEN New England Award*, sponsored by PEN New England and the *Boston Globe*, is given for the best book published in the calendar year preceding the deadline date, having some relation to New England—author, theme, plot, or locale. Children's books and anthologies are not eligible. One award of $2,000 is available annually.

Available to: No restrictions
Deadline: January 1
Apply to: L. L. Winship/PEN New England Award, above address for list of judges' names and addresses

Bread Loaf Writers' Conference
Middlebury College
Middlebury, VT 05753

Ⓡ The *Bread Loaf Writers' Conference* awards fellowships and scholarships to candidates applying to attend a session of the conference. Candidates for fellowships must have a first original book published within three years of filing their application. Scholarship candidates must have published in major literary periodicals or newspapers. One letter of nomination is required for each candidate and is due by March 1. Applications and supporting materials are due by April 1. Awards are announced in June.

Available to: Published writers
Deadlines: March 1 for nominations; April 1 for applications
Apply to: Above address

Ⓜ Bread Loaf also sponsors the *Bakeless Literary Publication Prizes*, an annual book series competition for new authors of literary works in poetry, fiction, and nonfiction. The prize supports emerging writers by sponsoring publication of their first books through Middlebury College/University Press of New England. Winners also receive fellowships to attend the Bread Loaf Writers' Conference. Send an SASE for complete guidelines.

Available to: Emerging writers
Deadline: Manuscripts accepted from January 1 to March 1
Apply to: The Bakeless Prizes, above address

Brody Arts Fund
California Community Foundation
606 South Olive Street, Suite 2400
Los Angeles, CA 90014-1526

Ⓜ Up to five fellowships of $5,000 each are awarded to emerging writers residing in Los Angeles County. Writers who are "rooted in and reflective of the diverse multicultural communities of Los Angeles County" are preferred. The awards rotate among disciplines; the next literature cycle will be in 1997.

Available to: Los Angeles County residents
Deadline: Inquire
Apply to: Above address

Bronx Council on the Arts
1738 Hone Avenue
Bronx, NY 10461

Ⓜ The *BRIO [Bronx Recognizes Its Own] Fellowships* offer $1,500 to Bronx artists in various disciplines including fiction, poetry, playwriting/screenwriting, and nonfiction literature. The Council also offers technical assistance to Bronx writers and is in the process of developing the Bronx Writers Center, a haven for writers in the Bronx. Write for complete guidelines and application forms.

Available to: Bronx residents
Deadline: February 15, 1996; inquire for 1997
Apply to: BRIO Fellowships, above address

John Carter Brown Library
Brown University
Box 1894
Providence, RI 02912

The John Carter Brown Library annually awards approximately fifteen *Research Fellowships*. The library is an outstanding collection of primary materials relating to virtually all aspects of the discovery, exploration, settlement, and development of the New World. Recipients of all Fellowships are expected to be in regular residence at the John Carter Brown Library and to participate in the intellectual life of Brown University. Therefore, preference may be given to applicants able to take up the fellowship during the course of the academic year. Fellowships are of two types:

Short-Term Fellowships, carrying stipends of $1,000 per month, are available for periods of two to four months. They are available to Americans and foreign nationals engaged in predoctoral, postdoctoral, or independent research.

Long-Term NEH Fellowships, each carrying a stipend of $16,000, are for six months. Applicants must be United States citizens or have resided in the United States for three years immediately preceding the term of the fellowship. Graduate students are not eligible for these fellowships.

Available to: See above
Deadline: January 15
Apply to: Research Fellowships, above address

Brown University
English Department
Box 1852
Providence, RI 02912

Ⓓ The *Jane Chambers Playwriting Award* offers $1,000 to a full-length play or a performance-art text by a woman. The winning script will also receive a rehearsed reading at the national conference of the Association for Theatre in Higher Education's Women and Theatre Program (which sponsors the award). Submitted work should "reflect a feminist perspective and contain a majority of roles for women." Experimentation with form is encouraged; no one-woman shows accepted. The winner must be available to attend the reading and part of the conference in late July/early August (travel expenses covered). Send an SASE for guidelines.

Available to: Women playwrights
Deadline: February 15
Apply to: Tori Haring-Smith, 6 Fireside Drive, Barrington, RI 02806

Bucknell Seminar for Younger Poets
Bucknell University
Lewisburg, PA 17837

(R) The Center for Poetry at Bucknell University offers ten fellowships to give seniors and talented undergraduate poets an opportunity to write and receive guidance from established poets during a seminar from June to July. Readings and workshops are offered. Tuition, room, board, and space for writing is provided.

> Available to: Juniors and graduating seniors from American colleges
> Deadline: March 1
> Apply to: Send an academic transcript, two recommendations, a ten- to twelve-page portfolio, and a letter of self-presentation to John Wheatcroft, Director, above address

Bush Foundation Artist Fellowships
E-900 First National Bank Building
332 Minnesota Street
Saint Paul, MN 55101

(M) Grants to selected artists to enable them to set aside time in which they can concentrate on the development of their artistic talent. The program includes writers (fiction, creative nonfiction, and poetry), scriptwriters (playwriting and screenwriting), visual artists, choreographers, and composers. Writers must meet certain prior publication requirements. Fellowships are for twelve to eighteen months, with a stipend of $36,000 each.

> Available to: Minnesota, North Dakota, South Dakota, and western Wisconsin residents (nonstudents) age 25 or older who have lived in the state for at least twelve of the preceding thirty-six months
> Deadline: Inquire
> Apply to: Above address

Witter Bynner Foundation for Poetry
PO Box 10169
Santa Fe, NM 87504

(P) The foundation offers grants in support of individual poets, poetry translation and the process of translation, developing an audience for poetry, and uses of poetry. All applicants must be sponsored by a nonprofit organization to be considered for grants. Requests for application forms are accepted from July 1 through January 28.

> Available to: See above
> Deadline: February 1
> Apply to: Above address

California Arts Council
Artists Fellowship Program
1300 I Street, Suite 930
Sacramento, CA 95814

(M) *Fellowships in Literature,* of $2,500 each, are given in recognition of outstanding artistic achievement to exemplary California writers every four years. The next literature cycle is 1996–97. Applicants must be legal residents of California for one year prior to the application deadline. Applications will be available in September 1996; write for further information.

> Available to: California residents
> Deadline: Inquire for 1996
> Apply to: Above address

California Library Association
717 K Street, Suite 300
Sacramento, CA 95814

Ⓒ The *John and Patricia Beatty Award* offers $500 for a children's or young adult book "high-lighting California, its culture, heritage and/or future. The California setting must be depicted authentically and must serve as an integral focus for the book." Any children's or young adult book set in California and published in the United States during the calendar year preceding the presentation of the award is eligible for consideration. This includes works of fiction as well as nonfiction.

Available to: No restrictions
Deadline: Inquire
Apply to: John and Patricia Beatty Award, above address

The Camargo Foundation
c/o Ricardo Bloch
West 1050 First National Bank Building
332 Minnesota Street
Saint Paul, MN 55101-1312

Ⓡ The Camargo Foundation offers fellowships consisting of a free residence in fully furnished, self-catering apartments in Cassis, France, to members of universities and college faculties, teachers in secondary schools, graduate students, and writers, photographers, visual artists and musicians who are in an advanced stage of a project that will benefit from residence near Marseilles and Aix-en-Provence. Applicants must be working on subjects in the humanities relating to French and/or Francophone culture. Candidates are asked to submit an application form, a *vita*, and a detailed description of the project they wish to complete in France. Three letters of recommendation are also required.

Available to: See above
Deadline: February 1
Apply to: Above address for informational brochure and application form

Cambridge Arts Council
57 Inman Street
Cambridge, MA 02139

Ⓜ *Arts Lottery Grants* are available for projects in the arts, humanities, interpretive sciences, and writing that take place in Cambridge, Massachusetts and publicly benefit the local community. Send an SASE for application and guidelines.

Available to: No restrictions
Deadline: October 15
Apply to: Arts Lottery Grants, above address

CANADA
The Canada Council—Writing and Publishing Section
350 Albert Street
Box 1047
Ottawa, Ontario K1P 5V8
Canada

Ⓜ The *Governor General's Literary Awards* of $10,000 (Canadian) each are given annually to Canadian authors of the best English-language and best French-language work in each of the following categories: children's literature (text and illustration), drama, fiction, poetry, nonfiction, and translation. The juries review all books by Canadian authors, illustrators, and translators published in Canada or abroad during the previous year. In the case of translation, the original work also must be a Canadian-authored title. All entries (books or bound galleys) must be received at the Canada Council by August 31. The books must have been published between October 1 and September 30. Books must be submitted by publishers and accompanied by a publisher's submission form, available from the Writing and Publishing Section. A sheet describing guidelines for publishers is also available.

Available to: Canadian citizens
Deadline: August 31
Apply to: Above address

CANADA
Canadian Authors Association
27 Doxsee Avenue North
Campbellford, Ontario K0L 1L0
Canada

Ⓜ The *Canadian Authors Association Literary Awards* are given "to honor writing which achieves literary excellence without sacrificing popular appeal." The awards are offered in four categories: prose fiction, prose nonfiction, poetry, and drama, published or produced by a Canadian in any medium in each calendar year. Each award carries a cash prize of $5,000 (Canadian) and is awarded annually.

Available to: Canadian citizens
Deadline: December 15
Apply to: Above address

Ⓒ The *Vicky Metcalf Award* is given for a body of work for children—fiction, nonfiction, poetry, or picture books—by any Canadian author. One prize of $10,000 (Canadian) is awarded annually.

Available to: Canadian citizens
Deadline: December 31
Apply to: Above address

Ⓒ The *Vicky Metcalf Short Story Award* of $3,000 (Canadian) is awarded annually for the best children's short story published in the previous year by a Canadian. An additional $1,000 (Canadian) will be awarded to the editor of the journal, magazine, or anthology in which the winning story appeared, provided the publication is Canadian.

Available to: Canadian citizens
Deadline: December 31
Apply to: Above address

CANADA
Canadian Science Writers' Association
PO Box 75 Station A
Toronto, Ontario M5W 1A2
Canada

Ⓙ The Canadian Science Writers' Association offers awards to honor outstanding contributions to science journalism in Canadian print and electronic media. Awards for print media are given annually in four categories: newspapers (2); magazines (2); trade publications (1); and books (2); as well as two electronic categories: radio (2); and television (2). A cash prize of $1,000 (Canadian) accompanies each award. In addition there is a $500 award to any student science writer who has a science article published in a Canadian university or college newspaper. One entry may be submitted in each category.

Available to: Canadian citizens or residents
Deadline: January 31
Apply to: CSWA Awards, above address, or fax 416-960-0528

CANADA
Le Conseil de la Vie Française en Amérique
56, rue St-Pierre, 1er étage
Québec, Québec G1K 4A1
Canada

(F)
(N)
The *Champlain Prize* is given for a work published in French by a North American resident. If the author is living outside the province of Québec, there is no restriction as to the subject matter. If the author lives in Québec the subject matter must be related to French-speaking people living as minorities in North America. The $1,500 (Canadian) prize is awarded annually, one year for a scholarly work, the next for a creative work.

Available to: French Americans or French Canadians
Deadline: December 31
Apply to: The Secretary, above address

CANADA
Délégation Générale du Québec
Services culturels
117, rue du Bac
75007 Paris
France

Le Prix France Québec Jean Hamelin has been given since 1965 for a literary work written in French and published in Québec or France during the preceding year. One prize of 5,000 French francs is awarded annually.

Available to: French-American or French-Canadian writers
Deadline: Inquire
Apply to: Above address

(F)
Le Prix Québec-Paris is awarded annually for a literary work written in the French language by a Canadian writer and published the preceding year in Canada or in France. The laureate receives $2,000 (Canadian), plus 4,000 French francs. Expenses for the winning author to travel to and stay in France will be paid by the French government.

Available to: Canadian or Québec writers
Deadline: Inquire
Apply to: Above address

CANADA
The Lionel Gelber Prize
Applause! Communications Inc.
110 Spadina Avenue, Suite 1007
Toronto, Ontario M5V 2K4
Canada

(N)
The *Lionel Gelber Prize* is an annual book award of $50,000 (Canadian) given to the author of the best book in the field of international relations. To be eligible the book must be published in the twelve months preceding October 31 and submitted by the publisher. Books must be published in English, or in English translation (in the case of translated titles, the copyright year of the translation into English must match the year of the prize). Also, books must be published in Canada, or be distributed in Canada through a recognized Canadian agency, though the author may be of any nationality. Write for additional information.

Available to: No restrictions
Deadline: July 1 (for titles to be published between July 1 and October 31, publishers may submit bound galleys or cirlox-bound typescript in lieu of a finished book).
Apply to: The Manager, above address

CANADA
Grain Magazine
Box 1154
Regina, Saskatchewan S4P 3B4
Canada

(M) The *Short Grain Writing Contest* annually offers a $500 first prize, a $300 second prize, and a $200 third prize in each of three categories: "Postcard Story," a work of fiction of up to 500 words; "Prose Poem," a lyric poem written as a prose paragraph of up to 500 words; and "Dramatic Monologue," a self-contained speech given by a single character in 500 words or less. The winning works will be published in *Grain*, a quarterly magazine published by the Saskatchewan Writers Guild. There is a $20 entry fee which includes a one-year subscription to *Grain*. Write for complete guidelines.

Available to: No restrictions
Deadline: January 31
Apply to: Short Grain Writing Contest, above address

CANADA
Stephen Leacock Associates
Box 854
Orillia, Ontario L3V 6K8
Canada

The *Stephen Leacock Medal for Humor* is given annually to promote Canadian writing of humor to a book published in the year preceding the presentation of the medal. The winning author receives the $5,000 Laurentian Bank of Canada cash award and the Stephen Leacock silver medal. To apply, send ten copies of the book, a $25 (Canadian) entry fee, and a photograph of the author.

Available to: Canadian citizens or landed immigrants
Deadline: December 30
Apply to: Mrs. Jean Dickson, Chairman, Award Committee, 203 Martin Drive, Orillia, Ontario L3V 3P4 Canada

CANADA
Leighton Studios for Independent Residencies
The Banff Centre for the Arts
PO Box 1020, Station 28
Banff, Alberta T0L 0C0
Canada

(R) Residency periods of one week to three months are available for established writers, composers, and visual artists based upon proven artistic achievement and project proposals. Juries are ongoing. Interested artists should apply at least six months prior to the starting date of the requested residency.

Available to: Established artists
Deadlines: Inquire
Apply to: Leighton Studios Registrar, above address

CANADA
Manitoba Arts Council
93 Lombard Avenue, Room 525
Winnipeg, Manitoba R3B 3B1
Canada

(M) *Creative Arts Grants* are available to writers of fiction and nonfiction and to playwrights in the following categories:

The *Major Arts Grant*, covering living expenses, project costs, and travel expenses, is available to support personal creative projects of six to ten months duration, with a maximum award of up to $25,000. The *Writers A Grant*, worth up to $10,000 for living expenses only, is available to support concentrated work on a major writing project by Manitoba writers who show a high standard of work and exceptional promise. The *Writers B Grant*, worth up to $5,000 for living expenses, is designed to assist published professional Manitoba writers in the early stages of their careers. The *Writers C Grant*, covering any combination of living, research, or travel expenses up to $2,000, is available to support a variety of developmental writing projects, particularly manuscript development by an emerging writer, and research and/or travel that is related to current work.

Available to: Published Manitoba writers
Deadline: Inquire
Apply to: Pat Sanders, Writing and Publishing Officer, above address

CANADA
Saskatchewan Writers Guild
PO Box 3986
Regina, Saskatchewan S4P 3R9
Canada

® The Saskatchewan Writers Guild offers residences to writers at three different colonies in Saskatchewan: Riverhurst Colony, Saint Peter's Abbey Colony, and Emma Lake Colony. Residence details (duration, season, deadlines, etc.) vary according to colony: the weekly fee is $100 (Canadian) at all three. Writers are limited to a month's retreat in a year. Write for additional information and guidelines.

Available to: No restrictions (though preference is given to applicants from Saskatchewan)
Deadline: Inquire
Apply to: Above address

CANADA
Société Saint-Jean Baptiste de Montréal
82, rue Sherbrooke Ouest
Montréal, Québec H2X 1X3
Canada

IN *Le Prix de Journalisme "Olivar-Asselin"* is given to an established journalist whose work has served "the superior interests of the province of Québec." One prize, of $3,000 (Canadian) and a medal, is awarded every three years (next in 1996). *By Internal Nomination Only.*

IN *Le Prix de Litterature "Ludger-Duvernay"* is given to an established writer whose work has served "the superior interests of the province of Québec." One prize, of $3,000 (Canadian) and a medal, is awarded every three years (next in 1997). *By Internal Nomination Only.*

IN *Le Prix de Théâtre "Victor-Morin"* is given to an established writer or player in the field of theater whose work has served "the superior interests of the province of Québec." One prize, of $3,000 (Canadian) and a medal, is awarded every three years (next in 1998). *By Internal Nomination Only.*

CANADA
Union des Ecrivains Québécois
1030 rue Cherrier
Bureau 510
Montréal, Québec H2L 1H7
Canada

Ⓕ *Le Prix Molson de l'Académie Canadienne-Française*, of $5,000 (Canadian), is given annually for a published novel by a French-Canadian national.

Available to: French-Canadian nationals
Deadline: June; inquire for exact date
Apply to: Le Prix Molson, above address

CANADA
West Coast Book Prize Society
1033 Dayle Street, #700
Vancouver, British Columbia V6E 1M7
Canada

The following five prizes, comprising the *British Columbia Book Prizes*, are awarded each spring for books published during the preceding calendar year. Each winner is awarded a cash prize of $1,500 (Canadian).

ⓒ The *Sheila A. Egoff Children's Prize* is awarded to the best book written for children sixteen years and younger. It is judged on content—of text or illustration—and originality. The author and/or illustrator must have lived in British Columbia or the Yukon for three of the past five years. The book may have been published anywhere.

Ⓝ The *Hubert Evans Nonfiction Prize* is awarded to the author of the best original nonfiction literary work (philosophy, belles lettres, biography, history, etc.). Quality of research and writing, as well as insight and originality, are major considerations in the judging of this prize. The writer must have lived in British Columbia or the Yukon for three of the last five years. The book may have been published anywhere.

The *Roderick Haig-Brown Regional Prize* is awarded to the author of the book which contributes most to the enjoyment and understanding of British Columbia. The book may deal with any aspect of the province (people, history, geography, oceanography, etc.) and must be original. Guide books, how-to books and fiction are not considered for this prize. The book may have been published anywhere, but the author must have lived in British Columbia for three of the last five years.

Ⓟ The *Dorothy Livesay Poetry Prize* is awarded to the author of the best work of poetry by a poet who has lived in British Columbia or the Yukon for three of the past five years. No anthologies or "best of" collections. The book may have been published anywhere.

Ⓕ The *Ethel Wilson Fiction Prize* is awarded to the author of the year's most outstanding work of fiction. The author must have lived in British Columbia or the Yukon for three of the past five years.

Available to: See above for residency restrictions
Deadline: December 31
Apply to: B.C. Book Prizes, above address

CANADA
Western Magazine Awards
3898 Hillcrest Avenue
North Vancouver, British Columbia V7R 4B6
Canada

Ⓙ The *Western Magazine Awards*, of $500 (Canadian) each, in eighteen categories, are given annually to writers of articles published in a western Canadian magazine during the previous year. Topics range from fiction to commentary, and usually deal with issues and experiences particular to the western region of Canada. A complete list of categories is available from the above address.

Available to: Canadian citizens and landed immigrants
Deadline: January 31
Apply to: Above address for entry form, guidelines, and fees

Carnegie Fund for Authors
1 Old Country Road
Carle Place, NY 11514

The Carnegie Fund offers grants-in-aid to qualified, published authors who have suffered a financial emergency as the result of illness or injury to the author, spouse, or dependent child, or who have suffered some equivalent misfortune. Grant amounts vary according to need.

Available to: Authors of books published commercially
Deadline: None
Apply to: Above address

Carnegie-Mellon University
Drama Department
Schenley Park
Pittsburgh, PA 15213

(D) The *Carnegie-Mellon Showcase of New Plays* offers a $1,000 stipend plus travel and housing to five playwrights who are invited to work for a week with a director and Equity company of actors on a full-length play or bill of related one-acts. The week culminates in two public script-in-hand performances. The program seeks "plays of risk; no subjects are taboo; all forms are acceptable; the more audacious and the richer the language, the better." Submissions are accepted only from agents or when accompanied by a letter of recommendations from the literary manager of a major theater.

Available to: No restrictions
Deadline: December 1
Apply to: Carnegie-Mellon Showcase of New Plays, above address

Carolina Quarterly
CB #3520 Greenlaw Hall
University of North Carolina
Chapel Hill, NC 27599-3520

(F)
(P) The *Charles B. Wood Award for Distinguished Writing* offers $500 for the best poem or short story by an emerging writer published during the year in *Carolina Quarterly*. All poems and short stories appearing in the quarterly by emerging writers are considered for the prize.

Available to: *Carolina Quarterly* contributors
Deadline: None
Apply to: Above address

Case Western Reserve University
Department of Theater Arts
10900 Euclid Avenue
Cleveland, OH 44106-7077

(D) The *Marc A. Klein Playwriting Award* offers $500, full production, and an additional $500 for housing and travel expenses for previously unpublished or unproduced full-length plays, and evenings of thematically related one-acts by a student currently enrolled at a U.S. college or university. Musicals and children's plays are not eligible. Write for additional information and entry form.

Available to: Students in American colleges and universities
Deadline: May 15
Apply to: The Marc A. Klein Playwriting Award, above address

C.C.S. Entertainment Group
433 North Camden Drive, Suite 600
Beverly Hills, CA 90210

Ⓓ The *Christopher Columbus Screenplay Discovery Awards* option screenplays for up to $10,000 through a monthly awards process. One screenplay will be selected monthly—if it meets quality standards—to receive rewrite notes and become a finalist in the *Screenplay Discovery of the Year*. First-, second-, and third-place winners in the yearly competition will be offered film rights options by Breaking In Productions and will receive a gift certificate to the Hollywood Film Institute. There is a $45 per script registration fee. Write for complete guidelines and release form.

Available to: No restrictions
Deadline: Last day of each month for monthly selection; December 1 for annual cycle
Apply to: Screenplay Discovery Awards, above address

Ⓕ The *Opus Magnum Discovery Awards* are given for completed, unpublished works of fiction
Ⓝ and nonfiction suitable for film adaptation. First-, second-, and third-place winners will be offered film rights options, up to $10,000 by Breaking In Productions. There is a $75 per book manuscript registration fee. Write for complete guidelines and release form.

Available to: No restrictions
Deadline: Last day of each month for monthly submissions
Apply to: Opus Magnum Discovery Awards, above address

C.E.C. International Partners
12 West 31st Street
New York, NY 10001-4415

ArtsLink Collaborative Projects offer grants of up to $6,000 (most grants are between $1,500 and $3,500) to enable creative artists, including writers and translators, to work with their counterparts in Central or Eastern Europe, the former Soviet Union or the Baltics on mutually beneficial collaborative projects that will enrich the artists' work and/or create new work that draws inspiration from the knowledge and experience gained in the country visited. Write for guidelines and application.

Available to: U.S. citizens or permanent residents
Deadline: February; inquire for exact date
Apply to: ArtsLink, above address

Centenary College of Louisiana
Department of English
PO Box 41188
Shreveport, LA 71134-1188

IN The *John William Corrington Award for Literary Excellence* offers $2,500 and a bronze plaque in honor of a lifetime achievement. The award is generally, though not necessarily, given to a Southern writer. The winner is chosen by a committee of the college's Student Government Association and the English faculty. There is no application process. *By Internal Nomination Only.*

Center for Book Arts
626 Broadway
New York, NY 10012

Ⓟ The Center for Book Arts *Poetry Chapbook Competition* offers a cash award of $500, a $500 reading honorarium, and publication of a letterpressed, limited-edition chapbook printed and bound by artists at the Center. Poets may submit one typescript of a collection of poems (sixteen to twenty-four pages) or one long poem of up to 500 lines. There is a $10 reading fee. Send an SASE for complete guidelines.

Available to: No restrictions
Deadline: December 31
Apply to: Poetry Chapbook Competition, above address

The Center for Foreign Journalists
11690-A Sunrise Valley Drive
Reston, VA 22091-1409

(J) The *Worth Bingham Prize,* of $10,000, honors newspaper or magazine investigative reporting of stories of national significance where the public interest is being ill-served. Entries may include a single story, a related series of stories, or up to three unrelated stories. Columns and editorials are eligible. Individual stories must have been published during the calendar year preceding the deadline; in the case of a series, at least half the individual stories must have been published during the contest year. Write for complete guidelines and entry form.

Available to: No restrictions
Deadline: February 15
Apply to: Worth Bingham Prize, above address

(J) The *Arthur F. Burns Fellowship* offers young journalists from the United States and Germany the opportunity to work and report from abroad. Ten journalists from the United States and ten from Germany are selected each year to work and travel in the others' country for two months. Fellows receive a $5,000 stipend to cover basic travel and living costs. American applicants must be working journalists in any news media, between the ages of twenty-one and thirty-three, with demonstrated journalistic talent and an interest in European affairs. Proficiency in German is not required but will be regarded favorably in the selection process. Write for complete application requirements.

Available to: See above
Deadline: March 1
Apply to: Burns Fellowship, above address

Center Press
PO Box 16452
Encino, CA 91416

(M) The *Masters Literary Award* annually offers a grand prize of $1,000 and publication with Center Press. Honorable mention awards are given quarterly in each of three categories: fiction, poetry and song lyrics, and nonfiction; the grand-prizewinner is selected from among the honorable mentions. All published and unpublished manuscripts are eligible. There is a $15 reading fee per entry. Send an SASE for guidelines and additional information.

Available to: No restrictions
Deadline: Ongoing (honorable mention awards are granted on March 15, June 15, September 15, and December 15)
Apply to: Masters Literary Awards, above address

The Center for Southern Studies
Jacksonville State University
228 Stone Center
Jacksonville, AL 36265

(D) The *Southern Playwrights Competition* offers $1,000 and a full-scale production for full-length plays that deal with the Southern experience and have not received Equity production. Write for guidelines and entry form.

Available to: Natives or residents of Alabama, Arkansas, Florida, Georgia, Kentucky, Louisiana, Mississippi, North Carolina, South Carolina, Tennessee, Virginia, or West Virginia
Deadline: February 15
Apply to: Steven J. Whitton, above address

Centrum
Fort Worden State Park
PO Box 1158
Port Townsend, WA 98368

® *Centrum Residency Program in Port Townsend, Washington* provides individual artists with a place to create, without distractions, in an isolated setting of incredible beauty. One-month residences, September through May, are offered in writing and other disciplines. Centrum provides individual cottages, a small stipend, and solitude. Families are welcome.

Available to: No restrictions
Deadlines: October 1
Apply to: Above address

Cerritos College
The Original Theatre Works
Burnight Center
11110 Alondra Boulevard
Norwalk, CA 90650-6298

Ⓓ The *Lee Korf Playwriting Awards* annually offer $750 plus production for plays. Work with multicultural themes is encouraged. Send an SASE for guidelines and application.

Available to: No restrictions
Deadline: January 1
Apply to: Lee Korf Playwriting Awards, Attention: Gloria Manriquez, above address

Chelsea Award Competition
c/o Richard Foerster, Editor
PO Box 1040
York Beach, ME 03910

Ⓕ

Ⓟ *Chelsea* awards two annual prizes of $500 for the best work of short fiction (7,500 words or less) and the best group of four to six poems (500 lines or less) selected in anonymous competitions. Only previously unpublished work will be eligible. The winning entries are published in *Chelsea*, and all work entered is considered for publication. An entry fee of $10 is required, for which entrants will receive a subscription to *Chelsea*. Send an SASE for guidelines.

Available to: No restrictions
Deadlines: June 15 for fiction; December 15 for poetry
Apply to: Above address; all other business should be directed to Box 773, Cooper Station, New York, NY 10276

The Chesterfield Film Company
100 Universal City Plaza, Building 447
Universal City, CA 91608

The *Chesterfield Film Company/Writer's Film Project*, sponsored by Amblin Entertainment and Universal Pictures, annually selects up to ten writers for a year-long screenwriting workshop in Los Angeles. Each writer chosen to participate receives a $20,000 stipend to cover living expenses and creates two original, feature-length screenplays during the year. The company intends to produce the best of the year's work. Writers meet in a workshop setting three to five times a week to consider story ideas, script outlines, and drafts of each screenplay. Current and former writing program students are encouraged to apply. There is a $37 application fee. Send an SASE for application materials.

Available to: No restrictions
Deadline: Inquire
Apply to: Writer's Film Project, above address

The Chicago Tribune
435 North Michigan Avenue
Chicago, IL 60611

(F) The *Nelson Algren Awards for Short Fiction* offer a first prize of $5,000 and three runners-up prizes of $1,000 for outstanding unpublished short stories by American writers. The winning stories will be published in the *Tribune*. Stories should be typed, double-spaced, and between 2,500 and 10,000 words. Enclose an SASE.

Available to: U.S. citizens
Deadline: January 31 (submissions not accepted prior to November 1)
Apply to: Nelson Algren Awards, Chicago Tribune Editorial Department, above address

(F) The *Heartland Prizes* award $5,000 for a novel and a book of nonfiction embodying the spirit
(N) of the nation's heartland. Eligible books are those published between August 1 and July 31 of the deadline year.

Available to: U.S. citizens
Deadline: July 31
Apply to: Heartland Prizes, above address

Children's Book Guild of Washington, D.C.
c/o Susan Hepler, President
2602 Valley Drive
Alexandria, VA 22302

[IN] The *Washington Post/Children's Book Guild Nonfiction Award* offers $1,000 annually to the author of an outstanding body of nonfiction work for children. There is no application process. *By Internal Nomination Only.*

Children's Literature Association
PO Box 138
Battle Creek, MI 49016

The Children's Literature Association offers two types of grants to scholars doing research in the field of children's literature. In each case it is expected that the research will lead to publication and make a significant contribution to the field.

(C) The *Children's Literature Association Research Fellowships*, of $250 to $1,000 each, are given to support any activity associated with serious literary criticism or original scholarship of children's literature. The awards may be used for transportation, living expenses, materials and supplies, but not for obtaining advanced degrees, for researching or writing a thesis or dissertation, for textbook writing or pedagogical projects.

(C) The *Margaret P. Esmonde Memorial Scholarship*, of $500, is given for proposals dealing with critical or original work in the fields of fantasy and science fiction for children and adolescents.

Available to: Scholars who have completed an advanced degree program
Deadline: February 1
Apply to: Dr. Dianne Johnson-Feelings, Department of English, University of South Carolina, Columbia, SC 29208

Cincinnati Playhouse in the Park
Box 6537
Cincinnati, OH 45206

(D) The *Lois and Richard Rosenthal New Play Prize* offers a $10,000 cash prize, production, and travel expenses and residence in Cincinnati for the playwright during production, for an unpublished full-length play that has not been produced professionally. Write for complete application procedures before submitting a manuscript.

Available to: No restrictions
Deadline: February 1
Apply to: Madeleine Pabis, Artistic Associate, Lois and Richard Rosenthal New Play
   Prize, above address

The Claremont Graduate School
160 East 10th Street
Claremont, CA 91711

(P)   The *Kingsley Tufts Poetry Award* offers a $50,000 prize for a book of poems, written in English
       and published during the calendar year. As part of the award program, the winner will
       spend one week in residence at the graduate school's Humanities Center. Books may
       be submitted by the author or, with the author's consent, by a publisher, agent, or other
       representative.

(P)   The *Kate Tufts Discovery Award, of $5,000,* is given to "an emerging poet whose work displays
       extraordinary promise." Entries are also considered for the *Tufts Prize*. Complete guide-
       lines and entry form are necessary for submission.

       Available to: American citizens or legally resident aliens
       Deadline: December 15
       Apply to: Kingsley Tufts and Kate Tufts Poetry Awards, above address

Clauder Competition for Excellence in Playwriting
PO Box 383259
Boston, MA 02238-3259

(D)   The *Clauder Competition for Excellence in Playwriting* biennially offers a first prize of $3,000
       and full production for full-length plays written by New England playwrights that have
       not been professionally produced. Runners-up will receive $500 and a staged reading.
       Write for guidelines.

       Available to: New England playwrights
       Deadline: June 30, 1997
       Apply to: Above address

The Cleveland Foundation
Suite 1400 Hanna Building
1422 Euclid Avenue
Cleveland, OH 44115-2001

(M)   The *Anisfield-Wolf Book Awards* are given "to recognize recent books which have made im-
       portant contributions to our understanding of racism or our appreciation of the rich
       diversity of human cultures." Two awards, of $5,000 each, are given annually to books
       written in English and published in the preceding calendar year. In the event that more
       than two winners are chosen in a given year, $10,000 is divided equally among the
       winning books. Copies of the published books should be sent directly to the panel of
       jurors. Write for jurors' names and addresses.

       Available to: No restrictions
       Deadline: January 31
       Apply to: Above address for list of current jurors

Cleveland State University
Poetry Center
Department of English
Rhodes Tower, Room 1815
1983 East 24th Street
Cleveland, OH 44115-2440

(P)   The *Poetry Center Prize* annually awards $1,000 and publication in the CSU Poetry Series for
       a volume of original poetry. Submission should consist of a book-length manuscript (50

to 100 pages) with the poet's name, address, and phone number appearing on the cover sheet only. Previously published collections, including self-published books, are not eligible. There is a $15 submission fee. Additional volumes for the series may be selected from the contest entries. Send an SASE for guidelines.

Available to: No restrictions
Deadline: March 1
Apply to: Poetry Center Prize, above address

Coalition for the Advancement of Jewish Education
261 West 35th Street, Floor 12A
New York, NY 10001

(F) The *David Dornstein Memorial Creative Writing Contest for Young Adult Writers* offers $1,000 and publication in CAJE's *Jewish Education News* for a short story on a Jewish theme or topic by a writer aged eighteen to thirty-five. Writers may submit one unpublished story of 5,000 words or less. Send an SASE for complete guidelines.

Available to: No restrictions
Deadline: December 31
Apply to: Annual Short Story Contest, above address

The Colonial Players
108 East Street
Annapolis, MD 21401

(D) The *Biennial Promising Playwright Award* is given for a full-length play or bill of two related one-acts suitable for an arena stage. Plays should have a two-set limit and a cast limit of ten. The winner is awarded $750, plus production (the playwright must be available to attend rehearsals). Send an SASE for guidelines.

Available to: Residents of Maryland, Delaware, Pennsylvania, Virginia, West Virginia, and the District of Columbia
Deadline: December 31, 1996; no manuscripts accepted before September 1, 1996
Apply to: Promising Playwright Award, above address

Colorado Council on the Arts and Humanities
750 Pennsylvania Street
Denver, CO 80203

(M) Several *COVision Recognition Awards in Literature* are offered annually to Colorado writers. Each recipient receives $4,000 with additional funds available for public presentations or exhibitions. Write for guidelines and application.

Available to: Colorado residents
Deadline: December 15
Apply to: COVision Recognition Awards, above address

Colorado Review
Department of English
Colorado State University
Fort Collins, CO 80523

(P) The *Colorado Prize* offers a $1,000 honorarium and publication by the University Press of Colorado for a book-length collection of poems. There is a $20 reading fee, which includes a subscription to the *Colorado Review*. Send an SASE for complete guidelines.

Available to: No restrictions
Deadline: January 1997; inquire for exact date
Apply to: Colorado Prize, above address

[IN] The *"Evil Companions" Literary Award*, of $500, is given annually to a writer living in, writing about, or with ties to the American West. The award is named for the self-proclaimed "Evil Companions," a group of Denver journalists in the 1950s and 1960s. The winner is chosen by a committee of individuals from the *Colorado Review,* the Tattered Cover Bookstore, and the Oxford Hotel. There is no application process. *By Internal Nomination Only.*

Columbia: A Magazine of Poetry and Prose
Columbia University
School of the Arts--Writing Division
404 Dodge Hall
New York, NY 10027

(F)
(P)
Columbia: A Magazine of Poetry and Prose awards a first prize of $250 for poetry and prose, plus publication for the best submissions. Short stories and excerpts from novels and literary nonfiction will be considered for the prose award. All genres of poetry may be submitted for the poetry award. Runners-up in both categories may be offered publication. A $7 entry fee is required (payable to *Columbia: A Magazine of Poetry and Prose*). Enclose an SASE for return of manuscripts.

Available to: No restrictions
Deadline: February 15, 1996; inquire for 1997
Apply to: Above address

Columbia College
72 East 11th Street
Chicago, IL 60605

(D) The *Theodore Ward Prize for Playwriting* annually awards $2,000 plus production for a professionally unproduced full-length play by an African-American writer. The winner will also receive transportation to Chicago and housing during the final week of rehearsal prior to the performance period. A second prize of $500 plus a staged reading is also offered. Write for guidelines.

Available to: African-American writers
Deadline: August 1 (no submissions accepted before May 1)
Apply to: Chuck Smith, Facilitator, Theodore Ward Prize for Playwriting, above address

Columbia University
Bancroft Prize Committee
202A Low Memorial Library
New York, NY 10027

(N) The *Bancroft Prizes* are given for books in the field of American history (including biography) and diplomacy. The awards are for books first published in the year preceding that of the award. Two awards of $4,000 each are given annually.

Available to: No restrictions
Deadline: November 1
Apply to: Bancroft Prizes, above address, with four copies of the book, and a nominating letter

Columbia University
The Freedom Forum Media Studies Center
2950 Broadway
New York, NY 10027

(J) Fellowships are given to media professionals from print and broadcast organizations and journalism and mass communications educators who wish to undertake major scholarly or professional projects which examine major issues and problems facing the mass media and society, in either a domestic or global context. Fellows are in residence at Columbia University for periods of three months to one academic year, receive a stipend based on salary needs or matching sabbatical support and a housing allowance, and are provided with office space as well as secretarial and research assistance. Fellowships are awarded at three levels: senior fellowships for mature individuals with substantial national reputations, fellowships for accomplished persons at midcareer, and research fellowships for those with five to eight years of experience. Contact the center for additional information and application procedures.

Available to: No restrictions
Deadline: February 1
Apply to: Residential Fellowship Program, above address

Columbia University
Graduate School of Journalism
2950 Broadway
New York, NY 10027

(J) The *Mike Berger Award* honors human interest newspaper reporting about the daily life of New York in the tradition of the late Meyer "Mike" Berger, a reporter for the *New York Times*. A cash prize is presented on Journalism Day at the Columbia University Graduate School of Journalism.

Available to: Newspaper journalists writing about New York
Deadline: February 15
Apply to: Mike Berger Award, above address

(J) The *Maria Moors Cabot Prizes* honor advancement of press freedom and distinguished contributions to inter-American understanding. The prizes are awarded to professional journalists for the body of their work and consist of a medal, an honorarium, and travel expenses to the ceremony at Columbia.

Available to: Print and broadcast journalists covering Central and South America for publications and broadcast outlets in the western hemisphere
Deadline: March 31
Apply to: Cabot Prizes, above address

(J) The *Knight-Bagehot Fellowships in Economics and Business Journalism* provide a nine-month course of study to improve the quality of reporting by expanding participants' understanding of business, finance, and economics. Up to eight fellowships are awarded annually, including tuition and a stipend. Applicants must have at least four years of professional experience, not necessarily in business and economics, and have published work that regularly appears in the United States or Canada.

Available to: See above
Deadline: March 1
Apply to: Terri Thompson, Director, Knight-Bagehot Fellowships, above address

(M) The *Pulitzer Prizes* are given to American authors for the most distinguished volume of original verse, fiction published in book form, biography or autobiography, produced play, book of nonfiction, and a book in American history to authors of any nationality. Prizes are also given for journalism published in United States daily or weekly newspapers. Several prizes of $3,000 each are awarded annually.

Available to: All candidates must be American with the exception of authors of books on American history.
Deadlines: July 1 and November 1 for books; February 1 for journalism; March 1 for plays
Apply to: The Pulitzer Prizes, above address

(J) The *Paul Tobenkin Award*, of $250, honors "outstanding achievement in the field of newspaper writing in the fight against racial and religious hatred, intolerance, discrimination, and every form of bigotry, reflecting the spirit of Paul Tobenkin."

Available to: Newspaper journalists writing for U.S. newspapers
Deadline: February 15
Apply to: Paul Tobenkin Award, above address

Columbia University
The Charles H. Revson Fellows
Program on the Future of the City of New York
New York, NY 10027

The *Revson New York Program* awards fellowships to those who have made a significant contribution to New York City or to another large metropolitan center and who can be expected to make even greater contributions in the future, after using Columbia University's instructional, research, and other resources for an academic year. Ten awards of a $16,000 stipend, four courses for credit, and an unlimited number of audited courses are given each year.

Available to: No restrictions
Deadline: February 1
Apply to: Above address

The Common Wealth Awards
c/o PNC Bank, Delaware, Trustee
222 Delaware Avenue
Wilmington, DE 19899

[IN] The *Common Wealth Awards*, of $25,000 each, are available in literature, the dramatic arts, mass communications, science and invention, government, public service, and sociology. Awards are given for a body of work, not for a specific project. Nominations are made by various nominating organizations recognized as umbrella organizations in each specific category; nominations by the public are not encouraged. *By Internal Nomination Only.*

Community Children's Theatre of Kansas City
c/o Mrs. Blanche Sellens
8021 East 129 Terrace
Grandview, MO 64030

(C)
(D) The *Margaret Bartle Annual Playwriting Award* offers a cash prize of $500 for an unpublished children's play suitable for trouping by the Community Children's Theatre of Kansas City. Plays (fifty-five to sixty minutes) must have no more than eight characters and be suitable for an elementary school age audience. Send an SASE for rules.

Available to: No restrictions
Deadline: January 31
Apply to: Above address

The Conference on Latin American History
Institute for Latin America
508 Lowder Building
Auburn University
Auburn University, AL 36849-5258

(N) The *Herbert Eugene Bolton Memorial Prize* offers $500 annually for the best book in English, published during the year previous to the award, on any significant aspect of Latin American history. The conference additionally awards several other prizes with lesser monetary stipends for articles on Latin American history. Inquire for further information.

Available to: No restrictions
Deadline: Inquire
Apply to: Dr. Michael Conniff, Executive Secretary, above address

Connecticut Commission on the Arts
227 Lawrence Street
Hartford, CT 06106

Ⓜ *Artist Fellowships* in the amounts of $2,500 and $5,000 are offered to Connecticut residents. Grants are on a two-year cycle with literary arts (poetry, fiction, and drama) plus choreography, music composition, and media arts (film, video, audio) given in even-numbered years. Write for complete guidelines.

Available to: Connecticut writers who have lived and worked in the state for four years
Deadline: February 1, 1996; inquire for 1998
Apply to: Linda Dente, Program Director, Artist Fellowships Program Director, above address

The Commission on the Arts maintains a roster of auditioned performing artists in dance, music and theater as well as poets, writers, and storytellers for public readings. Its *Arts Presentation Partnerships* program offers funding support to organizations which form partnerships to present events featuring roster artists (up to one-half the artist fee). New performing groups and writers are added to roster every year; nonprofit organizations, schools, and other civic groups are eligible to apply for funding.

Available to: Connecticut residents
Deadline: Inquire for exact date
Apply to: Above address

Contemporary Arts Educational Project
6026 Wilshire Boulevard
Los Angeles, CA 90036

Ⓜ The *American Awards for Literature International Award,* of $1,000, is given annually for a body of literary writing. The *American Awards for Literature* are also given in the categories of fiction, poetry, drama, and belles lettres, however these awards currently carry no cash stipend. Publishers may submit four copies of a book published during the calendar year.

Available to: No restrictions for the International Award; U.S. citizen for the fiction, poetry, drama, and belles lettres awards
Deadline: December 31
Apply to: American Awards for Literature, above address

The Continuum Publishing Group
370 Lexington Avenue
New York, NY 10017

The *Continuum Book Award* offers $10,000 for the best work received in Continuum's principal publishing areas: religious studies, literature and the arts, psychology and social thought, and women's studies. Manuscripts that are interdisciplinary in nature and that offer innovative and theoretical perspectives of wide-ranging cultural importance are the primary focus of the award. Manuscripts will be considered for the award twice yearly. Monies awarded represent an advance against royalties, and will be granted as often as a book is found to merit the award, but no more than once a year.

Available to: No restrictions
Deadlines: February 1 and September 1
Apply to: Continuum Book Award, above address

Cornell University
Department of English
Goldwin Smith Hall
Ithaca, NY 14853

(D)
(J)
The *George Jean Nathan Award for Dramatic Criticism* is given for the best piece of drama criticism written during the theatrical year (July 1 to June 30), whether it is an article, an essay, treatise, or book. Drama criticism that has been broadcast on television or radio is also eligible. One award of $5,000 and a silver medallion are given annually. Send an SASE for guidelines.

Available to: U.S. citizens
Deadline: Inquire
Apply to: George Jean Nathan Award, above address

Council on Foreign Relations
Office of Membership and Fellowship Affairs
58 East 68th Street
New York, NY 10021

(J)
(R)
The *Edward R. Murrow Fellowship* to reside at the council offices for nine months is available yearly to an American foreign correspondent for "sustained analysis and research," and the opportunity to interact with foreign policy experts. Stipend equals journalist's current salary up to $60,000 (prorated for nine months).

Available to: U.S. citizens serving abroad as journalists or those who have recently returned from a foreign post and who expect to return to a foreign post after the residence
Deadline: March 1
Apply to: Elise Lavis, Director of Membership and Fellowship Affairs, above address

Council for International Exchange of Scholars
3007 Tilden Street, NW, Suite 5M
Washington, DC 20008-3009

The council administers the *Fulbright Scholar Program* for advanced research and university lecturing in over 135 countries around the world. Some 1,000 grants are awarded annually to faculty and professionals in virtually all academic disciplines, including creative writing. Grant benefits vary by country, but usually include international travel, a monthly stipend, and other allowances depending on the host country. Applications are available in March from the above address.

Available to: U.S. citizens
Deadline: August 1 for all world areas. Special programs have other deadlines.
Apply to: Box NEWS, above address

A similar program for scholars from abroad for university lecturing and advanced research in the United States is administered in the United States by the Council. Interested non-U.S. citizens should inquire at the Fulbright agency or U.S. embassy in their home country.

The Crane-Rogers Foundation. *See* **Institute of Current World Affairs**

Crazyhorse
University of Arkansas at Little Rock
English Department
2801 South University
Little Rock, AR 72204-1099

(IN)
The *Crazyhorse Fiction Award* and the *Lynda Hull Memorial Poetry Award* offer $500 for the best short story and the best poem to appear in *Crazyhorse* during the calendar year. All

poems and short stories published in *Crazyhorse* are eligible for the awards. *By Internal Nomination Only.*

Crescent Films
1920 Abrams Parkway, No. 419
Dallas, TX 75214-3915

(D) The *Lone Star Screenplay Competition,* cosponsored by the Irving Texas Film Commission, offers a first-place prize of $500 and a second-place prize of $300 to both a Texas writer and a non-Texas writer for an original, feature length screenplay. The *Irving Film Commission Award for Best Script Suitable for Filming in Texas,* consisting of a $500 first prize and a $300 second-place prize, is also offered. Additionally, all winners are eligible to sign an option with Crescent Films to represent the screenplay for a period of one year (although this is not obligatory). Send an SASE for guidelines and entry form. There is a $35 entry fee.

Available to: No restrictions
Deadline: December 31
Apply to: Lone Star Screenplay Competition, above address

Cultural Arts Council of Houston/Harris County
1964 West Gray, Suite 224
Houston, TX 77019-4808

Artists' Project Grants offer up to $5,000 for Houston writers working on projects with a public dimension in either product or process that will benefit Houston's low- and moderate-income residents.

Available to: Houston residents
Deadline: Early fall
Apply to: Artists' Project Grants, above address

(M) *Creative Artist Awards,* of $5,000, are given in fiction, poetry, creative nonfiction, playwriting, and screenwriting to writers who have lived and worked in Houston. Award recipients are asked to perform a community service of their choice.

Available to: Houston residents
Deadline: Early fall
Apply to: Creative Artist Awards, above address

Cumberland Poetry Review
PO Box 120128
Acklen Station
Nashville, TN 37212

(P) The *Robert Penn Warren Poetry Prize* awards a $500 first prize, a $300 second prize, and a $200 third prize for unpublished poems. Prize winners and honorable mentions will be published in the *Cumberland Poetry Review.* Poets may enter as many as three unpublished poems of no more than 100 lines each that have not been submitted elsewhere. There is a $14 reading fee, which includes a one-year subscription to *Cumberland Poetry Review.* Write for the required entry form.

Available to: No restrictions
Deadline: March 1
Apply to: Above address

Cushwa Center for the Study of American Catholicism
614 Hesburgh Library
University of Notre Dame
Notre Dame, IN 46556

(N) Two *Publication Awards* are offered by the Cushwa Center and the University of Notre Dame Press for manuscripts dealing with the American Catholic experience or the Irish in

America. The award-winning manuscript in each category will be published by the University of Notre Dame Press, and their authors will receive a $500 advance on royalties. These awards are not limited to studies in any one discipline. Manuscripts from the humanities, the historical and social studies disciplines will be considered; unrevised dissertations normally will not be considered. Write for additional information and submission guidelines.

Available to: No restrictions
Deadline: December 15
Apply to: Publication Awards, above address

The Dayton Playhouse
1301 East Siebenthaler Avenue
Dayton, OH 45414

Ⓓ *The Dayton Playhouse FutureFest '97* will award $1,000 and possible production to previously unproduced and unpublished plays. Three full-scale selections, as well as three readers' theater selections, will be presented during FutureFest weekend, July 1997. A $1,000 prize will be awarded to the winning playwright. Send an SASE for guidelines before submitting manuscript.

Available to: No restrictions
Deadline: September 30 (no submissions accepted before August 1)
Apply to: Playwriting Competition, above address

The Deep South Writers Conference
c/o English Department
Box 44691
University of Southwestern Louisiana
Lafayette, LA 70504

Ⓓ The *Miller Award* offers a minimum of $500 biennially, in odd-numbered years, for full-length, unpublished plays that deal with an aspect of the English Renaissance and/or the life of Edward de Vere, Earl of Oxford. Plays should be readily adaptable for film or television.

Available to: No restrictions
Deadline: July 15, 1997
Apply to: Contest Clerk, Miller Award, above address

The Deep South Writers Conference sponsors several other competitions with lesser monetary prizes in short fiction, juvenile fiction, fantasy and science fiction, the novel, nonfiction, poetry, and drama. Send an SASE to DSWC for complete information and guidelines.

Delaware Division of the Arts
Carvel State Office Building
820 North French Street
Wilmington, DE 19801

Individual Artist Fellowships in literary art are available to Delaware residents. Fellowships are $2,000 for emerging professionals; $5,000 for established professionals.

Available to: Delaware residents
Deadline: March 1
Apply to: Write for guidelines and application to Barbara King, Fellowship Coordinator, above address

Delaware Theatre Company
200 Water Street
Wilmington, DE 19801-5030

(D) *Connections,* a biennial new play competition, awards a $10,000 first prize, plus a staged reading for a full-length play that deals with interracial dynamics in America. The Delaware Theatre Company will retain an option to produce the winning work in one of its two following seasons. Entries may utilize historical or contemporary settings; they may be dramas, comedies or musicals. Plays may not have received a full professional production. Write for guidelines.

Available to: No restrictions
Deadline: April 1, 1996; inquire for 1998
Apply to: Connections, above address

The Gladys Krieble Delmas Foundation
521 Fifth Avenue, Suite 1612
New York, NY 10175-1699

Predoctoral and postdoctoral grants for study in Venice and the Veneto are awarded annually for historical research on Venice and the former Venetian empire, and for study of contemporary Venetian society and culture. Disciplines of the humanities and social sciences are eligible areas of study, including (but not limited to) archaeology, architecture, art, bibliography, economics, history, history of science, law, literature, music, political science, religion, and theater. Applicants must be citizens or permanent residents of the United States and have some experience in advanced research. Grants range from $500 to $12,500. Funds are granted for research in Venice and the Veneto only, and for transportation to, from, and within the Veneto. Write for additional information and application.

Available to: U.S. citizens or permanent residents
Deadline: December 15
Apply to: Above address

Delta Kappa Gamma Society International
PO Box 1589
Austin, TX 78767-1589

(N) The *Educator's Award,* of $2,000, is given annually to the author of a book in recognition of "outstanding educational research and writings of women authors whose book may influence the direction of thought and action necessary to meet the needs of today's complex society." The book must be written in English by one or two women and copyrighted during the calendar year prior to the year in which the award is given. Write to above address for guidelines and additional information.

Available to: Female residents of the society's member countries: Canada, Costa Rica, El Salvador, Finland, Germany, Guatemala, Iceland, Mexico, the Netherlands, Norway, Sweden, the United Kingdom, and the United States (including Puerto Rico)
Deadline: February 1
Apply to: Above address

Eben Demarest Trust
3 Mellon Bank Center, Room 4000
Pittsburgh, PA 15259-0001

The *Eben Demarest Fund* makes one grant annually of approximately $10,000 to an artist or archaeologist who wishes to concentrate for a time on a chosen field without having to depend entirely on the sale of work or outside jobs. The beneficiary is chosen by a search committee. Unsolicited applications from individuals will not be accepted, but an application from some organization or institution for an unusually gifted person will be considered.

Available to: Preferably, but not necessarily, U.S. citizens
Deadline: June 1 for the following calendar year
Apply to: Above address, Attention: Laurie A. Moritz

DENMARK
Commission for Educational Exchange between Denmark and the U.S.A.
Fiolstraede 10, 2. Floor
DK 1171 Copenhagen K
Denmark

Candidates for the *Binational Commission (Fulbright) Scholarships* for study and research in Denmark should be university graduates with a specific research program. Grants cover maintenance and travel for graduate students as well as for postdoctoral or advanced research candidates.

Available to: U.S. citizens
Deadlines: October 31 for predoctoral students; August 15 for postdoctoral candidates
Apply to: For predoctoral applicants: Institute of International Education, 809 United Nations Plaza, New York, NY 10017; for postdoctoral applicants: Council for International Exchange of Scholars, 3007 Tilden Street, NW, Suite 5M, Washington, DC 20008-3009

DePaul University
Theatre School
2135 North Kenmore
Chicago, IL 60614-4111

(D) The *Cunningham Prize for Playwriting* awards $5,000 annually for an original full-length play, musical, or play for young audiences by a Chicago-area playwright. Submitted plays should "affirm the centrality of religion, broadly defined, and the human quest for meaning, truth and community." Write for guidelines.

Available to: Chicago-area playwrights (living within 100 miles of the Loop)
Deadline: September 1
Apply to: The Cunningham Prize Selection Committee, above address

Walt Disney Studios
500 South Buena Vista Street
Burbank, CA 91521-0880

The *Walt Disney Studios Fellowship Program* selects approximately ten to fifteen writers annually to work full-time at developing their craft at Disney. The one-year fellowship, beginning late-October, offers a salary of $30,000. Travel expenses and one month's housing will be given to fellows from outside the Los Angeles area. Applications from culturally and ethnically diverse new writers are encouraged. No previous film or television writing experience is necessary. Send for additional guidelines and application form.

Available to: No restrictions
Deadline: Submissions accepted April 1 through April 26, 1996; inquire for 1997
Apply to: Fellowship Program Administrator, above address

District of Columbia Commission on the Arts and Humanities
Stables Art Center
410 8th Street, NW, Fifth Floor
Washington, DC 20004

(M) The *Arts Education Projects Program* offers funds from $1,000 to $4,500 for programs that provide training and exposure in arts to young people, ages prekindergarten through twenty-one years, and reinforce the importance of the arts as basic to education. Projects that provide in-service training and arts curriculum development for teachers, and collaborative projects between a school and community facility are also eligible. Projects may take place in traditional school settings or community facilities, such as churches and arts and day care facilities. The commission encourages applicants to apply for projects that occur in the schools. Send for complete guidelines and application form.

Available to: District of Columbia residents
Deadline: June 30
Apply to: Arts Education Projects Program, above address

Ⓜ The *City Arts Projects Program* offers grants of $1,000 to $4,500 for programs that encourage the growth of quality arts activities throughout the city and make arts experiences accessible to District residents. Projects must provide exposure to the arts and arts experiences to the broader community or to persons traditionally underserved or separated from the mainstream due to geographic location, economic constraints, or disability. Send for complete guidelines and application form.

Available to: District of Columbia residents
Deadline: June 30
Apply to: City Arts Projects, above address

Ⓜ The *Grants-in-Aid Program* offers fellowships of $2,000 to writers of poetry, fiction, and creative nonfiction who can make a significant contribution to the arts and who can promote the arts in the District of Columbia through artistic excellence. Send for complete guidelines and application form.

Available to: District of Columbia residents
Deadline: June 30
Apply to: Grants-in-Aid Program, above address

Ⓜ The *Larry Neal Writers' Competition* awards prizes in the categories of poetry, fiction, and essay/criticism to District of Columbia writers.

Available to: District of Columbia residents
Deadline: Early April; inquire for exact date
Apply to: Larry Neal Writers' Competition, above address

The Djerassi Resident Artists Program
2325 Bear Gulch Road
Woodside, CA 94062-4405

Ⓡ The Djerassi Program offers accommodations on a beautiful 600-acre ranch one hour south of San Francisco, along with board and studio space to writers and other creative artists for periods of one month. Write, telephone, or fax for application guidelines.

Available to: Working writers
Deadline: February 15, 1996 (for the '97 season); inquire for 1997 deadline
Apply to: Above address, or fax 415-747-0105

Dobie-Paisano Project
The University of Texas at Austin
Main Building 101
Austin, TX 78712

Ⓡ An annual fellowship is available to writers, providing a stipend and free residence at Frank Dobie's ranch Paisano. Two six-month fellowships, with stipends of $7,200, will be awarded. Applicants will be required to submit a record of their personal achievements in writing, together with a brief outline of the work they expect to accomplish at Paisano.

Available to: Native Texans, persons currently living or previously residing in Texas, or persons whose published work has Texas as its subject
Deadline: Late January; inquire for exact date
Apply to: Audrey N. Slate, above address

DOMINICAN REPUBLIC
Altos de Chavon
Apartado Postal 140
La Romana
Dominican Republic

(R)   Altos de Chavon, a nonprofit center for the arts, offers three fourteen-week residences beginning in September, February, and June to artists. The majority of residents are visual artists, though writers are welcome. Residents are asked to pay a $100 registration fee (this covers the cost of transportation between the airport and the colony), a reduced rate of $300 a month, and to contribute artistically to the community by giving a reading, workshop, performance, or exhibit. Knowledge of Spanish is helpful.

      Available to: No restrictions (though preference is given to those whose work has been influenced by or is involved with Latin America and/or the Caribbean)
      Deadline: July 15
      Apply to: Artists in Residence Program, Altos de Chavon, c/o Parsons School of Design, 66 Fifth Avenue, New York, NY 10011

Dorland Mountain Arts Colony
PO Box 6
Temecula, CA 92593

(R)   Residences of one to two months are available. Dorland encourages applications from writers as well as other artists. Five rustic cabins on a 300-acre nature conservancy preserve offer quiet and privacy for concentrated work. Sample of work must be submitted with application form and resume. A donation of $150 a month is requested. Send a #10 SASE for application form and guidelines.

      Available to: No restrictions
      Deadlines: September 1 and March 1
      Apply to: Admissions Secretary, above address

The Dorset Colony
Box 519
Dorset, VT 05251

(R)   The *Dorset Colony House Residencies* are awarded to writers for intensive work periods of from one week to two months. Up to eight writers are in residence at a time. Requested fee of $95 per week, but ability to pay is not necessarily a determining factor in awarding residences. Writers are accommodated in private rooms in a turn-of-the-century historic house located in Dorset village, southern Vermont.

      Available to: No restrictions
      Deadline: Variable, fall and spring
      Apply to: John Nassivera, Director, above address; send letter of inquiry

The Dow Jones Newspaper Fund
PO Box 300
Princeton, NJ 08543-0300

(J)   The *High School Journalism Teacher of the Year* will select one teacher of the year and four distinguished advisers from applicants throughout the country. Candidates may be nominated by newspapers, press associations, colleges, or high school principals for their outstanding abilities as journalism teachers. The teacher of the year will then select the best journalism student attending his or her high school to receive a $1,000 scholarship for journalism study in college. A $500 scholarship will be similarly awarded to students of the distinguished advisers.

(J)   Candidates for the *High School Workshop Writing Competition* must be nominated by directors of High School Journalism Workshops for Minorities. Up to eight scholarships of $1,000 each will be awarded; all are renewable for the sophomore year in college based on continued interest in a journalism career, grades, and financial need. Students do not apply for these scholarships.

Available to: Minority students about to study journalism as undergraduates who attend above-mentioned workshop

Deadlines: Teacher of the Year, July 31; High School Workshop Writing Competition, none

Apply to: Program Director, above address, for information on where workshops will be held and for nomination forms for the Teacher-of-the-Year Competition

The Drama League of New York
165 West 46th Street, Suite 601
New York, NY 10036

(D) The Drama League produces the *Developing Artists Series*, which provides playwrights with a forum in which their work can be heard in an ongoing program of public readings of finished new scripts or works-in-progress.

Available to: No restrictions
Deadline: Scripts accepted year-round
Apply to: Artistic Director, D.A.S., above address

Dubuque Fine Arts Players
1321 Tomahawk Drive
Dubuque, IA 52003

(D) The *National One-Act Playwriting Contest* awards a $600 first prize, a $300 second prize, and a $200 third prize for unproduced, unpublished one-acts. All three prize winners may be produced. There is a $10 entry fee. Send an SASE for guidelines and entry form.

Available to: No restrictions
Deadline: January 31
Apply to: Jennie Stabenow, DFAP One-Act Playwriting Contest Coordinator, above address

Dumbarton Oaks
1703 32nd Street, NW
Washington, DC 20007

The *Bliss Prize Fellowship in Byzantine Studies* is intended to provide encouragement, assistance, and training to outstanding college seniors who plan to enter the field of Byzantine studies. The fellowship carries graduate school tuition and living expenses for two academic years, up to a maximum of $33,500 per year. It also includes summer travel (up to a maximum of $5,000) for the intervening summer to areas that are important for an understanding of Byzantine civilization and culture.

Fellowships are awarded to scholars who hold a doctorate (or appropriate final degree) or have established themselves in their field and wish to pursue research in Byzantine studies, Pre-Columbian studies, and landscape architecture. A stipend of $21,000 plus housing is available annually.

Junior Fellowships, with a stipend of $12,000 plus housing, are available to advanced graduate students who have completed all course work for their doctorate and wish to work on their dissertation or final project at Dumbarton Oaks.

Summer Fellowships, with a maintenance allowance of $150 per week plus housing, are available to scholars on any level of advancement.

Contact Dumbarton Oaks for application procedures.

Available to: No restrictions
Deadline: November 1
Apply to: Assistant Director, above address

Dungannon Foundation
131 East 66th Street, Suite 27
New York, NY 10021

[IN] The *Rea Award for the Short Story* offers $25,000 annually to "a writer who has made a significant contribution to the short story as an art form." Recipients are nominated and selected by a jury. *By Internal Nomination Only.*

Early Childhood Resources and Information Center of the New York Public Library
66 Leroy Street
New York, NY 10014

© The *Ezra Jack Keats New Writer Award,* of $1,000, is given biennially to a promising new writer of not more than six published children's books "that reflect the tradition of Ezra Jack Keats, a Caldecott Medal-winner whose books often featured multicultural settings and portrayed strong family relationships." Honorees need not have illustrated the book(s) nominated for the award; books must appeal to children ages nine and under. Publishers may submit books published in the two-year period preceding the award deadline. Write for guidelines. Next award: 1997

Available to: No restrictions
Deadline: Inquire
Apply to: Ezra Jack Keats New Writer Award, above address

East-West Center
1777 East-West Road
Honolulu, HI 96848

Ⓙ The *Jefferson Fellowship Program* annually makes available six awards for American and seven awards for Asian midcareer journalists, particularly news editors, radio/television news producers and news analysts, for briefings, seminars on major news issues, and the cultural background of the countries of the Asia-Pacific region. Awards are for eight weeks, including four weeks of travel in Asia or the Pacific for American journalists. Transportation to and from Hawaii, living expenses at the center, and travel expenses may be shared by the applicant's employing institution and the East-West Center.

Available to: U.S. midcareer journalists nominated by their news organizations
Deadline: September 15
Apply to: Director, Media Program, above address

Education Writers Association
1331 H Street NW, Suite 307
Washington, DC 20005

Ⓙ The *National Awards for Education Reporting* honor the best education reporting in the print and broadcast media during the calendar year. A $250 cash prize is awarded in each of twenty categories. There is a $1,000 grand prize for the best of the first-place winners. A $35 entry fee is required. Query above address for rules and entry blanks.

Available to: No restrictions
Deadline: Mid-January; inquire for exact date
Apply to: National Awards for Education Reporting, above address

Ⓙ The *National Fellowship in Education Reporting* offers an eight-week program of investigative study and travel for education journalists. The fellowships support up to twelve reporters to spend two months away from daily deadlines to pursue a special project in education. Fellows receive half-salary for the two-month study period; travel expenses; access to expert sources; editing assistance, if desired; the opportunity to work with other reporters at EWA regional meetings and National Seminar; and consultation with EWA staff about progress and problems during the project. Fellowships are open to full-time print or broadcast journalists who have been covering education for at least two years, have the endorsement of their employers, and can show that they have a likely outlet for the product of their study. Freelance writers may apply if they write about education for a substantial portion of their time and if they have an agreement with a media organization to publish or air stories resulting from the fellowship. Write for application guidelines.

Available to: Education journalists
Deadline: Early May; inquire for exact date
Apply to: National Fellowships in Education Reporting, above address

Eighth Mountain Press
624 Southeast 29 Avenue
Portland, OR 97214-3026

(P) The *Eighth Mountain Poetry Prize* offers $1,000 and publication for a book-length poetry manuscript by a woman writer. The biennial award, offered in even-numbered years, was established "in honor of the poets whose words envision and sustain the feminist movement, and in recognition of the importance of their contribution to literature." There is a $20 reading fee. Send an SASE for guidelines and further information.

Available to: Women poets
Deadline: Submission must be postmarked from January 1 to February 1, 1998
Apply to: Above address

ELF: Eclectic Literary Forum
PO Box 392
Tonawanda, NY 14150

(P) The *Ruth Cable Memorial Prize for Poetry* awards $500 and publication in *ELF* for a single poem of fifty lines or less. There is an $8 entry fee for the first three poems, and $3 for each additional poem. The entry fee includes a copy of *ELF*. Send an SASE for complete guidelines.

Available to: No restrictions
Deadline: March 31
Apply to: ELF Poetry Competition, above address

Elmira College
Theatre Department
Elmira, NY 14901

(D) The *Elmira College Playwriting Award* biennially offers $1,000 and full-scale production for an original full-length script. Write for guidelines.

Available to: No restrictions
Deadline: June 1, 1997
Apply to: Professor Fred Goodson, Theatre Program Chair, above address

Emporia State University
English Department
Emporia, KS 66801-5087

(P) The annual *Bluestem Award* offers $1,000 plus publication for a book-length collection of poems by a U.S. author. Manuscripts may include poems published previously in periodicals or anthologies but not in full-length single-author volumes. There is a $15 reading fee.

Available to: U.S. poets
Deadline: March 1
Apply to: Bluestem Award, above address

Maurice English Foundation for Poetry
2222 Rittenhouse Square
Philadelphia, PA 19103-5505

(P) The *Maurice English Poetry Award* is presented annually to an author in his or her sixth (or beyond) decade of life for a distinguished book of poems published during the preceding calendar year. It responds to the fact that a body of work by Maurice English did not appear in book form until his fifty-fifth year. The award carries a $1,000 honorarium with a request for a public reading in Philadelphia.

Available to: See above
Deadline: April 1
Apply to: Above address

The Ensemble Theatre
3535 Main Street
Houston, TX 77002

(D) The Ensemble Theatre, Houston's resident professional black company, annually sponsors the *George Hawkins Playwriting Contest* for short plays or musicals that illuminate the African-American experience for young people aged six to eight. First prize is a cash award of $500, production, and travel and housing to attend the final weeks of rehearsal. The second- and third-prizewinners will receive a staged reading. Send an SASE for guidelines and entry form.

Available to: African-American playwrights
Deadline: Inquire
Apply to: George Hawkins Playwriting Contest, above address

Epoch
Cornell University
251 Goldwin Smith
Ithaca, NY 14853-3201

(F) The *Baxter Hathaway Prize* annually awards a cash prize for prose or poetry, and publication in a special edition of *Epoch*. Details of the prize were currently under review at press (P) time. Send an SASE for updated information and revised guidelines.

Available to: No restrictions
Deadline: Inquire
Apply to: Baxter Hathaway Prize, above address

Evergreen Chronicles
PO Box 8939
Minneapolis, MN 55408-0939

(F) The *Evergreen Chronicles Novella Contest* offers $500 and publication in a special issue of *Evergreen Chronicles*, a journal of gay and lesbian literature. The contest is open to writers who have published no more than one novel or novella and whose work in some way speaks of the gay, lesbian, bisexual, or transgender experience. Send an SASE for guidelines.

Available to: See above
Deadline: September 30
Apply to: Evergreen Chronicles Novella Contest, above address

Experimental Television Center
109 Lower Fairfield Road
Newark Valley, NY 13811

The *Electronic Arts Grant Program* annually awards approximately twenty-five grants of up to $500 to New York State artists involved in the creation of audio, video, or computer-generated time-based works. Funds must be used to assist in the completion of work which is currently in progress. Eligible forms include film; audio and video as single or multiple-channel presentations; computer-based moving-imagery and sound works; installations and performances; and works for CD-Rom, multimedia technologies, and the Internet. Work must be innovative, creative, and approach the various media as art forms; all genres are eligible, including experimental, narrative, and documentary work. Write for guidelines and application form.

Available to: New York State writers
Deadline: March 15
Apply to: Electronic Arts Grant Program, above address

Fargo-Moorhead Community Theatre
Box 644
Fargo, ND 58107

Ⓓ The *FMCT National Playwright Competition* biennially awards $500, or $300 and production expenses, to one-act plays by American playwrights with a particular emphasis on the Midwestern experience. Plays must be unpublished and unproduced professionally, preferably with a small cast. The next competition will be held in 1997. Write for details.

Available to: U.S. residents
Deadline: July 1, 1997
Apply to: National Playwright Competition, Administrator, above address

Fellowship of Southern Writers
Arts and Education Council
PO Box 4203
Chattanooga, TN 37405

ⒾⓃ Four biennial awards, of $1,000 each, are given in recognition of distinguished achievement in Southern writing: the *Robert Penn Warren/Chubb American Fiction Prize*, the *Hillsdale Foundation Fiction Prize*, the *Hanes Poetry Prize*, and the *Cleanth Brooks Medal*. Winners must be writers who were born and raised in the South or resided there for a significant part of their lives, or those whose works, in character or spirit, embody aspects of the Southern experience. *By Internal Nomination Only.*

FC2
Illinois State University
Campus Box 4241
Normal, IL 61790-4241

Ⓕ The *National Fiction Competition*, cosponsored by Illinois State University and FC2 (Fiction Collective Two), offers publication to the author of an original book-length work of prose fiction (short stories, novellas, or novel) not previously published in book form. The manuscript should not exceed 400 double-spaced typed pages. A $15 reading fee and an SASE must accompany each manuscript. The winning author will be brought to the Illinois State University campus to give a reading and meet with students.

Available to: No restrictions
Deadline: November 15
Apply to: National Fiction Competition, above address

Fiction Collective Two
c/o English Department
University of Colorado
Boulder, CO 80309

Ⓕ The University of Colorado at Boulder and Fiction Collective Two invite submissions for the *Charles H. and N. Mildred Nilon Award for Excellence in Minority Fiction.* The contest is open to the following U.S. racial and ethnic minorities: African-American, Hispanic, Native American or Alaska native, and Asian or Pacific Islander. $1,000 plus publication is awarded for the winning English-language, book-length fiction (minimum 200 pages): novel, novella, or short story collection. Send an SASE for guidelines.

Available to: See above
Deadline: November 30
Apply to: Nilon Award, above address

The Fine Arts Work Center in Provincetown
24 Pearl Street
Provincetown, MA 02657

Ⓡ The Fine Arts Work Center in Provincetown "aims to help emerging artists and writers in the critical stage of their professional career by providing them with an opportunity to work independently in a congenial and stimulating environment." Fields of interest are limited to fiction writers, poets, playwrights, and visual artists. Fellows are admitted on the basis of work submitted. The program extends from October 1 through May 1. Grants-in-aid are awarded to those accepted. Send an SASE for brochure and application.

Available to: No restrictions
Deadline: February 1
Apply to: Director, above address

FINLAND
Finnish Literature Information Center
Marja-Leena Rautalin
Mariankatu 7A2
00170 Helsinki 17
Finland

Ⓣ Translation grants are offered annually for translators and publishers, authors of critical works, and regular contributors to literary magazines published outside Finland. Applications should specify the amount of grant required, how it should be used, describe the project and its expected duration, and give the name of the prospective publisher. Applications for grants toward the cost of translating scientific and scholarly journals, dissertations, textbooks, or technical literature will not be considered. Projects should be concerned with the advancement of Finnish, Finland-Swedish, and Lapp literature abroad and for the translation of works by Finnish writers.

Available to: No restrictions
Deadline: April 1
Apply to: Director, above address

Florida Division of Cultural Affairs
Department of State
The Capitol
Tallahassee, FL 32399-0250

Ⓜ *Individual Fellowships,* of $5,000, are given to Florida writers in the categories of poetry, fiction, children's literature (through the Literature Program), and playwriting (through the Theatre Program). Applicants must have lived in the state of Florida for twelve consecutive months at the time of application. Write for complete guidelines.

Available to: Florida residents
Deadline: January 25
Apply to: Above address

Florida Studio Theatre
1241 North Palm Avenue
Sarasota, FL 34236

(D) The *American Shorts Contest* offers $500 and production for the best very short play (five pages or less) on a specified theme (the theme is announced each year in January). Up to twelve other plays will be selected as well for production as part of an evening of short works. Write for guidelines.

Available to: No restrictions
Deadline: Inquire for theme and deadline
Apply to: American Shorts Contest, above address

The Folger Shakespeare Library
201 East Capitol Street, SE
Washington, DC 20003

Folger Institute Programs offers *Grants-in-Aid* for participation in institute seminars to doctoral candidates and faculty from the institute's affiliated universities: American, Amherst, Catholic, Columbia, CUNY Graduate School and University Center, Delaware, Duke, Emory, George Mason, George Washington, Georgetown, Harvard, Howard, Johns Hopkins, Maryland-Baltimore County, Maryland-College Park, Massachusetts-Amherst, New York, North Carolina, North Carolina State, Pennsylvania, Pennsylvania State, Princeton, Rochester, Rutgers, St. Andrews, South Carolina, SUNY at Buffalo, Vanderbilt, Virginia, West Virginia, William and Mary, and Yale.

Available to: No restrictions
Deadlines: September 1 for fall semester; January 1 for spring semester
Apply to: Folger Institute, above address

Folger Library and NEH Fellowships
a) *Short-term Fellowships* (postdoctoral) offer up to $1,700 a month for a term of one to three months, and are available from July to June yearly.
b) *Folger Long-term Fellowships* and *National Endowment for the Humanities Senior Fellowships* (postdoctoral) offer stipends of up to $1,700 per month and $30,000 respectively for terms from six to nine months to senior scholars who have made significant contributions in their fields of research.

Available to: No restrictions
Deadlines: March 1 for short-term fellowships; November 1 for long-term fellowships
Apply to: Committee on Research Fellowship, c/o Carol Brobeck, above address

[IN] The *O. B. Hardison, Jr., Poetry Prize* awards $2,000 annually to a U.S. poet who has published at least one book within the last five years, has made important contributions as a teacher, and is committed to furthering the understanding of poetry. The prize was named to honor the memory of the former director of the Folger Shakespeare Library. *By Internal Nomination Only.*

The Formalist
320 Hunter Drive
Evansville, IN 47711

(P) The *Howard Nemerov Sonnet Award* offers $1,000 and publication in the *Formalist* for an original, unpublished sonnet. Writers may enter as many sonnets as they wish; there is a $2 per sonnet entry fee. Eleven other finalists will be published as well. Send an SASE for competition rules.

Available to: No restrictions

Deadline: June 15, 1996; inquire for 1997
Apply to: Howard Nemerov Sonnet Award, above address

Foundation for Iranian Studies
4343 Montgomery Avenue, Suite 200
Bethesda, MD 20814-4401

The foundation offers an annual prize of $1,000 for the best Ph.D. dissertation in the field of Iranian Studies. Students completing their dissertations between July 1, 1995, and June 30, 1996, are eligible to apply for the 1996 prize; the 1997 prize is for work completed between July 1, 1996, and June 30, 1997. Dissertations must be nominated by the author's advisor and be accompanied by the dissertation committee's letter of acceptance.

Available to: Ph.D. candidates in Iranian Studies
Deadline: August 1
Apply to: Above address

Four Way Books
PO Box 607
Marshfield, MA 02050

(P) The Four Way *Award Series in Poetry* offers $1,500 and publication of a book-length collection of poems by a U.S. poet who has already published at least one collection of poems. The award includes a reading in New York's CCS Reading Series. There is a $15 entry fee. Send an SASE for complete guidelines.

Available to: U.S. poets
Deadline: April 30
Apply to: Above address

(P) The Four Way *Intro Series in Poetry* offers $1,000 and publication of a book-length collection of poems by a U.S. poet who has not previously published a book of poetry. The award includes a reading in New York's CCS Reading Series. There is a $15 entry fee. Send an SASE for complete guidelines.

Available to: U.S. poets
Deadline: April 30
Apply to: Above address

The French-American Foundation
41 East 72nd Street, 2nd Floor
New York, NY 10021

(T) The *French-American Foundation Translation Prize* annually awards $5,000 for the best translation of a work from French into English published in the United States in the past year. All categories of prose are eligible, with the exception of technical, scientific and reference works, and children's literature. All translations must be submitted by publishing houses, not by individual translators. Please note that at press time, continued funding for the prize was uncertain.

Available to: No restrictions
Deadline: April 15
Apply to: Ellen Pope, above address

Friends of American Writers
c/o Kay O'Connor
15237 Redwood Lane
Libertyville, IL 60048

(C) The *Friends of American Writers Young People's Literature Award* offers two prizes of $800 annually for the best books written for young people from toddler to high school age.

Available to: Inquire for guidelines
Deadline: December 15
Apply to: Above address

Friends of the Chicago Public Library
400 South State Street, 10S-7
Chicago, IL 60605

(M) The *Carl Sandburg Literary Arts Awards* offer four awards, of $1,000 each, in the categories of poetry, fiction, nonfiction, and children's literature to Chicago-area residents or native Chicago writers who have published a book between June 1 and May 31 of the award year. Publishers or authors must submit two copies of the book.

Available to: Chicago-area residents or native Chicagoans
Deadline: August 1
Apply to: Chair, Carl Sandburg Literary Arts Awards, above address

The Fund for Investigative Journalism
1755 Massachusetts Avenue, NW, No. 324
Washington, DC 20036

(J) The Fund for Investigative Journalism "makes grants to writers to enable them to probe abuses of authority or the malfunctioning of institutions and systems which harm the public." The reports supported by the fund have been published in newspapers, magazines, as books, or have been broadcast. Some 700 grants totaling more than $600,000 have been awarded, primarily to free-lance investigative writers. No tuition support.

Available to: Anyone with a publisher's or producer's commitment
Deadline: No fixed date
Apply to: Anne Grant, Executive Director, above address

George Washington University
Department of English
Washington, DC 20052

(F)
(P) The *Jenny McKean Moore Fund for Writers* and George Washington University jointly engage a creative writer (a poet for 1996–97, a fiction writer for 1997–98) to teach two semesters at the university, and provide for a salary of approximately $40,000. A writing sample and a resume must accompany applications, as well as an SASE. The visiting lecturer is required to reside in Washington during the academic year.

Available to: No restrictions
Deadline: November 15
Apply to: Above address

Georgia Council for the Arts
530 Means Street, NW, Suite 115
Atlanta, GA 30318

Individual Artist Grants of up to $5,000 are awarded to writers based on merit and potential career benefit. Writers must be legal residents of Georgia for at least one year immediately prior to the application date. Applications cannot be made by students.

Available to: Georgia residents
Deadline: April 1
Apply to: Above address

Georgia State University Review
Georgia State University
PO Box 1894
Atlanta, GA 30303-3083

Ⓕ
Ⓟ The *GSU Review Writing Contest* offers a $1,000 prize for an unpublished story and an $800 prize for an unpublished poem. The winning entries will be published in the *Georgia State University Review*. Short story manuscripts should not exceed 10,000 words. Poets may submit up to three poems with no length limit. There is a reading fee of $10 for each story or group of three poems. Send an SASE for complete guidelines.

Available to: No restrictions
Deadline: April 30
Apply to: Writing Contest, above address

GERMANY
The Art Society (Künstlergilde)
Hafenmarkt 2
D-73728 Esslingen
Germany

Ⓜ The *Andreas-Gryphius Prize* is given for the best essay, novel, or poem which deals with the particular problems of the German culture in Eastern Europe. One award of DM 15,000 is available annually, as well as three awards of DM 7,000 each.

Available to: No restrictions
Deadline: Inquire
Apply to: Above address

Ⓟ The *Nikolaus-Lenau Prize of the Art Society* is awarded annually as part of an anonymous competition. A prize of DM 12,000 is offered for the three best poems in the German language.

Available to: No restrictions
Deadline: Inquire
Apply to: Nikolaus-Lenau Prize of the Art Society, above address

GERMANY
Stadt Buxtehude
Kulturabteilung
Stavenort 5
D 21614 Buxtehude
Germany

[IN] The *Buxtehude Bulle,* founded by the city of Buxtehude, is a literary prize awarded for the best children's book (for ages twelve to eighteen) published in Germany during the preceding year. One prize of DM 10,000 is awarded annually. *By Internal Nomination Only.*

GERMANY
DAAD (German Academic Exchange Service)
Jagerstrasse 23
D 10117 Berlin
Germany

Ⓡ The *Artists-in-Berlin Program* (*Berliner Künstlerprogramm*) invites approximately fifteen to twenty internationally known artists, as well as qualified young sculptors, painters, writers, composers, and filmmakers to spend twelve months in Berlin where they have the opportunity to continue their work undisturbed and to participate actively in the cultural life of the city.

Available to: No restrictions
Deadline: December 31 of each year
Apply to: Artists-in-Berlin Program, German Academic Exchange Service, 950 Third Avenue, New York, NY 10022.

DAAD also awards short-term grants for study, research, and information visits to Germany for scholars and Ph.D. candidates. Contact German Academic Exchange Service, at above address, for additional information.

GERMANY
German Academy for Language and Literature
Alexandraweg 23
64287 Darmstadt
Germany

IN The *Friedrich-Gundolf Prize* for the dissemination of German culture abroad is awarded to persons who have distinguished themselves in disseminating German culture abroad. A brochure can be requested under separate cover. One award of DM 20,000 is available annually. *By Internal Nomination Only.*

IN The *Johann-Heinrich-Voss Prize for Translation* is awarded annually for an outstanding lifetime achievement in translation into German. One award of DM 20,000 is available annually. *By Internal Nomination Only.*

GERMANY
Goethe Prize of the City of Frankfurt
Römerberg 23
60311 Frankfurt am Main
Germany

IN The *Goethe Prize of the City of Frankfurt* is given to a writer whose creative work has shown a continuation of Goethe's ideals and thoughts. One award of DM 50,000 is available every three years. *By Internal Nomination Only.*

GERMANY
Institut für Europaische Geschichte
Alte Universitätsstrasse 19
D-55116 Mainz
Germany

Grants for advanced study and research in Germany in the fields of modern and contemporary European history and the history of European religion with regard to the Reformation. Candidates must be university graduates. Several grants of DM 16,602 to DM 20,340, depending upon the academic degree of the applicant, are available annually.

Available to: Nationals of all countries, including U.S. citizens
Deadlines: Inquire
Apply to: For European history awards: Professor Heinz Duchhardt, Abteilung für Universalgeschichte, above address; for history of European religion awards: Professor H. Gerhard May, Abteilung für Abendländische Religionsgeschichte, above address

GERMANY
Kulturamt der Stadt Pforzheim
Neues Rathaus Marktplatz 1
75158 Pforzheim
Germany

The *Reuchlin Prize* is awarded by the city of Pforzheim every two years for an outstanding work in the humanities, written in the German language. One cash prize of DM 15,000 is awarded.

Available to: No restrictions
Deadline: Inquire
Apply to: Reuchlin Prize, above address

The Getty Grant Program
401 Wilshire Boulevard, Suite 1000
Santa Monica, CA 90401-1455

The J. Paul Getty Postdoctoral Fellowships in the History of Art and the Humanities are given to advance the understanding of art and its history by supporting the work of outstanding scholars at the early stages of their careers. The program especially encourages research that explores connections among the humanistic disciplines. A maximum of fifteen fellowships with stipends of $30,000 each are awarded for twelve-month periods.

Available to: Scholars whose doctorate (or the equivalent qualification in countries outside the United States) has been conferred between January 1, 1990, and January 1, 1996
Deadline: November 1
Apply to: Above address

Senior Research Grants provide opportunities for teams of scholars to pursue collaborative research for projects that offer new explanations of art and its history. Collaborations that foster a cross-fertilization of ideas and methodologies are particularly encouraged. Teams may consist of two or more art historians or museum curators, or of an art historian and one or more scholars from other disciplines. Applications for the development of basic research tools, such as computers, databanks, and art historical reference works, are not eligible. Stipends vary according to the needs of the project.

Available to: No restrictions
Deadline: November 1
Apply to: Above address

Gibbs Smith, Publisher
PO Box 667
Layton, UT 84041

(P) The *Peregrine Smith Poetry Competition* awards a $500 prize plus publication by Gibbs Smith, Publisher, for a book-length manuscript of poems, forty-eight to sixty-four typewritten pages. Submissions must be accompanied by a $15 reading fee and an SASE.

Available to: No restrictions
Deadline: Submissions accepted in the month of April only
Apply to: The Peregrine Smith Poetry Competition, above address

Gilman School
5407 Roland Avenue
Baltimore, MD 21210

(F)
(P) The *Reginald S. Tickner Writing Fellowship,* of $12,000, is awarded annually to a serious poet or fiction writer for the academic year. Responsibilities include teaching creative writing, directing a speakers' series, advising the literary magazine, and working one-to-one with students on their writing. Gilman School is an independent boys' school with coordinated classes with Bryn Mawr School and Roland Park Country School. Send an SASE for application guidelines.

Available to: No restrictions
Deadline: Applications considered from January 3 to February 5
Apply to: Meg Tipper, above address

Glimmer Train Press
812 Southwest Washington Street, No. 1205
Portland, OR 97205

(F) *Glimmer Train's Short Story Award for New Writers* offers $1,200 and publication in *Glimmer Train* for a short story by a writer whose fiction has not been published in a nationally distributed publication with a circulation of over 5,000. The first runner-up will receive $500. All applicants will receive the issue of *Glimmer Train* in which the winners are announced. Each entry may include up to two short stories between 1,200 and 8,000 words each. There is a $11 reading fee per entry. Send an SASE for complete guidelines and further information.

Available to: See above
Deadline: Submissions accepted in February and March and again in August and September
Apply to: Short Story Award for New Writers, above address

The Dick Goldensohn Fund Projects
175 Fifth Avenue, Suite 2245
New York, NY 10010

(J) The *Dick Goldensohn Fund* annually awards grants up to $5,000 (with an average of $1,500) to reporters, editors, and free-lance writers, or others working on innovative journalistic projects. The Fund's goal is "to foster journalistic undertakings that investigate abuses of the public trust, spotlight overlooked aspects of contemporary life, or promote social, political, and economic justice." Send an SASE for grant proposal procedure and details.

Available to: No restrictions
Deadline: March 1
Apply to: Above address

Goshen College
1700 South Main Street
Goshen, IN 46526

(D) The *Goshen College Peace Playwriting Contest* seeks unproduced, unpublished one-acts exploring a contemporary peace theme for its biennial competition. The winning entry will be awarded $500, production, and room and board for the playwright to attend rehearsals and/or production.

Available to: No restrictions
Deadline: December 31, in odd-numbered years
Apply to: Lauren Friesen, Director of Theatre, above address

Great Lakes Colleges Association
2929 Plymouth Road, Suite 207
Ann Arbor, MI 48105-3206

(F)
(P) The *New Writer Awards* are given in recognition of excellence for the best first book in the field of poetry and fiction published during the previous year. As soon as possible after publication of the book, each winning author is committed to make a visit to a number of the GLCA colleges, where he/she will receive recognition and participate in whatever promotional activities the colleges can arrange. The author will receive from each of the colleges visited an honorarium of at least $300, room and board, and transportation costs. Two awards, one poetry and one fiction, are available annually. Entries may be submitted by publishers only. Each publisher is limited to one entry in poetry and one in fiction.

Available to: No restrictions
Deadline: February 28

Apply to: Mark Clark, Director, GLCA New Writer Awards, GLCA Philadelphia Center, North American Building, 121 South Broad Street, Suite 700, Philadelphia, PA 19107

John Simon Guggenheim Memorial Foundation
90 Park Avenue
New York, NY 10016

Fellowships are given for research in any field of knowledge or creative work in any of the arts. Candidates should already have demonstrated exceptional capacity for productive scholarship or exceptional creative ability in the arts. The awards are ordinarily given for one year, but requests for periods as short as six months will be considered. About 152 awards, which averaged $28,105 in 1995, are available annually to scholars and artists in the U.S. and Canada competition.

Available to: U.S. and Canadian citizens or permanent residents
Deadline: October 1
Apply to: Above address

Hadassah Magazine
50 West 58th Street
New York, NY 10019

(F)   The *Harold U. Ribalow Prize* is given annually for an outstanding work of fiction on a Jewish theme. Any book of fiction first published in English in the calendar year preceding the prize year is eligible (books published in 1995 are eligible for the 1996 prize). The prize consists of $1,000 and publication of an excerpt in *Hadassah*.

Available to: Published authors of Jewish fiction
Deadline: Submissions accepted January 1 through April 1
Apply to: Harold U. Ribalow Prize, above address

The Hambidge Center
PO Box 339
Rabun Gap, GA 30568

(R)   Residency fellowships, from two weeks to two months, are available to artists in all fields. Every year the Center awards some seventy fellowships, with eight artists in residence at any one time. Each fellow is provided with a private cottage and a common evening meal. Send an SASE for further information and an application.

Available to: No restrictions
Deadline: January 31
Apply to: Send an SASE to Residence Program, above address

Harian Creative Books
47 Hyde Boulevard
Ballston Spa, NY 12020

(F)   The *Workshop Under the Sky Writing Award* is given for a previously unpublished manuscript of fiction, 3,000 to 20,000 words in length. Established as well as unpublished writers are eligible. "We wish to encourage writing with a social context without being preachy. Preference is for writing of resolution rather than revolution. Obscenity and violence are not encouraged." The award consists of publication and multiple copies, as well as $500, $300, $200, and several $100 prizes, if warranted by the quality of the entry. Send an SASE for complete guidelines.

Available to: No restrictions
Deadline: September 1
Apply to: Workshop Under the Sky Writing Award, above address

Harrisburg Area Community College
Rose Lehrman Arts Center, 213-E
1 HACC Drive
Harrisburg, PA 17110

(P)   The *Wildwood Prize in Poetry* offers $500 and publication in *Wildwood Journal* for an original, unpublished poem of 100 lines or fewer. Poets may submit up to three poems for consideration. There is a $5 reading fee. Send an SASE for guidelines.

   Available to: No restrictions
   Deadline: Submissions accepted from September 30 through November 30
   Apply to: T.H.S. Wallace, Director, Wildwood Prize in Poetry, above address

Harvard Review
Poetry Room
Harvard College Library
Cambridge, MA 02138

[IN]   The *Daniel A. Pollack-Harvard Review Prize* awards $1,000 annually to the author of a book of poetry, fiction, or literary nonfiction that has been discussed in the *Harvard Review*. By *Internal Nomination Only.*

[IN]   The *Ignatz and Berthe Zitomirsky Prize for Excellence in Reviewing*, awards $500 annually to the author of the best piece of criticism published in the *Harvard Review*. *By Internal Nomination Only.*

Harvard University Press
79 Garden Street
Cambridge, MA 02138

(N)   The *Robert Troup Paine Prize*, of $3,000, is given every four years to the best manuscript on a predesignated subject that has been accepted for publication by Harvard University Press in the preceding four years. The subject for the period January 1, 1994, to December 31, 1997, is the history of natural sciences. Authors will be paid royalties as well as the $3,000 prize.

   Available to: Authors whose manuscripts are book-length, unpublished, and original
   Deadline: December 31, 1997
   Apply to: Robert Troup Paine Prize, Michael G. Fisher, Science Editor, above address

HBO New Writers Project
Wavy Line Productions
2049 Century Park East, Suite 4200
Los Angeles, CA 90067

   The *HBO New Writers Project* is designed to encourage and cultivate a diverse new generation of multicultural writing and performing talent. The Project will select twenty-five scripts (one-act plays, solo performance pieces, short screenplays, or original half-hour teleplays, not to exceed sixty pages) for participation in a writers workshop sponsored by Home Box Office, in conjunction with Wavy Line Productions, with the intention that these works will be nurtured for further stage, television, or film development. Write for complete guidelines and application form.

   Available to: No restrictions
   Deadline: February 1
   Apply to: Steve Kaplan, above address

The Headlands Center for the Arts
944 Fort Barry
Sausalito, CA 94965

(R)   The Headlands Center, located in a national park, offers residences of one to six months for artists in all disciplines from certain states in the United States and abroad. (Eligible states, based on 1995 funding, currently include California, North Carolina, and Ohio; this may change in subsequent years.) Live-out, eleven-month residences are also available to Bay Area artists exclusively. Live-in residences include a monthly stipend of $500 and free housing; live-out residences for Bay Area artists include a $2,500 stipend and studio space. Residents are encouraged to interact with fellow artists and the environment.

Available to: Bay Area artists and residents of selected states
Deadline: June; inquire for exact date
Apply to: Above address

Hedgebrook
2197 East Millman Road
Langley, WA 98260

(R) Residences of one week to three months are available to women writers of diverse cultural backgrounds in six individual cottages on thirty wooded acres on Whidbey Island, near Seattle. Residence includes free room and board. Send an SASE for application form.

Available to: Women writers
Deadlines: September 30 for winter and spring; April 1 for summer and fall
Apply to: Above address

Heekin Group Foundation
PO Box 1534
Sisters, OR 97759

(F) The *James Fellowship for Novel-in-Progress* offers $3,000 to each of two writers who have never been published in the novel. Writers should submit the first fifty to seventy-five pages of their work-in-progress. There is a $20 application fee. Send an SASE for the required application and further information.

Available to: No restrictions
Deadline: December 1
Apply to: James Fellowship for Novel-in-Progress, above address

(C) The *Mary Molloy Fellowship for Children's Working Fiction* offers $2,000 to a writer who has never published a children's novel. Writers should submit the first thirty-five to fifty pages of their work-in-progress. There is a $20 application fee. Send an SASE for the required application and further information.

Available to: No restrictions
Deadline: December 1
Apply to: Heekin Group Foundation, Children's Literature Division, PO Box 209, Middlebury, VT 05753

(N) The *Siobhan Fellowship for Nonfiction Essay,* of $2,000, is offered to a writer who has never published a nonfiction essay. Writers should submit essay of 2,500 to 10,000 words. There is a $20 application fee. Send an SASE for the required application and further information.

Available to: No restrictions
Deadline: December 1
Apply to: Heekin Group Foundation, Nonfiction Division, PO Box 3385, Stamford, CT 06905

(F) The *Tara Fellowship in Short Fiction* offers $1,500 to each of two writers who have published five or fewer short stories in national publications. Writers may submit stories from 2,500 to 10,000 words. There is a $20 application fee. Send an SASE for the required application and further information.

Available to: No restrictions
Deadline: December 1
Apply to: Tara Fellowship in Short Fiction, above address

Helicon Nine Editions
9000 West 64th Terrace
Merriam, KS 66202

(F) The *Willa Cather Fiction Prize* offers a $1,000 award and publication by Helicon Nine Editions for an original, unpublished manuscript of fiction (a novella or short story collection) between 150 and 300 double-spaced pages. Work that has been previously published in magazines or anthologies may be included. There is a $15 reading fee. Send for complete guidelines.

(P) The *Marianne Moore Poetry Prize* offers a $1,000 award and publication by Helicon Nine Editions for an original, unpublished poetry manuscript of at least fifty pages. Work that has been previously published in magazines or anthologies may be included. There is a $15 reading fee. Send for complete guidelines.

Available to: No restrictions
Deadline: May 1
Apply to: Literary Prizes, above address

Hemingway Days Festival
PO Box 4045
Key West, FL 33041

[IN] The *Conch Republic Prize for Literature* is awarded to an author whose life's work reflects the daring and creative spirit of Key West. The award is made annually, and includes $1,000 and transportation and lodging so that the recipient can accept the award during the Hemingway Days Festival, held in honor of the Nobel laureate the third week in July. *By Internal Nomination Only.*

Hemingway Days Young Writers' Scholarships offer two unrestricted $1,000 scholarships to college-bound high school juniors and seniors who exhibit exceptional talent in the craft of writing. At least one of the scholarships will be awarded to a Florida resident, while the second is open to any student living in the United States. Applicants should send an SASE for information and required entry form.

Available to: College-bound high school juniors and seniors
Deadline: May 1
Apply to: Above address

(F) The *Hemingway First Novel Contest* offers $1,000 and literary representation for one year with a top New York agent to any writer who has never had a novel published. Writers must submit a copy of the completed novel along with a one- to five-page synopsis of the novel. There is a $20 entry fee. Send an SASE for guidelines and the required entry form.

Available to: No restrictions
Deadline: May 1
Apply to: Hemingway First Novel Contest, above address

(F) The *Hemingway Short Story Competition* offers a $1,000 first prize and two $500 runner-up prizes for short stories of any form or style, 3,000 words or less. The competition is open to writers whose fiction has not appeared in a nationally distributed publication with a circulation of over 5,000. There is a $10 reading fee. Send an SASE for guidelines.

Available to: No restrictions
Deadline: June 1
Apply to: Above address

Hemingway Western Studies Center
Boise State University
1910 University Drive
Boise, ID 83725

The *Rocky Mountain Artists'/Eccentric Book Competition* offers $500 and standard sales royalties for multiple-edition works (100 to 1,000 copies) relating to public issues, such as race, religion, gender, or the environment. The purpose of the annual contest is to "encourage the creation of beautiful, terrifying, intriguing and ingenious, as well as inexpensive books." Works with special relevance to Rocky Mountain audiences are preferred. Authors and artists may submit publication proposals. Works may consist of text and/or visual content.

Available to: U.S. writers
Deadline: Proposals accepted from September 1 through December 1
Apply to: Above address

The Heritage Foundation
214 Massachusetts Avenue, NE
Washington, DC 20002

Ⓙ The *Lawrence Wade Journalism Fellowship* is awarded annually to a journalism student or student journalist who best exemplifies the high ideals and standards of the late Lawrence Wade. The winning fellow receives a ten-week salaried internship at The Heritage Foundation in Washington and a $1,000 cash scholarship. Applicants must be enrolled full-time in an accredited college or university, working toward an undergraduate or graduate degree. It is not necessary to be studying or majoring in journalism or a related communications field. Write for complete application guidelines.

Available to: See above
Deadline: March 1
Apply to: Selection Committee, Lawrence Wade Journalism Fellowship, above address

Highlights for Children
803 Church Street
Honesdale, PA 18431

Ⓒ *Highlights for Children* sponsors an annual *Fiction Contest*. Previously unpublished short stories (for readers ages nine to twelve, a maximum of 900 words; for readers up to age eight, a maximum of 500 words) will be considered for three cash prizes of $1,000. All entries will be considered for regular publication with payment at regular rates. Stories should not include violence. For current category and details, send an SASE for guidelines.

Available to: No restrictions
Deadline: Submissions accepted January 1 through February 28
Apply to: Fiction Contest, above address

Ⓒ The *Highlights Foundation Scholarship Program* enables writers with a serious interest in writing for children to attend the Highlights Foundation Writers Workshop at Chautauqua. Awards vary in amount and requirements and will be awarded at the discretion of the Highlights Foundation Scholarship Committee. Query for guidelines.

Available to: Children's writers who have not previously attended the workshop
Deadline: Apply between December 15 and March 15
Apply to: Selection Committee, PO Box 686, Honesdale, PA 18431

The Sidney Hillman Foundation
c/o UNITE!
1710 Broadway
New York, NY 10019-5299

(J)
(N)
The *Sidney Hillman Foundation Prize Awards* for outstanding contributions dealing with themes relating to the ideals of Sidney Hillman, including "the protection of individual civil liberties, improved race relations, a strengthened labor movement, the advancement of social welfare and economic security, greater world understanding and related problems." Contributions may be in the fields of daily or periodical journalism, nonfiction, radio and television, and must have been published or produced in the current year. Several prizes of $1,000 each are awarded annually.

Available to: No restrictions
Deadline: January 15
Apply to: Jo-Ann Mort, Executive Director, above address

Hilton-Long Poetry Foundation
PO Box 21607
Detroit, MI 48221

(P)
The *Naomi Long Madgett Poetry Award* offers a cash prize of $500 and publication by Michigan State University Press as part of its Lotus Poetry Series for a volume of poems by an African-American poet. Send an SASE for guidelines.

Available to: African-American poets
Deadline: April 1
Apply to: Constance Withers, above address

The Historic New Orleans Collection
533 Royal Street
New Orleans, LA 70130-2179

(N)
The *General L. Kemper Williams Prizes in Louisiana History* are given annually for the best published and unpublished works of nonfiction dealing with Louisiana history. An award of $1,000 and a plaque are given for the best published book or article; $500 and a plaque are given for the best manuscript.

Available to: No restrictions
Deadline: February 1
Apply to: Chair, General L. Kemper Williams Prize Committee, above address

History of Science Society
University of Washington
Box 351330
Seattle, WA 98195

(N)
The *Pfizer Award* is given for the best book on the history of science in English (either as its original language or in translation) published during the preceding three years. One award of $2,500 is given annually.

Available to: No restrictions
Deadline: April 15
Apply to: Keith R. Benson, Executive Secretary, above address

(N)
The *Henry and Ida Schuman Prize* awards $250 annually for an original essay by a graduate student on the history of science and its cultural influences.

Available to: Graduate students
Deadline: April 15
Apply to: Keith R. Benson, Executive Secretary, above address

The George A. and Eliza Gardner Howard Foundation
Box 1956
Brown University
Providence, RI 02912

The *George A. and Eliza Gardner Howard Foundation* seeks to aid the personal development of promising individuals at the crucial middle stages of their careers. Nominees should have the rank of assistant or associate professor or their nonacademic equivalents. Support is intended to augment paid sabbatical leaves.

The foundation awards four to eight fellowships each year, with stipends of $18,000 for one-year terms for independent projects in fields selected on a rotational basis each year that the awards are made. For 1997–98 fellowships in history, including the history of science and archaeology, and political science will be offered. Fellowships are not available for work leading to an academic degree or for private study. Candidates must be nominated by a representative of an affiliated college or university, a professional critic, editor, or the director of a professional society.

> Available to: Candidates should normally be between the ages of twenty-five and forty-five
> Deadlines: October 15 for nominations; November 30 for completed applications with supporting materials
> Apply to: Henry F. Majewski, Administrative Director, above address

L. Ron Hubbard's Writers of the Future Contest
PO Box 1630P
Los Angeles, CA 90078

Ⓕ L. Ron Hubbard's *Writers of the Future Contest* is an international search for new and amateur writers of science fiction, fantasy, or horror short stories (under 10,000 words) or novelettes (under 17,000 words). Quarterly prizes: first place, $1,000; second place, $750; third place, $500. Annual grand prize $4,000. Submissions must be unpublished; no entry fee is required. Entrants retain all rights.

> Available to: Writers who have not professionally published a novel or short novel, more than three short stories, or more than one novelette
> Deadlines: December 31, March 31, June 30, and September 30
> Apply to: Send SASE to above address for rules

The Hudson Review
684 Park Avenue
New York, NY 10021

IN The *Bennett Award* is given to honor a writer of significant achievement whose work has not received the full recognition it deserves, or who is at a critical stage in his or her career—a stage at which a substantial grant might be particularly beneficial to furthering creative development. One prize of $20,000 is awarded biennially. The next award will be given in 1996. *By Internal Nomination Only.*

Hudson River Classics, Inc.
Box 940
Hudson, NY 12534

Ⓓ HRC's *Annual Playwriting Contest* offers $500, a staged reading, and room, board and travel to attend performances for an unpublished evening-length work (either a full-length play or a series of one-acts). HRC prefers work by New York State playwrights. There is a $5 entry fee.

> Available to: No restrictions, though New York State playwrights preferred

Deadline: June 1
Apply to: Annual Playwriting Contest, above address

Humboldt State University
English Department
Arcata, CA 95521-8299

(F) The *Raymond Carver Short Story Contest* annually awards $500 plus publication in *Toyon*, the HSU literary journal, to the best submitted short story, under twenty-five typed pages. A second prize of $250 is offered. No previously published work will be accepted. Writers should submit two copies of their manuscript and a $10 entry fee per story, payable to Raymond Carver Short Story Contest. The author's name should appear on a cover sheet only. For a list of winners include an SASE.

Available to: Writers living in the United States
Deadline: November 1
Apply to: Raymond Carver Short Story Contest, above address

ICELAND
Ministry of Culture and Education
Solvholsgata 4
IS-150 Reykjavik
Iceland

One award is offered for advanced study and research in the language, literature, and history of Iceland at the University of Iceland. Grants are given for a period of eight months, which includes tuition plus a cash stipend (currently $900 a month for eight-and-one-half months).

Available to: U.S. citizens
Deadline: October 31
Apply to: Institute of International Education, U.S. Student Programs Division, 809 United Nations Plaza, New York, NY 10017

Idaho Commission on the Arts
Box 83720
Boise, ID 83720-0008

At press time, the commission was restructuring its grant programs for artists and writers. The following programs may continue to be offered: *Fellowship Grants*, of $5,000, awarded to individual artists in fields including literature, theater, and media; *Sudden Opportunity Awards*, which offer up to $1,000 to support activities relevant to an artist's work and/or career; *Worksites Awards*, which offer up to $5,000 for artists wishing to work as apprentices with a master or artists seeking a residence at an artist colony; and the *Writer in Residence Program*, which provides $10,000 over a two-year term during which time the writer gives twelve readings or workshops in selected Idaho communities.

Available to: Idaho residents of one year prior to application; inquire for age requirements
Deadline: Inquire
Apply to: Literature Director, above address

Illinois Arts Council
James R. Thompson Center
100 West Randolph, Suite 10-500
Chicago, IL 60601-3298

(M) Artists' fellowships are offered in alternating years to Illinois writers of poetry and prose, and playwriting/screenwriting. Poetry and prose fellowships are offered in odd-numbered years; playwriting/screenwriting in even. The number and the amount of the fellowships vary from year to year. Write for guidelines before submitting manuscript.

Available to: Illinois writers
Deadline: September 1
Apply to: Communication Arts Program (poetry and prose) or Performing Arts Program (playwriting/screenwriting), above address

Ⓜ *Special Assistant Grants* are available to poets, prose writers, and playwrights as the budget allows. These are open-deadline, project-specific grants with a $1,500 maximum request which must be matched one-to-one with either cash or in-kind contributions.

Available to: Illinois writers
Deadline: Open (proposals accepted beginning July 1 for activities occurring between September 1 and August 31 of following year)
Apply to: Communication Arts Program (for poetry and prose) or Performing Arts Program (playwriting)

Indiana University-Purdue University at Indianapolis
National Youth Theatre Playwriting Competition
525 North Blackford Street
Indianapolis, IN 46202

Ⓓ The *IUPUI National Youth Theatre Playwriting Competition* biennially presents awards to the top ten finalists for professionally unproduced plays for youth. Four cash awards of $1,000 each will be received by the top four playwrights whose scripts will be showcased in polished readings at the National Youth Theatre Symposium held on the IUPUI campus. Send an SASE to receive contest and submission guidelines. Submissions must be accompanied by an official entry form.

Available to: No restrictions
Deadline: September 1, 1996, and 1998
Apply to: W. Mark McCreary, Youth Theatre Playwriting Competition, above address

The Ingersoll Prizes
The Ingersoll Foundation
934 Main Street
Rockford, IL 61103

ⅠⓃ The *T. S. Eliot Award for Creative Writing* and the *Richard M. Weaver Award for Scholarly Letters* are awarded annually to honor "authors of abiding importance" and to call public attention to their works. Authors "of international eminence in literature and humanities whose works affirm the moral principles of Western Civilization" are considered for $20,000 awards. *By Internal Nomination Only.*

Institute of Current World Affairs
The Crane-Rogers Foundation
4 West Wheelock Street
Hanover, NH 03755

One or two fellowships are awarded per year to individuals of high quality and unusual promise from varied academic and professional backgrounds, to observe and study firsthand particular foreign cultures of contemporary significance. Full support, including living and traveling expenses, is provided. Awards are not made to support work toward academic degrees or to underwrite specific programs of research as such, but are aimed at providing the opportunity to acquire a thorough knowledge and understanding of the forces at work in the chosen area. Duration of fellowships is two years.

Available to: Persons under age thirty-six
Deadline: None
Apply to: Peter Bird Martin, Executive Director, above address

Institute of Early American History and Culture
Box 8781
Williamsburg, VA 23185-8781

(N) The *Jamestown Prize* is offered for the best book-length scholarly manuscript on early American history or culture before circa 1815, or on the related history of the British Isles, Europe, West Africa, or the Caribbean during the same period. The prize competition is open only to authors who have not previously published a book. One award of $1,500 plus publication is available annually.

Available to: No restrictions
Deadline: None
Apply to: Editor of Publications, above address

The Institute for Humane Studies
George Mason University
4084 University Drive, Suite 101
Fairfax, VA 22031-6812

The *Assistance Fund for Professionals* offers grants of up to $1,000 to advanced students and young professionals pursuing careers in journalism, writing (fiction or nonfiction), film, or publishing. Grant recipients must provide a report of how the money was used and to what effect.

Available to: Seniors, graduate students, or young professionals
Deadline: Ongoing
Apply to: Assistance Fund for Professionals, above address

The *Humane Studies Fellowships* offer up to $18,500 in tuition and stipend to talented graduate and undergraduate students in the social sciences, humanities, jurisprudence, journalism, and related fields who intend to pursue academic or other intellectual careers, including public policy and journalism, and who have demonstrated an interest in classical liberal principles and the advancement of a free society of responsible individuals.

Available to: Graduate students, junior or senior undergraduates
Deadline: December 30
Apply to: Humane Studies Fellowships, above address

(D)
(F) *IHS Film & Fiction Scholarships* offer up to $10,000 in tuition and stipend to talented graduate students pursuing a Master of Fine Arts (M.F.A.) in film, fiction writing, or playwriting who have demonstrated an interest in classical liberal, or libertarian, principles.

Available to: Graduate students in the creative arts
Deadlines: January 15 (first stage); March 1 (second stage)
Apply to: Film & Fiction Scholarships, above address

The *Liberty in Film and Fiction Summer Seminar* awards places to undergraduates and graduate students worth $1,000. Places are open to students studying literature, cinema, drama, writing, and related areas. Students selected to attend are awarded full tuition, room and board, and are provided with study material and books.

Available to: Undergraduate and graduate students
Deadline: April 14, 1996; inquire for 1997
Apply to: Liberty in Film and Fiction Summer Seminar, above address

Institute of Industrial Engineers
25 Technology Park
Norcross, GA 30092

(N) The *IIE-Joint Publishers Book-of-the-Year Award* is given for an outstanding book directly concerned with one or more areas of industrial engineering. Entries must have been published in the United States or Canada in the year prior to the award presentation. One prize of at least $500 is awarded annually.

Available to: No restrictions
Deadline: Inquire
Apply to: IIE-Joint Publishers Book-of-the-Year Award, above address

(N) The *Outstanding IIE Publication Award* is given for the outstanding current original publication which has appeared in any IIE sponsored or cosponsored medium. The award is made to the author, or authors, of that published work which is judged to be a meritorious contribution to the profession of industrial engineering. A $2,500 cash award will be presented to the recipient at the International Industrial Engineering Conference.

Available to: IIE members
Deadline: Inquire
Apply to: Outstanding IIE Publication Award, above address

The *IIE Transactions Award* promotes excellence in industrial engineering research and applications by recognizing the best paper published in the "Feature Applications" department of *IIE Transactions*. A $1,000 cash prize is presented at the International Industrial Engineering Conference.

Available to: IIE members
Deadline: Inquire
Apply to: IIE Transactions Award, above address

Institute of International Education
U.S. Student Programs Division
809 United Nations Plaza
New York, NY 10017

The *Fulbright and Other Grants for Graduate Study Abroad* are available in academic fields and the creative and performing arts. One requirement is a proficiency in the language of the country to which they apply. The grants will cover the costs of international travel, tuition, living allowance, and health insurance.

Available to: U.S. citizens
Deadline: October 23
Apply to: Above address

Institute for the Study of Diplomacy
1316 36th Street, NW
Washington, DC 20007

(J) The *Edward Weintal Prize for Diplomatic Reporting* offers a cash award to reward initiative, hard digging, and bold thinking in the coverage of American diplomacy and foreign policy. The competition is open to both print and broadcast media. There is no standard entry form. A nomination should include clips (print media) or cassettes and transcript (broadcast media), a cover letter, and biographical material on the nominee.

Available to: No restrictions
Deadline: Mid-January; inquire for exact date
Apply to: Weintal Prize, above address

Inter-American Press Association Scholarship Fund
2911 NW 39th Street
Miami, FL 33142

(J) Scholarships are available to journalists in the print media between the ages of twenty-one and thirty-five for advanced study and research for six to nine months in Latin America. Candidates must have a well-defined program which will enable them to return to their country to carry forward the work of promoting understanding among the Americas.

Four grants of $10,000 each are awarded annually. The program also brings Latin American journalists to study in Canada or the United States.

Available to: U.S. and Canadian residents only
Deadline: December 31
Apply to: Above address

Intermedia Arts
425 Ontario Street, SE
Minneapolis, MN 55414

The *Intermedia Arts/McKnight Interdisciplinary Fellowship Program* annually awards five fellowships, of $12,000 each, to writers working in interdisciplinary forms who "exhibit an established commitment to exploring the changing relationships between artistic disciplines, diverse cultural forms and/or traditional expressions. Interdisciplinary work may be defined as work that fuses, integrates or explores the boundaries between at least two distinct art disciplines." Applicant must reside in Iowa, Kansas, Minnesota, Nebraska, North Dakota, South Dakota, or Wisconsin. Each grant recipient also receives an additional $2,000 to conduct or carry out an activity during a period of two years following the fellowship award that will promote their artistic development. Send an SASE for guidelines and application.

Available to: Residents of Iowa, Kansas, Minnesota, Nebraska, North Dakota, South Dakota, and Wisconsin
Deadline: November; inquire for exact date
Apply to: McKnight Interdisciplinary Fellowships, above address

INTERNATIONAL
The Abiko Quarterly
8-1-8 Namiki
Abiko-shi
Chiba-ken 270-11
Japan

Ⓕ
Ⓟ
The *Abiko Quarterly International Poetry and Fiction Contests* offer prizes of 100,000 Japanese yen (approximately $1,090) each for an unpublished poem and short story. The winning poem and story will be published in the *Abiko Quarterly*, an English-language journal of poetry, prose, and James Joyce studies published in Japan. Poets should send two copies of no more than three poems of fewer than 100 lines each. Short story writers should send a typed, double-spaced story of 5,000 words or less. For both contests, include a separate card with name and address, and a self-addressed envelope with two international reply coupons for notification (do not send U.S. postage). There is a $10 reading fee.

Available to: No restrictions
Deadline: December 31
Apply to: International Poetry and Fiction Contests, above address

INTERNATIONAL
Arvon Foundation
Kilnhurst, Kilnhurst Road
Todmorden, Lancashire OL14 6AX
England

Ⓟ
The *Arvon International Poetry Competition,* cosponsored by Duncan Lawrie Limited and the *Observer*, biennially awards one first prize of £5,000, five prizes of £500 each, and ten prizes of £250. All prize-winning entries will be published in an anthology. Competitors may submit as many entries as they wish, provided that each poem is accompanied by the entry fee ($7 in 1995; inquire for 1997). All poems must be written in English. Write for guidelines and entry form.

Available to: No restrictions
Deadline: Inquire (next award given in 1997)
Apply to: International Poetry Competition, above address

INTERNATIONAL
Biennale Internationale de Poésie
Chaussée de Wavre, 150
1050 Brussels
Belgium

☒IN *Le Grand Prix des Biennales* of 150,000 Belgian francs (approximately $4,000) is attributed by an international jury to a poet chosen for the worldwide significance of his or her work. The next award is given in Liège, Belgium, in September 1996. *By Internal Nomination Only.*

INTERNATIONAL
Simone and Cino del Duca Foundation
10, rue Alfred de Vigny
75008 Paris
France

☒IN The *Cino del Duca World Prize* is awarded in October of each year to encourage and promote a writer of any nationality whose work constitutes a message of humanity. The author's work should be of a scientific or literary nature. *By Internal Nomination Only.*

INTERNATIONAL
English Center of International PEN
7 Dilke Street
London SW3 4JE
England

Ⓕ The *UNESCO/PEN Short Story Prize* is awarded every two years for short stories of up to 1,500 words written in English by writers whose native language is not English. There is a $3,000 first prize, a $2,000 second prize, and a $500 third prize. Write for complete guidelines.

Available to: See above
Deadline: December 1996 (inquire for exact date)
Apply to: UNESCO/PEN Short Story Prize, above address

INTERNATIONAL
Federation Internationale des Traducteurs
Secretariat Permanent
Heiveldstraat 245
B-9040 SINT-Amandsberg (Ghent)
Belgium

Three international translation prizes are awarded by the FIT, for which American translators must apply through the American Translators Association.

Ⓣ The *Pierre-François Caille Memorial Medal* is awarded once every three years during an FIT congress for "promoting the standing and reputation of the translating profession on an international level." The recipient must be a member of an FIT member society; in the United States, this is the American Translators Association.

Ⓣ The *Astrid Lindgren Translation Prize* is awarded once every three years during an FIT congress; for "promoting the translation of works written for children."

Ⓣ The *Carl-Bertil Nathhorst Translation Prize* is awarded once every three years for "promoting translation, improving the quality thereof and drawing attention to the role of the translator in bringing the peoples of the world together." One-half of this award is for literary translation, one-half for scientific translation. Translators must be sponsored by a member society of FIT; in the United States, this is the American Translators Association.

Available to: Translators sponsored by a member society of FIT
Deadline: Six months in advance of an FIT congress; query American Translators Association for date
Apply to: American Translators Association, 1800 Diagonal Road, Suite 220, Arlington, VA 22314-2840, Attention: Walter Bacak

INTERNATIONAL
International League of Antiquarian Booksellers
Bibliographical Prize Secretary
Konrad Meuschel
Hauptstrasse 19A
D-53604 Bad Honnef/Rhine
Germany

IN   The *International League of Antiquarian Booksellers' Bibliography Prize* is awarded to the author of the best work, published or unpublished, of learned bibliography or research into the history of the book or of typography, and books of general interest on the subject. One prize of $10,000 is given every four years. The next award will be given in 1998.

Available to: No restrictions
Deadline: For 1998, December 31, 1996
Apply to: Above address

INTERNATIONAL
The Irish Times Ltd
10-16 D'Olier Street
Dublin 2
Ireland

IN   The *Irish Times Irish Literature Prizes*, of IR £5,000 each, are awarded biennially in three categories: fiction, nonfiction prose, and poetry. The authors must have been born in Ireland or be Irish citizens, although they may live in any part of the world. *By Internal Nomination Only.*

IN   The *Irish Times International Fiction Prize* awards IR £7,500 biennially to the author of a work of fiction written in English and published in Ireland, the United Kingdom, or the United States. There is no application process; nominations are submitted by a Screening Panel, consisting of literary editors and critics, based in Ireland, Europe and America. The next prizes will be awarded in 1997. *By Internal Nomination Only.*

INTERNATIONAL
Journalists in Europe
33, rue du Louvre
75002 Paris
France

J   The *Journalists in Europe* program gives journalists the opportunity to acquire first-hand
R   experience of European countries, to explore the ties between them and between Europe and the rest of the world, and to see how the European Union and its institutions work. The program lasts eight months, from October to June. Participants are based in Paris at the headquarters of the Centre de formation et perfectionnement des journalistes (CFPJ). Candidates must be between twenty-five and thirty-five years of age, be currently working journalists with at least four years' full-time experience, and should have a working knowledge of English and French. Write for complete information.

Available to: See above

Deadline: January 15
Apply to: Above address

INTERNATIONAL
The Mitchell Prizes
The Burlington Magazine
14-16 Duke's Road
London WC1H 9AD
England

The *Mitchell Prize for the History of Art* annually awards $15,000 to the author(s) of books in English which have made outstanding and original contributions to the study and understanding of the visual arts. Publications are assessed in terms of their scholarly, literary, and critical merit. Books must be published within the calendar year preceding the deadline. Publishers are asked to send titles of books they wish to nominate.

The *Eric Mitchell Prize* annually awards $5,000 for an outstanding first book of art history by a promising scholar. Other criteria and requirements are the same as for the Mitchell Prize.

Available to: No restrictions
Deadline: April 30
Apply to: Caroline Elam, above address

INTERNATIONAL
Alexander S. Onassis Public Benefit Foundation
56, Amalias Avenue
GR-105 58 Athens
Greece

Ⓓ The Alexander S. Onassis Foundation *International Competition* offers a first prize of $250,000, a second prize of $200,000, and a third prize of $150,000 for a new and original theatrical play "which deals with the problems facing man on the threshold of the twenty-first century." Plays may be written or translated into English, French, German, Greek, Italian, or Spanish. All submissions must be unpublished and unproduced. The foundation reserves the right to publish in Greek (at its own expense) the three winning plays and distribute up to 2,000 free copies of each work. The foundation also reserves the right (without royalties) to offer the three winning plays for performance to serious theatrical troupes in Athens or Salonica. Playwrights should submit three copies of their work by June 30, 1996.

Available to: No restrictions
Deadline: June 30, 1996
Apply to: Athens Cultural Center, above address

INTERNATIONAL
The Royal Exchange Theatre Company
St. Ann's Square
Manchester M2 7DH
England

Ⓓ The *Mobil Playwriting Competition* awards a £10,000 first prize for full-length plays in English, with possible production. A second prize of £5,000 and a third prize of £3,000 are also offered. Guidelines for the next competition are currently under review; do not submit a manuscript without querying first.

Available to: No restrictions
Deadline: Inquire
Apply to: Mobil Playwriting Competition, above address

INTERNATIONAL
Juan Rulfo Prize
Avenida Juárez 975
Guadalajara, Jalisco 44280
Mexico

(M) The *Juan Rulfo International Latin American and Caribbean Prize for Literature* awards $100,000
for a body of work by a native of Latin America or the Caribbean who writes in Spanish,
Portuguese, or English; or a native of Spain or Portugal who writes in Spanish or Portuguese. Any writer who has produced noteworthy work in the genres of poetry, novel,
drama, short story, or essay is eligible. The prize is funded by a group of twelve Mexican
government agencies, universities, and businesses. Nominations may be made by cultural or educational institutions, associations, or groups interested in literature. Nom-
inators should send the writer's curriculum vitae and additional supporting documents.

Available to: See above
Deadline: June 30
Apply to: Awards Committee, above address

INTERNATIONAL
Swedish Information Service
Bicentennial Fund
One Dag Hammarskjold Plaza, 45th Floor
New York, NY 10017

The Swedish Bicentennial Fund for the exchange of qualified persons from the United States
and Sweden provides opportunity for study and contact, for three- to six-week periods,
for persons who are in a position to influence public opinion and contribute to the
development of their society in areas of current concern. Approximately ten grants,
usually equal to 20,000 Swedish crowns each, are awarded annually. The grant is intended to partially cover transportation and living expenses for no less than three
weeks. The study project must be carefully defined, and should include a detailed plan
for achieving specific goals. Applicants who have visited Sweden many times previously
will be considered only in exceptional cases. Two letters of recommendation are required.

Available to: U.S. citizens or permanent residents
Deadline: The first Friday in February
Apply to: Write to above address for application form and guidelines

INTERNATIONAL
Amaury Talbot Fund
Barclays Bank Trust Company Ltd.
Octagon House
PO Box 27
Gadbrook Park, Northwich
Cheshire CW9 7RE
United Kingdom

(N) The *Amaury Talbot Fund Annual Prize*, of approximately £600, is given for the most valuable
work of anthropological research relating to Africa published in the calendar year for
which the prize is being awarded. First preference is given to works relating to Nigeria,
second preference to works relating to West Africa as a whole, and then to works relating
to the rest of Africa. Two copies of the work in question must be submitted; these are
not returnable.

Available to: No restrictions
Deadline: March 31, for work published in the previous calendar year
Apply to: Above address, quoting reference 66/61/888

INTERNATIONAL

UNESCO
International Book Award
c/o International Book Committee, Book and Copyright Division
Place de Fontenoy
75700 Paris
France

IN The *International Book Award* recognizes outstanding services rendered by a person or institution to the cause of books in such fields as authorship, publishing, production, book design, translation, library services, bookselling, encouragement of the reading habit, and promotion of international cooperation. Selection of the recipient is made by the International Book Committee on the basis of a majority vote of its members. *By Internal Nomination Only.*

International Quarterly
PO Box 10521
Tallahassee, FL 32303-0521

M The *Crossing Boundaries Writing Awards* offers four prizes of $500 each and publication in *International Quarterly* for poetry, fiction, nonfiction, and "crossing boundaries," a category that includes "atypical work and innovative or experimental writing." Translations into English are also accepted. There are no length requirements for poetry. The reading fee for poetry is $10 for a maximum of five poems. Writers in all other categories should submit a manuscript of no more than 5,000 words with a $10 entry fee. Send an SASE for complete guidelines.

Available to: No restrictions
Deadline: February 1
Apply to: Crossing Boundaries Awards, above address

International Reading Association
800 Barksdale Road
PO Box 8139
Newark, DE 19714

C The *International Reading Association Children's Book Awards* are given to authors whose early work shows unusual promise for a career in children's literature. The awards are given for a first or second book published during the calendar year, in any country and any language, and selection focuses on books of fiction or nonfiction of high literary quality. Three prizes of $500 each are awarded annually: one for literature for younger children (ages four to ten), one for literature for older children (ages ten to sixteen and up), and one for informational work.

Available to: Beginning authors of any nationality
Deadline: December 1
Apply to: Executive Offices, above address

The *Outstanding Dissertation of the Year Award*, of $1,000, is given annually for dissertations in reading or related fields. Studies using any research approach (ethnographic, experimental, historical, survey, etc.) are encouraged. Each study will be assessed in the light of this approach, the scholarly qualification of its report, and its significant contributions to knowledge within the reading field.

Available to: Doctoral candidates
Deadline: October 1
Apply to: Outstanding Dissertation of the Year Award, c/o Research Division, above address

82

The *Helen M. Robinson Award,* of $500, is given annually to assist doctoral students at the early stages of their dissertation research. Applicants must be members of the International Reading Association.

Available to: IRA members
Deadline: June 15
Apply to: Research Division, above address

© The *Paul A. Witty Short Story Award* offers $1,000 to an author of an original short story published for the first time during the calendar year in a periodical for children. The story should serve as a literary standard that encourages young readers to read periodicals.

Available to: No restrictions
Deadline: December 1
Apply to: Executive Offices, above address

International Research and Exchanges Board
1616 H Street, NW
Washington, DC 20006

Individual advanced research grants are available in all disciplines with an emphasis on projects in the humanities and social sciences. Grants are awarded for a period of two to twelve months for research in Central and Eastern Europe (Albania, Bosnia Hercegovina, Bulgaria, Croatia, the Czech Republic, Estonia, Hungary, Latvia, Lithuania, Macedonia, Poland, Romania, Slovakia, Slovenia, and the Federal Republic of Yugoslavia); Eurasia (Armenia, Azerbaijan, Belarus, Georgia, Kazakhstan, Kyrgyzstan, Moldova, Russian Federation, Tajikistan, Turkmenistan, Ukraine, and Uzbekistan); and Mongolia. Candidates normally must have U.S. citizenship or permanent residency, advanced graduate student status or a Ph.D., and command of the host-country language sufficient for advanced research. Grants vary according to the country of study and academic level, and normally cover round-trip airfare and visa fees, dollar stipend, stipend for host country room and board, local research allowance, excess baggage allowance, and, in some cases, support for accompanying family members. Other programs include research residences, language training and development, short-term travel grants, and special projects.

Available to: See above
Deadline: Varies by program; preliminary inquiries are encouraged
Apply to: Above address

International Society for Animal Rights
421 South State Street
Clarks Summit, PA 18411

Ⓝ The *Animal Rights Writing Award,* of $500, is given annually to the author of an exceptional book and/or article that advances the cause of animal rights. Full-length submissions may be fiction, nonfiction, or for children. The work must have been published in English. In the event of two awards in one year, each author will receive $250; if no submission is considered deserving, an award will not be given. Write for guidelines.

Available to: No restrictions
Deadline: September 1; submit five copies
Apply to: Helen Jones, Chairperson, Reviewing Committee, Animal Rights Writing Award, above address

The International Women's Media Foundation
1001 Connecticut Avenue, NW, Suite 1201
Washington, DC 20036

Ⓙ The *Courage in Journalism Award* recognizes journalists who have demonstrated extraordinary qualities pursuing the craft of journalism under difficult or dangerous circumstances.

The award consists of $2,000 and a crystal eagle, presented at ceremonies in New York City.

Available to: U.S. and international women journalists
Deadline: Inquire
Apply to: Sherry Rockey, Executive Director, above address

Intersection for the Arts
446 Valencia Street
San Francisco, CA 94103

Ⓜ The *Joseph Henry Jackson Award* is given to the author of an unpublished work-in-progress of fiction, nonfiction, short fiction, or poetry. One award of $2,000 is given annually.

Available to: Residents of northern California or Nevada (for three consecutive years prior to deadline date), twenty to thirty-five years of age
Deadline: January 31
Apply to: Above address

Ⓜ The *James D. Phelan Award* is offered to bring about a further development of native talent in California. The award is given for an unpublished work in progress of fiction (novel or short stories), nonfictional prose, poetry, or drama. One award of $2,000 is given annually.

Available to: Native-born Californians, twenty to thirty-five years of age
Deadline: January 31
Apply to: Above address

Ⓝ A *Special Award for Nonfiction,* of $1,000, is given to nonfiction writers who apply for either the Jackson or the Phelan award, but are not selected as winners. No separate application is required for this award.

The Iowa Review
308EPB
University of Iowa
Iowa City, IA 52242

The *Tim McGinnis Memorial Award,* in the amount of $500, is given irregularly by the *Iowa Review*. All work published in the *Review* is eligible for the award. There is no separate application process. Send an SASE for more information.

Available to: Contributors to the *Iowa Review*
Deadline: None
Apply to: Above address

Iowa State University
Department of English
203 Ross Hall
Ames, IA 50011-1201

The *Pearl Hogrefe Fellowship* is granted once each year to support beginning graduate study in creative writing. The fellowship, for a nine-month academic year, includes the cost of tuition plus a stipend of $875 a month. Write for application guidelines.

Available to: No restrictions
Deadline: January 31
Apply to: Above address

Iowa Woman
PO Box 680
Iowa City, IA 52244-0680

Ⓜ The *Iowa Woman Writing Contest* offers a first prize of $500 and a second prize of $250 to women writers of poetry, short fiction, and creative nonfiction. Winning entries will be published in *Iowa Woman*. Women writers should send no more than three poems, or one story or essay of 6,500 words or less. The reading fee is $15 per entry; additional submissions are $5 each, with a maximum of nine poems, three stories, or three essays. Send an SASE for complete guidelines.

Available to: Women writers
Deadline: Submissions accepted from November 15 to December 30
Apply to: Writing Contest, above address

IRELAND
The Tyrone Guthrie Centre
Annaghmakerrig
Newbliss
County Monaghan
Ireland

(R) The Tyrone Guthrie Centre offers one-week to three-month residences throughout the year to writers who have shown "evidence of sustained dedication and a significant level of achievement." Overseas writers are expected to pay the whole cost of residences, though the center does offer assistance in obtaining grants from cultural institutions in the writer's home country. Write for guidelines.

Available to: Established writers
Deadline: None
Apply to: Above address, or fax: 353-47-54380

Irish American Cultural Institute
One Lackawanna Place
Morristown, NJ 07960

(M) The *Irish American Cultural Institute Literary Awards* are given to encourage excellence among Irish writers who write in Irish or English. Any writer resident in Ireland with published works of fiction, poetry, or drama is eligible. Prizes are awarded biennially, a total of $15,000 a year. For details, contact the institute.

Available to: Residents of Ireland
Deadline: August 1
Apply to: Above address, or fax: 201-605-8875

ISRAEL
Mishkenot Sha'ananim
PO Box 8215
Jerusalem 91081
Israel

(R) Residences are available to writers throughout the year in a historical building. Residents are asked to contribute to the cost of their stay: $40 for a studio, $99 for a room, $147 for two rooms, $200 for three rooms. Prices are per night on a bed and breakfast basis. A few grants are available based on the nature of the work to be done in Israel. Write for further information, guidelines, and financial possibilities at least two months in advance of preferred dates of residence.

Available to: No restrictions
Deadline: Apply two months prior to preferred dates of residence
Apply to: Above address

ITALY
The Harvard University Center for Italian Renaissance Studies
Villa I Tatti
Via di Vincigliata 26
50135 Firenze FI
Italy

The Harvard University Center for Italian Renaissance Studies offers up to fifteen fellowships each academic year. These fellowships are available for postdoctoral scholars doing
advanced research in any aspect of the Italian Renaissance and are normally reserved
for scholars in the early stages of their careers, and for candidates whose projects require
their presence in Florence. The maximum grant will be no higher than $30,000; most
grants will be considerably less.

Available to: No restrictions
Deadline: October 15
Apply to: Villa I Tatti, Harvard University, University Place, 124 Mount Auburn Street,
Cambridge, MA 02138-5762. Please send original to the address in Italy above, and
a duplicate to the Villa I Tatti office at Harvard.

ITALY
Premi Feltrinelli
c/o Accademia Nazionale dei Lincei
Via Lungara 10
00165 Rome
Italy

IN The *Antonio Feltrinelli International Prize* is awarded to persons distinguishing themselves in
the arts and sciences. The prize is international, given to both Italians and foreigners,
and is awarded annually in rotation of subjects in the following fields: moral and historical sciences, physical sciences, medicine, the visual and performing arts, and letters
(which includes all forms of literature). The prize consists of a cash award of 200 million
lire (about $150,000). *By Internal Nomination Only.*

The Ivar Theater
1605 North Ivar Street
Los Angeles, CA 90028

D The *Inner City Cultural Center Competition* offers cash awards ($1,000 first prize, $500 second
prize, $250 third prize) or a paid professional internship with a film studio for one-acts,
translations, adaptations, or plays for young audiences. Fully mounted productions
(with a maximum running time of forty minutes, a small cast, and minimal sets) compete
in a series of elimination rounds. Translations and adaptations must be of unpublished
work. Write for guidelines.

Available to: No restrictions
Deadline: July 22, 1996; inquire for 1997
Apply to: Inner City Cultural Center Competition, above address

Rona Jaffe Foundation
c/o Private Founding Associates
345 East 80th Street
New York, NY 10021

IN The *Rona Jaffe Foundation Writers' Awards* offers several grants to women writers of fiction
and poetry. Grants are based on the writer's financial need, with a maximum award of
$7,500. There is no application process. *By Internal Nomination Only.*

Alice James Books. *See* **alicejamesbooks.**

JAPAN
Association of International Education
Information Center
4-5-29 Komaba
Meguro-ku
Tokyo 153
Japan

The *Monbusho Scholarships*, tenable in Japan, to university graduates, with preference to candidates in the fields of Japanese culture and science, or those for whom study in Japan is considered to enhance the value of their specific program. Grants for up to two years, covering tuition, transportation costs, and a stipend of 183,500 yen per month, are available annually.

Available to: U.S. citizens
Deadline: Varies; contact Japanese Embassy or nearest Consulate
Apply to: Consulate General of Japan for candidate's own area. Information can also be obtained from Japan Information Center, Consulate General of Japan, 299 Park Avenue, 18th Floor, New York, NY 10171

JAPAN
The Japan Foundation
New York Office
152 West 57th Street, 39th Floor
New York, NY 10019

Fellowships are offered to writers and other artists who wish to pursue creative projects in Japan and to exchange opinions with Japanese specialists. Fellowships are tenable in Japan for periods of two to six months during the Japanese fiscal year (April 1, 1996, to March 31, 1997) and are not normally renewable. Fellows receive stipends and other related living expenses. Tuition and fees may also be paid. Airfare to and from Tokyo will be provided for the fellow only.

Available to: U.S. citizens and permanent residents. All others apply to the Tokyo office: The Japan Foundation, Ark Hills Building, 21st Floor, 1-12-32 Akasaka, Minatyo-ku, Tokyo 107, Japan
Deadline: December 1
Apply to: Above address or nearest Consulate General of Japan office for Artist Fellowship application

JAPAN
The Donald Keene Center of Japanese Culture
407 Kent Hall
Columbia University
New York, NY 10027

(T) The *Friendship Commission Prize for the Translation of Japanese Literature* awards two prizes of $2,500 each for the best book-length translations of Japanese literature into English by an American translator. The translations may be of any works of Japanese literature from the classical, premodern and modern periods. Manuscripts, works-in-progress, and books published in the last two years may be submitted by eligible translators or their publishers. No translations of history or criticism are eligible.

Available to: American translators of book-length fiction, drama, literary essays, memoirs, and poetry
Deadline: December 31
Apply to: Above address

The Jerome Foundation
West 1050, First National Bank Building
332 Minnesota Street
Saint Paul, MN 55101

The *Jerome Foundation Travel and Study Grant Program* offers up to $4,000 twice yearly for travel in the United States and up to $5,000 for foreign travel to artists and art administrators in any discipline (including all literary and dramatic arts) to support a period of significant professional development through travel and study.

Available to: Residents of the Twin Cities metropolitan area
Deadlines: May 1 and October 1
Apply to: Above address

Jewel Box Theatre
3700 North Walker
Oklahoma City, OK 73118

Ⓓ The Jewel Box Theatre *Playwriting Award* offers $500 and possible production, to an unproduced, full-length play of "strong ensemble nature with an emphasis on character rather than spectacle." Write for complete guidelines and entry form.

Available to: No restrictions
Deadline: January 15
Apply to: Playwriting Award, above address

Jewish Book Council
15 East 26th Street
New York, NY 10010

Ⓜ The *National Jewish Book Awards* are given annually for published books, widely distributed in the United States, which are of literary merit and of Jewish interest. Awards of $750 are in the following categories: anthropology, autobiography/memoir, children's literature, contemporary Jewish life, fiction, the Holocaust, Israel, scholarship, illustrated children's books, Jewish folklore, Jewish history, Jewish thought, Sephardic studies, and the visual arts.

Available to: No restrictions
Deadline: Inquire
Apply to: Above address

Jewish Community Center
3505 Mayfield Road
Cleveland Heights, OH 44118

Ⓓ The *Dorothy Silver Playwriting Competition* offers a prize of $1,000 and a staged reading of the winning play at the JCC Theatre in Cleveland ($500 is awarded on announcement of the award and an additional $500 on or around the date of the reading, to help cover travel and "in-residence" expenses for the playwright). Submissions must be original works, suitable for full-length presentations; they must be previously unproduced at the time of submission and deal directly with the Jewish experience. The JCC Theatre will have permission to perform the first fully staged production of the winning script following the staged reading, without payment of additional royalties.

Available to: Playwrights whose previously unproduced entries deal with the American Jewish experience
Deadline: December 15
Apply to: Elaine Rembrandt, Director, JCC Theatre, above address

The Lyndon Baines Johnson Foundation
2313 Red River Street
Austin, TX 78705

A limited number of *Grants-in-Aid of Research,* ranging from $500 to $2,000, are available semi-annually for research at the Lyndon B. Johnson Library. The grant periods are September 1 through February 28, and March 1 through August 31. The funds are for the purpose of helping to defray living, travel, and related expenses incurred while conducting research at the Johnson Library. Prior to submitting a grant-in-aid proposal, it is strongly recommended that applicants write to the chief archivist of the library at the above address to obtain information about materials available in the library on the proposed research topic.

Available to: Scholars and graduate students
Deadlines: July 31 for the period September through February; January 31 for the period March through August
Apply to: Executive Director, above address

The Chester H. Jones Foundation
PO Box 498
Chardon, OH 44024

Ⓟ The *National Poetry Competition* offers prizes of $1,000, $750, $500, $250, $100, and $50, plus publication in the foundation anthology. Competitors may submit no more than ten poems ($2 entry fee for the first poem, $1 after that). All poems must be written in English and not have been previously published or broadcast. Send an SASE to the above address for an entry form and brochure.

Available to: U.S. and Canadian citizens and residents
Deadline: March 31
Apply to: National Poetry Competition, above address

Alfred Jurzykowski Foundation
21 East 40th Street
New York, NY 10016

The *Alfred Jurzykowski Foundation Awards* are granted to scholars, writers, composers, musicologists, and artists for significant career achievements in the arts and sciences, and to emphasize Polish contributions to the intellectual and artistic life of mankind. Awards are also made for translations of Polish literature into other languages. Individuals may not apply; scholarly and cultural institutions, members of the Cultural Advisory Committee of the foundation, and experts in respective fields may submit nominations. Candidates should be of Polish ethnic background, except candidates for the translation award. Currently nine awards of $6,000 each are given annually; the translation awards are $3,000 each.

Available to: For translators, no restrictions; for all other awards, people of Polish ethnic background
Deadline: Inquire
Apply to: By nomination only; for further information, contact the Cultural Advisory Committee, 15 East 65th Street, New York, NY 10021

Kalliope, a journal of women's art
Florida Community College at Jacksonville
3939 Roosevelt Boulevard
Jacksonville, FL 32205

Ⓟ The *Sue Saniel Elkind Poetry Contest* offers $1,000 plus publication in *Kalliope* for the best unpublished poem, up to forty lines, written by a woman. The entry fee is $3 per poem, or four poems for $10. Send an SASE for guidelines.

Available to: Women
Deadline: November 1
Apply to: Sue Saniel Elkind Poetry Contest, above address

Kappa Tau Alpha
University of Missouri
School of Journalism, Box 838
Columbia, MO 65205

Ⓝ The *Frank Luther Mott KTA Research Award,* of $1,000, is given annually to the author of a published book concerned with journalism research. Applicants should submit six copies of the book (carrying a 1996 copyright for the 1997 award).

Available to: No restrictions
Deadline: January 15
Apply to: Dr. Keith Sanders, Executive Director, above address

John F. Kennedy Library Foundation
JFK Library
Columbia Point
Boston, MA 02125-3313

The *Hemingway Research Grants,* ranging from $200 to $1,000, are offered to five to ten scholars and writers, to help defray living, travel, and related costs incurred while doing research in the Hemingway Collection. Grant applications are evaluated on the basis of expected utilization of the Hemingway Collection, the degree to which projects address research needs in Hemingway or related studies, and the qualifications of applications.

Available to: No restrictions (though preference is given to dissertation research by Ph.D. candidates)
Deadline: March 15
Apply to: Hemingway Research Grants, above address

The *Kennedy Library Research Grants,* ranging from $500 to $1,500, are offered to between fifteen and twenty scholars and students, to help defray living, travel, and related costs incurred while doing research in the textual and nontextual holdings of the library. Grant applications are evaluated on the basis of expected utilization of available holdings of the library, the degree to which they address research needs in Kennedy period studies, and the qualifications of the applicants.

Available to: No restrictions (though preference is given to dissertation research by Ph.D. candidates)
Deadlines: March 15 for spring grants; August 15 for fall grants
Apply to: William Johnson, Chief Archivist, above address

The *Marjorie Kovler Research Fellowship,* of $2,500, is intended to support a scholar in the production of a substantial work in the area of foreign intelligence and the presidency or a related topic.

Available to: No restrictions
Deadline: March 15
Apply to: William Johnson, Chief Archivist, above address

The *Arthur M. Schlesinger, Jr., Research Fellowship,* of $5,000, is intended to support scholars in the production of substantial works on the foreign policy of the Kennedy years, especially with regard to the western hemisphere, or on Kennedy domestic policy, especially with regard to racial justice and to the conservation of natural resources. The fellowship may be awarded to a single individual or divided between two recipients.

Available to: No restrictions
Deadline: August 15
Apply to: William Johnson, Chief Archivist, above address

The *Abba P. Schwartz Research Fellowship*, of $3,100, is intended to support a scholar in the production of a substantial work in the areas of immigration, naturalization, or refugee policy.

Available to: No restrictions
Deadline: March 15
Apply to: William Johnson, Chief Archivist, above address

The *Theodore C. Sorensen Research Fellowship*, of $3,600, is intended to support a scholar in the production of a substantial work in the areas of domestic policy, political journalism, polling, or press relations.

Available to: No restrictions
Deadline: March 15
Apply to: William Johnson, Chief Archivist, above address

Robert F. Kennedy Awards
1206 30th Street, NW
Washington, DC 20007

(F) The *Robert F. Kennedy Annual Book Award*, of $2,500, will be given for the best book of fiction or nonfiction published during the previous year. Four copies of each book submitted (N) should be accompanied by a letter of introduction or press release, and an entry blank. There is a $25 handling fee per entry.

Available to: Published authors of fiction and nonfiction
Deadline: Early January; query for exact date
Apply to: Merrill Warshoff, above address

(J) Nine *Robert F. Kennedy Journalism Awards for Outstanding Coverage of the Problems of the Disadvantaged*, of $1,000 each, are available annually in the categories of print (newspaper, magazine), cartoons, television, radio, photojournalism, international print, international broadcast, international radio, and international photojournalism. At the discretion of the awards committee, an additional grand prize of $2,000 may be awarded to the most outstanding of the seven category winners. The competition is open to both professional and student journalists (college undergraduates), whose entries will be judged separately. Query for guidelines.

Available to: See above
Deadline: The last Friday in January
Apply to: Erin P. Scully, Director, above address

The Kennedy Center
American College Theatre Festival
Washington, DC 20566-0001

The Kennedy Center American College Theater Festival (KC/ACTF) holds several regional festivals with workshops each year. Every college and university theater is eligible and encouraged to participate. Through the festivals, regional finalists are invited to Washington to take part in a two-week, noncompetitive festival at the Kennedy Center, including transportation, lodging, and a per diem. The following awards, which comprise the *Michael Kanin Playwriting Awards Program*, are available to student playwrights whose plays are produced as part of the festival.

(D) The *Anchorage Press Theatre for Youth Playwriting Award* is given for a festival student-written play on a theme appealing to young people from kindergarten through twelfth grade. The award consists of a cash prize of $1,000 and a fellowship to either the New Visions/ New Voices festival at the Kennedy Center or, in alternate years, the Bonderman/IUPUI festival in Indianapolis. In addition Anchorage Press will publish the winning play, lease it for production, and send the author royalty moneys on his or her behalf.

Ⓓ The *Fourth Freedom Forum Playwriting Award* is given for the best plays written on the themes of world peace and international disarmament. The first place award consists of a $5,000 cash prize and a fellowship to the Sundance Playwrights Laboratory. A second place award of $2,500 is also given. Grants of $1,500 and $1,000 will be made to the theater departments of the colleges and universities producing the first- and second-place winners, respectively.

Ⓓ The *KC/ACTF College Musical Theater Award* is given for outstanding achievement in the creation of a work for the musical theater by college and university students. First prize: $1,000 for lyrics, $1,000 for music, $1,000 for book, $1,000 to the institution producing the musical. The musical must be produced by a college or university participating in the ACTF. Fifty percent of the creative team must be students.

Ⓓ The *Lorraine Hansberry Award* is presented for the best written play by a student on the subject of the black experience. The first prize consists of a $2,500 cash prize, a fellowship to the Shenandoah Playwrights Retreat, and publication of the play by Dramatic Play Service. The second prize is $1,000. Grants of $750 and $500 will be made to the theater departments of the college or university producing the play.

Ⓓ The *National AIDS Fund Award for Playwriting* is given for the best new collegiate writing concerning the personal and social implications of HIV/AIDS. The winner will receive a cash award of $2,500 and a fellowship to attend the Bay Area Playwrights Festival in San Francisco.

Ⓓ The *National Student Playwriting Award* is given for the best production written by a full-time graduate or undergraduate student who is a participant in the regional festivals. The award consists of a cash prize of $2,500, membership in the Dramatists Guild, production at the Kennedy Center, a publication contract with royalties through Samuel French, and a three-week fellowship to the Mount Sequoyah New Play Retreat.

Ⓓ The *Short Play Awards Program* recognizes two or three outstanding productions of short plays in U.S. colleges each year, with consideration for presentation at the national festival at the Kennedy Center. The award consists of a cash prize of $1,000, publication and catalog listing by Samuel French, and membership in the Dramatist Guild. A short play is defined as a play of one act without intermission that, within itself, does not constitute a full evening of theater.

Available to: College and university students
Deadline: December 1
Apply to: Contact the above address for application procedures for the festival and awards program

Kent State University
Department of English
PO Box 5190
Kent, OH 44242-0001

Ⓟ The *Stan and Tom Wick Poetry Prize,* of $1,000, is given for a first book of poems in English by a writer who has not previously published a book of poetry. The winning collection will be published by Kent State University Press. Manuscripts should be between forty-eight and sixty-eight pages; the poet's name must not appear within the manuscript. Submissions should include a cover sheet with the applicant's name, address, telephone number, and title of the manuscript. There is a $10 reading fee for each submission.

Available to: No restrictions
Deadline: May 1
Apply to: Stan and Tom Wick Poetry Prize, above address

Kentucky Arts Council
31 Fountain Place
Frankfort, KY 40601

Ⓜ Kentucky artists' fellowships, of $5,000, are available every other year to Kentucky residents in areas including poetry, fiction, and playwriting.

> Available to: Kentucky residents
> Deadline: September 15 (in even-numbered years)
> Apply to: Write for application to Fellowships Director, above address, in June 1996

Kentucky Foundation for Women
The Heyburn Building, Suite 1215
Louisville, KY 40202

Grants are available biennially to women writers in Kentucky whose work "focuses on a feminist, not feminine, consciousness." The Foundation seeks to support writers "who describe the realities of women's lives, who experiment in style and substance, analyze language, or who are working to enlarge the feminist literary and historical heritage." *Project Grants*, of $3,000 and $5,000, are awarded for specific projects; *Process Grants*, of $3,000 and $5,000, are awarded for the on-going creative process of persons who have a track record of producing work in line with KFW goals; *Encouragement Grants*, of $1,000, are also awarded to encourage an applicant who has not received a full grant. Write for further information and complete guidelines.

> Available to: Feminist writers who live or work in Kentucky or whose work directly affects the lives of women in Kentucky
> Deadline: October 1, 1996
> Apply to: Above address

KOREA
The Korean Culture and Arts Foundation
Literature & Fine Arts Department
1-130, Dongsoong-dong, Chongro-ku
Seoul 110-510
Korea

Ⓣ The *Korean Literature Translation Award* biennially offers a $50,000 grand prize for the best published translation from Korean into another language. Two work-of-merit prize winners will receive $10,000 each. If no work is deemed of sufficient merit for the grand prize, the finest entry will be awarded $30,000. The publisher of the grand-prizewinning book will receive $10,000. Submissions may be in any literary genre (collections of poems, short stories, plays, literary criticism, novels, various types of anthologies). Write for additional information and guidelines.

> Available to: No restrictions
> Deadline: 1997; inquire for exact date
> Apply to: Korean Literature Translation Award, above address

Kosciuszko Foundation
15 East 65th Street
New York, NY 10021-6595

Scholarships and grants are available for candidates specializing in the Polish language, literature, and history; for "research and publication of scholarly books on topics pertaining to Polish history and culture and such other programs and activities as are designed to acquaint Americans in general with the Polish cultural heritage." Grants range from $500 to $1,500 and may be used in the United States or Poland. Send an SASE for application information. Graduate and postgraduate research grants are also available to university faculty for research in Poland.

Available to: U.S. residents and permanent resident Poles
Deadline: Inquire
Apply to: Grants Office, above address

Lake Forest College
555 North Sheridan Road
Lake Forest, IL 60045

(N) The *Bross Prize* will be given to the best book on the relation between any discipline or any topic of investigation and the Christian religion. The award is given every ten years. The next award will be in 2000. At least $20,000 will be awarded in one to three prizes. Three typewritten copies of each manuscript must be submitted or the author will be asked to assume the copying costs.

Available to: No restrictions
Deadline: Summer, 2000
Apply to: Bross Prize, Religion Department, above address

Latin American Writers Institute
Hostos Community College
500 Grand Concourse
Bronx, NY 10451

(F) The *Latino Literature Prize* offers $1,000 in both poetry and fiction to Latino writers living in the United States who have published a book in the year preceding the award deadline.
(P) Books may be written in Spanish or English or in bilingual format. Translations are not eligible. Writers or their publishers should submit four copies of their book and a brief biography.

Available to: Latino writers living in the United States
Deadline: February 28
Apply to: Latino Literature Prize, above address

Ledig House International Writers' Colony
43 Letter S Road
Ghent, NY 12075

(R) Residences of two weeks to two months are available to writers in all fields during two sessions: April through June and mid-August through October. Applications are accepted at any time and should include a letter of recommendation, a biographical sketch, a non-returnable copy of recent published work, and a one-page description of work to be undertaken at Ledig House. Ledig also offers residences to art critics, curators, and art historians from the end of July to mid-August. Write for further details.

Available to: English speaking writers
Deadline: Ongoing
Apply to: The Executive Director, above address

The Leeway Foundation
PO Box 30065
Philadelphia, PA 19103

The *Leeway Grants to Individual Women Artists* are awarded annually to women who reside in Bucks, Chester, Delaware, Montgomery, or Philadelphia County of Pennsylvania and are twenty-five years or older. Each year grants are awarded in a selected discipline. Literary grants were awarded in 1995 (four writers received $14,000 each). Contact the foundation for guidelines and deadlines for the next round of literature grants.

Available to: Women residents of Bucks, Chester, Delaware, Montgomery, or Philadelphia County, Pennsylvania

Deadline: Inquire
Apply to: Above address

The *Bessie Berman Grant* is given "to recognize and promote the advancement of mature, dedicated women artists who are fifty years old or older and live in the Philadelphia area." The grant is awarded annually for excellence in the same discipline as the Leeway Grants for that year.

Available to: Women residents of Bucks, Chester, Delaware, Montgomery, or Philadelphia County, Pennsylvania
Deadline: Inquire
Apply to: Bessie Berman Grant, above address

Lincoln College
300 Keokuk Street
Lincoln, IL 62656

(P) The *Billee Murray Denny Poetry Contest* awards a $1,000 first prize, a $500 second prize, and a $250 third prize for an unpublished poem under 100 lines. Applicants may submit up to three unpublished poems at $10 per poem title (include an SASE with submission).

Available to: No restrictions
Deadline: May 31
Apply to: Billee Murray Denny Poetry Contest, c/o Janet Overton, above address

Literary Arts
720 SW Washington, Suite 745
Portland, OR 97205

(M) *Oregon Literary Fellowships,* which range from $500 to $2,000, are awarded to Oregon writers in two categories: emerging writers and published writers. The intention of the fellowships is to help those in need of funds to initiate, develop, or complete a literary project in the areas of poetry, drama, fiction, literary nonfiction, and young readers' literature. The *William Stafford Fellowship in Poetry,* of $2,000, is awarded to the best poetry manuscript among all those submitted for the Emerging Writers Fellowship. Write for complete guidelines.

Available to: Oregon writers
Deadline: June 30, 1996; inquire for 1997
Apply to: Oregon Literary Fellowships, above address

(M) The *Oregon Book Awards* consist of the *Hazel Hall Award for Poetry,* the *H. L. Davis Award for Fiction,* the *Frances Fuller Victor Award for Creative Nonfiction,* and *the Mary Jane Carr Award for Young Readers' Literature.* Each award includes a cash prize of $1,000 and is given to outstanding Oregon authors for works published during the twelve months ending March 31. Publishers, authors, or friends may nominate books by Oregon residents. Write for complete guidelines.

Available to: Oregon residents
Deadline: March 31
Apply to: Oregon Book Awards, above address

Live Oak Theatre
200 Colorado Street
Austin, TX 78701

(D) Live Oak Theatre's *Harvest Festival of New American Plays* offers $1,000 plus full production with royalties, and travel and room and board to attend the fall festival of staged readings for the best full-length American play. Live Oak Theatre also awards the *Larry King Playwriting Award for Best Texas Playwright,* of $500. Send an SASE for guidelines.

Available to: U.S. citizens and, for the Larry King Award, residents of Texas

Deadline: Inquire
Apply to: Tom Byrne, Literary Manager, above address

The Gerald Loeb Awards
John E. Anderson Graduate School of Management at UCLA
PO Box 951481
Los Angeles, CA 90095-1481

(J) The *Gerald Loeb Awards* recognize distinguished work in business and financial journalism. Entries must be postmarked on or before February 15 and must have been published in a commercial American publication during the previous calendar year. Awards of $1,000 are made to writers in six categories: large newspapers, medium-sized newspapers, small newspapers, magazines, commentary, and deadline/beat writing. Publishers also receive a plaque.

Available to: Writers for American commercial publications
Deadline: February 15 for material published during the preceding calendar year
Apply to: Above address

The Loft
Pratt Community Center
66 Malcolm Avenue Southeast
Minneapolis, MN 55414

(M) The *Loft-McKnight Awards of Distinction* offer $10,500 to Minnesota poets and fiction/literary nonfiction writers with significant publication credits. Two awards are given annually; poets are honored in even-numbered years; prose writers in odd-numbered years. Send an SASE for complete guidelines.

Available to: Minnesota residents
Deadline: Mid-November; query for exact date
Apply to: Loft-McKnight Awards of Distinction, above address

The *Loft-McKnight Awards* annually offer $7,500 to each of eight Minnesotan poets and creative prose writers. Send an SASE for complete guidelines.

Available to: Minnesota residents
Deadline: Mid-November; query for exact date
Apply to: Loft-McKnight Awards, above address

Longwood College
Department of English
Farmville, VA 23901

[IN] The *John Dos Passos Prize for Literature* is given annually to a writer with a substantial publication record. The committee is especially interested in writers in "mid-career whose work is experimental in nature, wide in scope, and/or consonant with the work of the author for whom the prize is named." A medal for literary achievement and a cash prize of $1,000 are awarded each year. *By Internal Nomination Only.*

Los Angeles Times Book Prizes
Times Mirror Square
Los Angeles, CA 90053

[IN] The *Los Angeles Times Book Prizes* are given in the following categories: fiction, poetry, history, biography, current interest, science-and-technology, first fiction (the *Art Seidenbaum Award*), and for a body of work by a writer living in or writing on the American West (the *Robert Kirsch Award*). To be eligible, books must have been published in English in the United States between August 1 and July 31. The winner in each category receives $1,000 and a citation. *By Internal Nomination Only.*

Louisiana State Arts Council
Louisiana Division of the Arts
PO Box 44247
Baton Rouge, LA 70804

(M) Two fellowships of up to $5,000 are given annually to Louisiana writers of poetry, fiction, and nonfiction. Applications must have been residents of Louisiana for at least two years prior to the application date. Write for the required application and further guidelines.

Available to: Louisiana residents
Deadline: Postmarked by March 1
Apply to: Above address

The Louisville Review
Department of English
315 Humanities
University of Louisville
Louisville, KY 40292

(F)
(P) The *Louisville Review* offers $500 and publication for poetry and fiction. Writers may submit seven pages of poetry and twenty pages of fiction, along with an SASE and a $10 entry fee. Only previously unpublished work will be considered.

Available to: No restrictions
Deadline: December 31
Apply to: Above address

Love Creek Productions
c/o Cynthia Granville
79 Liberty Place
Weehawken, NJ 07087-7014

(D) The *Short Play Festival* selects up to fifty-two finalists yearly to receive a mini-showcase production in New York City. The best in competition receives a cash prize. Entries should contain at least two characters, be under forty minutes long, unpublished, and unproduced in New York City in the past year. Authors must enclose a permission letter for Love Creek to produce their play if chosen and should state if an Equity showcase is acceptable. Several times yearly Love Creek also presents minifestivals on specified themes with cash prizes. Send an SASE for minifestival schedules, themes, and deadlines.

Available to: No restrictions
Deadline: October 1 for Short Play Festival
Apply to: Short Play Festival or Minifestivals, above address

The Amy Lowell Poetry Travelling Scholarship
Choate, Hall & Stewart
Exchange Place, 34th Floor
Boston, MA 02109

(P) The *Amy Lowell Poetry Travelling Scholarship* awards approximately $29,000 annually to an American-born poet to enable that person to spend one year outside the continent of North America in whatever place the recipient feels will most advance his/her work in poetry. Although it is not a requirement of the scholarship, applicants are strongly advised to note that recipients in recent years have been published poets who have reached a professional standing. Write for application guidelines.

Available to: U.S. citizens
Deadline: October 15
Apply to: F. Davis Dassori, Jr., above address

Lullwater Review
Emory University
Box 22036
Atlanta, GA 30322

(P) The *Lullwater Prize for Poetry* awards $500 and publication in the *Lullwater Review*. Poets may submit up to five poems. All submissions will be considered for publication. There is an $8 reading fee, which includes a copy of the *Lullwater Review*. Send an SASE for complete guidelines.

    Available to: No restrictions
    Deadline: Early March; inquire for exact date
    Apply to: Lullwater Prize for Poetry, above address

Lynchburg College
Department of English
Lynchburg, VA 24501

(R) Each semester, the *Richard H. Thornton Writer-in-Residence* program selects a fiction writer, playwright, or poet to spend eight weeks in residence at Lynchburg College in Virginia. The writer receives a stipend of $8,000 and is provided with housing and meals at the college. Although considerable time is reserved for the writer's own work, the resident must also teach a weekly seminar to advanced level undergraduate writers, give one public reading on campus, and visit classes as a guest speaker.

    Available to: Writers with at least one published book and evidence for effective teaching
    Deadlines: Candidates should apply by March 1 for fall term residences and by September 1 for spring term residences
    Apply to: Send resume and cover letter outlining qualifications to Tom Allen, Thornton Chair, Richard H. Thornton Writer-in-Residence, above address

John D. and Catherine T. MacArthur Foundation
140 South Dearborn Street
Chicago, IL 60603

[IN] The *MacArthur Fellows Program* provides unrestricted fellowships to exceptionally talented and promising individuals who have given evidence of originality, dedication to creative pursuits, and capacity for self-direction. MacArthur Fellows receive an income, ranging from $30,000 to $75,000 annually, over five years so that they may have the time and freedom to fulfill their promise by devoting themselves to their own endeavors at their own pace. There is no application process. *By Internal Nomination Only.*

Research and Writing Grants for Individuals, ranging from $10,000 to $65,000, are awarded semi-annually "to broaden and strengthen the community of writers and scholars engaged in policy-oriented work on international peace and security; to encourage the reconceptualization of security issues in light of the fluidity of international events, and to encourage attention to new developments that have not been adequately understood as peace and security issues; and to foster integrated consideration of emerging relationships among economic, social, political, technological, and environmental aspects of global change." Write for additional information and application guidelines.

    Available to: No restrictions
    Deadlines: February 1 and August 1
    Apply to: Grants for Research and Writing, above address

John J. McCloy Fund
American Council on Germany
14 East 60th Street
New York, NY 10022

(J) The *John J. McCloy Fund* of the American Council on Germany offers journalism fellowships for American journalists to spend approximately a month in Germany. Fellowships cover the cost of transatlantic airfare, local ground transportation, and a per diem.

Available to: American and German professional journalists
Deadline: Inquire for exact date
Apply to: Above address for information; for applications contact Robert Petretti, Graduate School of Journalism 501B, Columbia University, New York, NY 10027

The MacDowell Colony
100 High Street
Peterborough, NH 03458

(R) *MacDowell Colony Fellowships* help to support residences at the colony in Peterborough, New Hampshire, for writers and other artists to concentrate on creative work without interruption. Studios, room, and board are provided; residences are up to eight weeks. For further information or forms, write to the above address.

Available to: Writers, visual artists, composers, filmmakers, architects, and interdisciplinary artists
Deadlines: January 15 for May to August; April 15 for September to December; September 15 for January to April
Apply to: Above address

The Madison Review
Department of English
University of Wisconsin
600 North Park Street
Madison, WI 53706

(F)
(P) The *Madison Review/Phyllis Smart Young Prize in Poetry* and the *Madison Review/Chris O'Malley Fiction Award* are given annually for the best group of three poems and the best short story submitted during the month of September. Each award carries a cash prize of $500 and publication in the *Madison Review*. Multiple or previously published submissions are ineligible. There is a $3 entry fee. Send an SASE for complete guidelines.

Available to: No restrictions
Deadline: September 30
Apply to: Phyllis Smart Young Prize in Poetry or Chris O'Malley Fiction Award, above address

Maine Community Foundation
PO Box 148
Ellsworth, ME 04605

The *Martin Dibner Memorial Fellowship for Maine Writers Fund* offers one or two grants in the $500 to $1,000 range for the professional development of Maine writers, particularly those who are just becoming established in their craft. Attendance at writing workshops, or assistance with living expenses while finishing a manuscript, are two examples of the kinds of projects eligible for support. Write for further information and guidelines.

Available to: Maine writers
Deadline: Applications must reach the above address by March 15
Apply to: Martin Dibner Memorial Fellowship Fund, above address

Manhattan Theatre Club
453 West 16th Street
New York, NY 10011

Ⓓ *Playwriting Fellowships,* of $10,000, are offered annually to New York-based playwrights, age thirty-five or younger, who have completed their formal education and can demonstrate financial need. Writers from diverse cultural groups are encouraged to apply. The fellowship includes a commission for a new play, production assistantship, and a one-year residence at MTC. Send an SASE for deadlines and eligibility requirements before applying.

   Available to: New York-based playwrights, age thirty-five or younger
   Deadline: Inquire for exact date
   Apply to: Paige Evans, Literary Manager, above address

Marin Arts Council
251 North San Pedro Road
San Rafael, CA 94903

Ⓜ The *Individual Artists Grants Program* offers grants to Marin County writers in poetry, fiction, and others kinds of creative prose. There will be no literary grants in 1996; they will resume in 1997. Send an SASE for an application form and guidelines.

   Available to: Marin County residents
   Deadline: Inquire in the fall of 1996
   Apply to: Above address

Maryland State Arts Council
601 North Howard Street
Baltimore, MD 21201

Ⓜ *Individual Artist Awards,* of $1,000, $3,000, and $6,000, are available in odd-numbered years to Maryland residents age eighteen and up in areas including fiction, poetry, and playwriting.

   Available to: Maryland residents at least eighteen years old, not including students
   Deadline: October 1996 for 1997 grants; inquire for exact date
   Apply to: Write for application to Tim Toothman for drama, Charles Camp for fiction and poetry, above address

Massachusetts Cultural Council
120 Boylston Street, 2nd Floor
Boston, MA 02116

Ⓜ *Artist Grants,* of $7,500 each, are given to Massachusetts writers in categories that rotate annually. Grants in fiction and poetry will be offered in 1996; grants in playwriting will be given in 1997. Writers who are eighteen years or older, have lived in Massachusetts for the past three consecutive years, and who are not enrolled in a related degree-granting program are eligible to apply. Write for guidelines and application.

   Available to: Massachusetts writers
   Deadline: Fall; inquire for exact date
   Apply to: Artist Grants Program, above address

Massachusetts Institute of Technology
Building 9, Room 315
Cambridge, MA 02139-4307

Ⓙ Six *Knight Science Journalism Fellowships* are awarded annually to U.S. print and broadcast journalists whose primary work is informing broad audiences about recent developments in technology and science and their wider social effects. The fellowships are open to freelance journalists as well as to employees of news-gathering organizations. The fellowships involve full-time residence at MIT for the academic year; fellows receive a stipend of $26,000, plus a relocation allowance of up to $2,000. Write for further information and application.

Available to: See above
Deadline: March 1
Apply to: Knight Science Journalism Fellowships, above address

Medieval Academy of America
1430 Massachusetts Avenue
Cambridge, MA 02138

Ⓝ The *John Nicholas Brown Prize* awards $500 annually for a first-published book in the field of medieval studies. Books with a publication date three years prior to the submission year are eligible.

Available to: Residents of North America
Deadline: November 1
Apply to: Above address

Ⓝ The *Van Courtlandt Elliott Prize* awards $300 annually for a first article on a medieval topic, published in any journal, of not less than five pages. Articles with a publication date one year prior to the submission year are eligible.

Available to: Residents of North America
Deadline: November 1
Apply to: Above address

Ⓝ The *Haskins Medal* is presented annually to the author of a book written within the broad field of medieval studies that is judged to be a work of outstanding importance and distinction. Books are eligible if the publication date is one to five years prior to the submission year.

Available to: Residents of North America
Deadline: November 1
Apply to: Above address

Michigan Author Award
Alpena County Library
211 North First Street
Alpena, MI 49707

Ⓜ The *Michigan Author Award*, of $1,000, is given for an outstanding body of work by a Michigan resident, a longtime Michigan resident who has recently relocated, or an author whose works are identified with Michigan because of their subject. Writers are cited for a published body of fiction, nonfiction, and/or poetry, consisting of three or more titles, which may be either adult or juvenile. Nominations may be made by librarians, publishers, or individuals. Write for the required application.

Available to: See above
Deadline: June 30
Apply to: Above address

Michigan Council for the Arts. *See* **Arts Foundation of Michigan**

Michigan Quarterly Review
The University of Michigan
3032 Rackham Building
Ann Arbor, MI 48109-1070

(F)   The *Lawrence Foundation Prize* annually awards $1,000 for the best short story published in the *Michigan Quarterly Review* during the previous calendar year. The magazine's editorial board chooses the winner.

Available to: *Michigan Quarterly Review* contributors

Midland Community Theatre
2000 West Wadley
Midland, TX 79705

(D)   The *McLaren Memorial Comedy Playwriting Competition* is a nationwide contest for original, unproduced comedy scripts of any length. The prize is a staged "Reader's Theatre" production at Midland Community Theatre, a cash stipend of $400, and accommodations in Midland for the rehearsal period and during the play's production. The playwright retains all rights to the work submitted. A $5 entry fee per script is required.

Available to: No restrictions
Deadline: January 31
Apply to: McLaren Memorial Comedy Playwriting Competition, above address

Mid-List Press
4324 12th Avenue South
Minneapolis, MN 55407-3218

(M)   The Mid-List Press *First Series Awards for the Novel, Poetry, Short Fiction, and Creative Nonfiction* offer publication and a $1,000 advance against royalties to a writer who has never published a book in that genre (a chapbook is not considered a book of poetry). Novels, collections of short fiction, and creative nonfiction manuscripts must be at least 50,000 words in length; poetry manuscripts must be at least sixty-five pages in length. There is a $10 reading fee in each category. Please send a #10 SASE for guidelines and an entry form.

Available to: Unpublished writers
Deadline: Submissions accepted October 1 to February 1 for novels and poetry; April 1 to July 1 for short fiction and creative nonfiction
Apply to: Above address

Midwest Theatre Network
5031 Tongen Avenue NW
Rochester, MN 55901

(D)   The *Rochester Playwright Festival* offers four to eight awards of $1,000 each (contingent on funding) and full production at one of seven cooperating theaters for unpublished work (full-length plays, collections of one-acts, musicals, experimental works) that has not received professional production. Send an SASE for guidelines and entry form.

Available to: No restrictions
Deadline: November 30, 1996; inquire for 1997
Apply to: Play Competition, above address

Milkweed Editions
430 First Avenue North, Suite 400
Minneapolis, MN 55401

(F)   The *Annual Milkweed National Fiction Prize* offers $2,000 over and above any advances, royalties, or other payments agreed upon in the contractual arrangement negotiated at the time of acceptance, to the best work of fiction accepted for publication by a writer not previously published by Milkweed Editions. Manuscripts should be one of the following: a novel, a collection of short stories, one or more novellas, or a combination of short stories and one or more novellas. All manuscripts submitted to Milkweed will automatically be considered for the prize. Send an SASE for fiction guidelines before submitting.

Available to: No restrictions
Apply to: Above address

© The *Milkweed Prize for Children's Literature* offers $2,000 over and above any advances, royalties, or other payment agreed upon in the contractual arrangement negotiated at the time of acceptance, to the best manuscript for children ages eight to twelve accepted for publication by a writer not previously published by Milkweed Editions. Manuscripts of novels or biographies are acceptable; collections of stories are not eligible, nor is the retelling of a legend or folktale. Milkweed is looking for manuscripts of high literary quality that "embody humane values and that contribute to cultural understanding." Send an SASE for children's literature guidelines.

Available to: No restrictions
Apply to: Above address

Mill Mountain Theatre
One Market Square SE
Roanoke, VA 24011-1437

Ⓓ The *Mill Mountain Theatre New Play Competition* annually awards $1,000, a staged reading with possible production, and a travel stipend and residence housing for an unproduced, unpublished play. Playwrights may submit one play, preferably with a cast of no more than ten. Send an SASE for complete guidelines.

Available to: U.S. residents
Deadline: January 1 (no submissions accepted before October 1)
Apply to: Jo Weinstein, Literary Manager, above address

The Millay Colony for the Arts
PO Box 3
Austerlitz, NY 12017-0003

Ⓡ The Millay Colony for the Arts provides workspace, meals, and sleeping accommodations for qualified writers, composers, and visual artists for a period of one month. It can accommodate five artists year-round in the Ellis studio and the four barn studios. Samples of work must accompany applications. Send an SASE for application, or e-mail to: application@millaycolony.org

Available to: No restrictions
Deadlines: February 1 for residences from June to September; May 1 for residences from October to January; September 1 for residences from February to May
Apply to: Gail Giles, Assistant Director, above address

The Milton Center
Kansas Newman College
3100 McCormick Avenue
Wichita, KS 67213

IN The *Milton Center Prize* annually awards $10,000 to a writer "who has produced a significant body of work within the Christian tradition." There is no application process. The Chrysostom Society, a group of twenty Christian writers founded by the Milton Center in 1986, nominates and selects the winner each year. *By Internal Nomination Only.*

The Milton Center also awards two postgraduate fellowships to "new writers of Christian commitment." The fellowships include a $6,000 stipend plus living expenses. Fellows are expected to complete their first book-length manuscript while in residence for the academic year, and to work eight hours per week in the Milton Center office. The Center offers assistance in placing manuscripts with publishers and agents, as well as providing a supportive community in which to work. Write for further information and application.

Available to: New writers of Christian commitment
Deadline: February 1
Apply to: Postgraduate Fellowships, above address

Minnesota Monthly
15 South Ninth Street, Suite 320
Minneapolis, MN 55402

(F)
(N)
The *Tamarack Award* offers $500 and publication in *Minnesota Monthly,* the magazine of Minnesota Public Radio, for an unpublished work of fiction or creative nonfiction by a resident of the upper midwest. Residents of Iowa, Michigan, Minnesota, North Dakota, South Dakota, and Wisconsin may submit one unpublished story, a novel excerpt, essay, or memoir of up to 3,500 words. Send an SASE for complete guidelines.

Available to: Residents of Iowa, Michigan, Minnesota, North Dakota, South Dakota, and Wisconsin
Deadline: May 19, 1996; inquire for 1997
Apply to: Tamarack Award, above address

Minnesota State Arts Board
400 Sibley Street, Suite 200
Saint Paul, MN 55101-1928

Artist Assistance Fellowship Grants, of $6,000, are given annually for new works, advanced study, and works-in-progress. Short-term *Career Opportunity Grants,* which range from $100 to $1,000, are also awarded three times a year.

Available to: Minnesota residents
Deadlines: October for fellowships; August, December, and April for Career Opportunity Grants
Apply to: Above address

Mississippi Arts Commission
239 North Lamar Street, Suite 207
Jackson, MS 39201

(M)
Fellowships in Literary Arts, of $5,000 each, are given to Mississippi artists in categories that alternate each year. The next cycle for poets and fiction writers will be in 1997-98. Write for further information.

Available to: Mississippi residents
Deadline: March 1, 1997
Apply to: Above address

Mississippi Review
The Center for Writers
University of Southern Mississippi
Box 5144
Hattiesburg, MS 39406-5144

(F)
The *Mississippi Review Prize in Short Fiction* awards $1,000 and publication in the *Mississippi Review* for an unpublished story. Up to fifteen runners-up will also be announced and published. Writers can submit two unpublished stories of no more than twenty-five pages each. There is a $10 entry fee per story. Send an SASE for complete guidelines.

Available to: No restrictions

Deadline: March 31
Apply to: Prize in Short Fiction, above address

The Missouri Review
University of Missouri, Columbia
1507 Hillcrest Hall, UMC
Columbia, MO 65211

(M) The *Editors' Prize Awards* offer $1,000 and publication annually for an essay and a short story, and $500 for poetry. All entries must be typed and double-spaced, stories and essays no more than twenty-five pages in length and poems no more than ten pages in length. There is a $15 entry fee.

Available to: No restrictions
Deadline: October 15
Apply to: Editors Awards, above address.

(F)   The *William Peden Prize* offers $1,000 annually for the best fiction published in the *Missouri Review*. The *Tom McAfee Discovery Feature in Poetry* offers an award of $125 to $250 once
(P)   or twice a year for the best group of poems to be published in the *Missouri Review* by a poet who has not yet published a book. Write for submission guidelines.

Available to: Writers published in the *Missouri Review*

Mixed Blood Theatre Company
1501 South 4th Street
Minneapolis, MN 55454

(D) The Mixed Blood Theatre Company sponsors the *Mixed Blood versus American Playwriting Competition*. The competition seeks unproduced plays, though applicants must have had one work previously staged or workshopped professionally or by an educational institution. The winner of the contest will receive a cash prize of $2,000 and a full production at Mixed Blood. Query for submission details; include an SASE. Contest is open to the first 300 submissions received.

Available to: No restrictions
Deadline: March 15
Apply to: Mixed Blood versus America, above address

Modern Language Association of America
10 Astor Place
New York, NY 10003

(N) The *Morton N. Cohen Award* offers $1,000 in odd-numbered years for an important collection of letters published in the two-year period preceding the award. The winning collection will be "one that provides readers with a clear, accurate, and readable text; necessary background information; and succinct and eloquent introductory material and annotations. The edited collection should be in itself a work of literature." Editors can apply regardless of the fields they and the authors of the letters represent; membership in the MLA is not required. To enter, send a letter of nomination and four copies of each eligible volume.

Available to: No restrictions
Deadline: May 1, 1997
Apply to: Morton N. Cohen Award, above address

(N) The *Katherine Singer Kovacs Prize* offers $1,000 annually for the best book published in English in the field of Latin American and Spanish literatures and cultures.

Available to: No restrictions

Deadline: May 1
Apply to: Katherine Singer Kovacs Prize, above address

Ⓝ The *James Russell Lowell Prize* of $1,000 is awarded annually to a member of the MLA who has published an outstanding literary or linguistic study, a critical edition of an important work, or a critical biography. Nominations may be made by publisher or author. To enter, send six copies of the work and a letter of nomination.

Available to: Members of the MLA only
Deadline: March 1
Apply to: James Russell Lowell Prize, above address

Ⓝ The *Howard R. Marraro Prize* and the *Aldo and Jeanne Scaglione Prize in Italian Literary Studies* jointly award $1,000 every even-numbered year to the author of a distinguished book- or essay-length scholarly study on any phase of Italian literature or comparative literature involving Italian. Nominations may be made by publisher or author. To enter, send four copies of the work and a letter of nomination.

Available to: Members of the MLA who have published works in this field
Deadline: May 1
Apply to: Howard R. Marraro Prize, above address

The *Kenneth W. Mildenberger Prize* awards $500 annually to the author of a research publication in the field of teaching foreign languages and literatures. To enter, send four copies of the work.

Available to: No restrictions
Deadline: May 1
Apply to: Kenneth W. Mildenberger Prize, above address

Ⓝ The *Modern Language Association Prize for a Distinguished Scholarly Edition* awards $1,000 and a certificate in odd-numbered years. For the current award, the committee solicits submissions of editions published in 1995 or 1996. A multivolume edition is eligible if at least one volume has been published during that period. An edition should be based on an examination of all available relevant textual sources; the source texts and the edited text's deviations from them should be fully described; the edition should employ editorial principles appropriate to the materials edited, and those principles should be clearly articulated in the volume; the text should be accompanied by appropriate textual and other historical contextual information; the edition should exhibit the highest standards of accuracy in the presentation of its text and apparatus; and the text and apparatus should be presented as accessibly and elegantly as possible. To enter, send four copies of the work.

Available to: No restrictions
Deadline: May 1, 1997
Apply to: MLA Prize for a Distinguished Scholarly Edition, above address

Ⓝ The *Modern Language Association Prize for a First Book* awards $1,000 for the first book-length scholarly publication by a current member of the association. The book must be a literary or linguistic study, a critical edition of an important work, or a critical biography. To enter send six copies of the book and a letter identifying the work and confirming the author's membership in the MLA.

Available to: MLA members
Deadline: May 1
Apply to: MLA Prize for a First Book, above address

Ⓝ The *Modern Language Association Prize for Independent Scholars* for distinguished published research in the fields of modern languages and literatures, including English, will be awarded annually to a person who, at the time of publication of the work, was not enrolled in a program leading to an academic degree and did not hold a tenured, tenure-track, or tenure-accruing position in a postsecondary educational institution. Tenure is understood as any comparable provision for job security in a postsecondary educational institution. The award will consist of a certificate, a check of $1,000, and a year's membership in the association. To enter a work, send six copies of the work and a completed application form.

Available to: No restrictions
Deadline: May 1
Apply to: MLA Prize for Independent Scholars, above address

Ⓝ The *Aldo and Jeanne Scaglione Prize for Comparative Literary Studies* awards $1,000 annually for an outstanding scholarly work in the field of comparative literary studies involving at least two literatures by a member of the association. Works of literary history, literary criticism, philology, and literary theory are eligible, as are works dealing with literature and other arts and disciplines, including cinema. To enter, send four copies of the book and a letter confirming the author's membership in the MLA.

Available to: MLA members
Deadline: May 1
Apply to: Aldo and Jeanne Scaglione Prize for Comparative Literary Studies, above address

Ⓝ The *Aldo and Jeanne Scaglione Prize for French and Francophone Studies* awards $1,000 annually for an outstanding scholarly work in the field of French or Francophone linguistic or literary studies by a member of the association. Works of literary history, literary criticism, philology, and literary theory are eligible for consideration. To enter, send four copies of the book and a letter confirming the author's membership in the MLA.

Available to: MLA members
Deadline: May 1
Apply to: Aldo and Jeanne Scaglione Prize for French and Francophone Studies, above address

Ⓣ The *Aldo and Jeanne Scaglione Prize for Literary Translation* awards $1,000 each even-numbered year for an outstanding translation into English of a book-length literary work; in odd-numbered years, the prize will honor an outstanding translation into English of a book-length work of literary history, literary criticism, philology, or literary theory. Translators need not be members of the association. For each year's prize, books published during the preceding biennium are eligible to compete. To enter, send five copies of the book and a letter of nomination.

Available to: No restrictions
Deadline: May 1
Apply to: Aldo and Jeanne Scaglione Prize for Literary Translation, above address

Ⓝ The *Aldo and Jeanne Scaglione Prize for Studies in Germanic Languages and Literatures* offers $1,000 biennially for an outstanding scholarly work on the linguistics or literatures of the Germanic languages, including Danish, Dutch, German, Icelandic, Norwegian, Swedish, and Yiddish, by a member of the association. Works of literary history, literary criticism, philology, and literary theory are eligible for consideration. The prize is awarded each even-numbered year. To enter, send four copies of the book and a letter confirming the author's membership in the MLA.

Available to: MLA members
Deadline: Inquire for 1996
Apply to: Aldo and Jeanne Scaglione Prize for Studies in Germanic Languages and Literatures, above address

Ⓝ The *Aldo and Jeanne Scaglione Prize for Studies in Slavic Languages and Literatures* offers $1,000 biennially for an outstanding scholarly work on the linguistics or literatures of the Slavic languages by a member of the association. Works of literary history, literary criticism, philology, and literary theory are eligible for consideration; books that are primarily translations will not be considered. The prize will be awarded each odd-numbered year beginning in 1995. To enter, send four copies of the book and a letter confirming the author's membership in the MLA.

Available to: MLA members
Deadline: Inquire for 1997
Apply to: Aldo and Jeanne Scaglione Prize for Studies in Slavic Languages and Literatures, above address

(N) The *Mina P. Shaughnessy Prize* awards $500 annually to the author of a research publication in the field of teaching the English language and literature. To enter, send four copies of the work.

Available to: No restrictions
Deadline: May 1
Apply to: Mina P. Shaughnessy Prize, above address

Money for Women/Barbara Deming Memorial Fund
PO Box 40-1043
Brooklyn, NY 11240-1043

The Fund provides grants to feminists active in the arts "whose work speaks for peace and social justice and in some way sheds light upon the condition of women or enhances self-realization." Most grants and awards are for under $1,000. The *Gerty, Gerty, Gerty in the Arts, Arts, Arts Award,* named after Gertrude Stein, is given for "outstanding work by a lesbian whose work gives voice to a lesbian sensibility or confronts homophobia." The *Fannie Lou Hamer Award* is given to a woman "whose work combats racism and celebrates women of color." Send an SASE for application form.

Available to: Feminists active in the arts
Deadlines: December 31 and June 30
Apply to: Above address

Montana Arts Council
316 North Park Avenue, Suite 252
Helena, MT 59620

Ten *Individual Artists Fellowships,* of $2,000 each, are available each year to Montana residents age eighteen and up in areas including fiction and nonfiction.

Available to: Montana residents age 18 and up
Deadline: April; inquire for exact date
Apply to: Write for application in January to Director of Artists Services, above address

The Jenny McKean Moore Fund for Writers. *See* **George Washington University**

Mount Sequoyah New Play Retreat
c/o University of Arkansas
Department of Drama
619 Kimpel Hall
Fayetteville, AR 72701

(D) The *Mount Sequoyah New Play Retreat* annually offers residence fellowships to six playwrights at the retreat's three-week developmental workshop. Fellows are provided with room and board and personal writing time combined with workshop sessions in which plays are developed with participating directors and a resident acting company under the supervision of the retreat's staff of directors and produced playwrights. Each play receives a public staged reading. Send an SASE for additional information and guidelines.

Available to: No restrictions
Deadline: February 1
Apply to: Roger Gross, Retreat Director, above address

The Mountaineers Books
1001 SW Klickitat Way, Suite 201
Seattle, WA 98134

(N) The *Barbara Savage "Miles from Nowhere" Memorial Award* is given in even-numbered years for an outstanding unpublished book-length manuscript of a nonfiction, personal-adventure narrative. The prize consists of a $3,000 cash award, plus publication and a $12,000 guaranteed advance against royalties. Send an SASE for details.

Available to: No restrictions
Deadline: October 1, 1996
Apply to: Margaret Foster, Editor-in-Chief, Barbara Savage "Miles from Nowhere" Memorial Award, above address

Mudfish
184 Franklin Street
New York, NY 10013

(P) The *Mudfish Poetry Prize* offers $500 and publication in *Mudfish*, a journal of art and poetry published by Box Turtle Press. There is a reading fee of $7 for up to three poems; $2 is required for each additional poem. All entries will be considered for publication. Write for complete guidelines.

Available to: No restrictions
Deadline: Mid-November; inquire for exact date
Apply to: Mudfish Poetry Prize, above address

Municipal Art Society of New York
457 Madison Avenue
New York, NY 10022

[IN] The *Brendan Gill Prize*, consisting of a cash award and an engraved Steuben crystal vessel, is given annually to recognize the creator of a "work of art which best captures the energy, vigor and verve of New York City." The award is open to all artistic disciplines, including writing. *By Internal Nomination Only.*

Museum of Science
Science Park
Boston, MA 02114

The *Bradford Washburn Award*, $10,000 and a gold medal, is presented annually to an individual who has made "outstanding contributions toward public understanding of science, its importance, its fascination, and the vital role it plays in all of our lives." The award honors a writer or lecturer of national or international influence, and is not meant to reward specific research, technical accomplishment, or teaching although it may be given to an outstanding teacher or research worker who also was a highly effective writer or lecturer. There is no application process and the committee does not consider self-nominees. Presentation is made at the annual dinner in the autumn.

Available to: Writers, lecturers, or scientists of any nationality
Deadline: Inquire for nomination procedures
Apply to: Bradford Washburn Award, Community Relations Dept., above address

National Association of Science Writers
PO Box 294
Greenlawn, NY 11740

(J) The *Science-in-Society Awards* are given "to recognize investigative and interpretive reporting about the sciences and their impact for good and bad." Three awards, of $1,000 each, are offered in the following categories: newspapers, magazines, and television and radio. Write for guidelines and entry blank.

Available to: No restrictions
Deadline: July 1
Apply to: Above address

National Association for Women in Education
1325 18th Street, NW, No. 210
Washington, DC 20036-6511

The *Women's Research Awards* are designed to encourage and support excellence in research by, for, and about women. Research considered for the awards may be on any topic relevant to the education and personal and professional development of women and girls. The research may be historical, philosophical, experimental, evaluative, or descriptive. Two awards, of $750 each, are given: one in a graduate student competition and one in an open competition for persons at any career/professional level. Send for complete guidelines.

Available to: Women
Deadline: October 1
Apply to: Women's Research Awards Committee, Anna Roman-Koller, Ph.D., University of Pittsburgh School of Medicine, Dept. of Pathology, 701 Scaife Hall, Pittsburgh, PA 15261

The National Book Awards
c/o National Book Foundation
260 Fifth Avenue, Room 904
New York, NY 10001

Ⓜ The *National Book Awards* recognize American literary excellence in three categories: fiction, nonfiction, and poetry. Each winner receives a cash prize of $10,000; runners-up receive awards of $1,000. Eligible books must be published in the United States between December 1 and November 30 of the award year and may be nominated by their publishers only.

Available to: American authors
Deadline: July 15

National Endowment for the Arts
Literature Program
Nancy Hanks Center
1100 Pennsylvania Avenue, NW
Washington, DC 20506

Grants are available to create new opportunities for artists to expand and develop audiences and to assist existing organizations to broaden arts programs through a variety of projects. One program, "Residencies for Writers and Reading Series," funds organizations to pay writers' fees for readings and workshops.

Fellowships are available to published creative writers of exceptional talent, in poetry, fiction, creative nonfiction, and translation, to enable them to set aside time for writing, research, or travel, and generally to advance their careers. The fellowships are currently $20,000 for creative writing and $10,000 or $20,000 for translation, depending on the length and scope of the project.

Available to: U.S. citizens
Deadlines: Vary; write for specific information
Apply to: Above address

110

(D) The *Theater Program* should be contacted for details of fellowships and organizations sponsoring residences for playwrights. Write to the Theater Program at the above address.

(R) The *United States/Japan Artist Exchange Fellowships* are awarded each year to five American artists in various disciplines, including literature. Fellowships are awarded to outstanding midcareer practicing creative artists who show promise of becoming leaders in their fields. These are six- to nine-month residences in Japan.

Available to: U.S. citizens and permanent U.S. residents
Deadline: Varies according to type of artist; inquire
Apply to: Office of International Activities, above address

(R) The *U.S./Canada/Mexico Creative Artists' Residencies Program* offers residencies of two consecutive months in Canada or Mexico to U.S. creative artists, including writers. Visiting artists meet with artists in their field and participate in activities that benefit the host community during the stay (such as master classes, workshops, or readings). Proficiency in Spanish is not required for Mexican residencies.

Available to: U.S. citizens and permanent U.S. residents
Deadline: Inquire
Apply to: Partnerships/Planning and Stabilization Cluster, above address

National Endowment for the Humanities
1100 Pennsylvania Avenue, NW
Washington, DC 20506

Fellowships and grants for research, editing, and writing in the humanities are available to writers through the Division of Research. These grants are made for scholarly writing rather than for works of fiction. The Division of Public Programs, through the Media Program, makes scriptwriting grants to non-profit organizations for production of radio or television programs on subjects central to the humanities. The humanities include language, linguistics, literature, history, jurisprudence, philosophy, archaeology, comparative religion, ethics, the history, criticism, and theory of the arts, those aspects of the social sciences which have humanistic content and employ humanistic methods, and the study and application of the humanities to the human environment with particular attention to the relevance of the humanities to the current conditions of national life.

Available to: U.S. citizens and permanent residents
Deadline: Inquire
Apply to: Above address (specify division); or request the brochure "Overview of Endowment Programs" for information on more than thirty-five funding possibilities at NEH

National Federation of Press Women
4510 West 89th Street
Prairie Village, KS 66207-2282

(J) The *Helen Miller Malloch Scholarships*, of $1,000, are available to women college students who wish to complete communications studies for a degree in an accredited course or NFPW professionals who wish to study further in a special area or who desire to improve skills. Scholarships provide support for one year with money being sent to university or college to apply to tuition or other expenses. The NFPW also offers $1,000 scholarships to professional members seeking a graduate journalism degree and $500 scholarships to graduating high school seniors who plan to pursue the study of journalism and to a junior or senior woman communications student. Send a #10 SASE for additional information and application form.

Available to: Women who are entering college, are junior or senior college students, graduate students seeking a degree in journalism, or professional journalists who wish to obtain further education

Deadline: May 1
Apply to: Professional Education Scholarships, above address

National Foundation for Advancement in the Arts
800 Brickell Avenue
Miami, FL 33131

The *Arts Recognition and Talent Search Program,* for young people involved in the arts, is a
program of the National Foundation for Advancement in the Arts. Applicants must be
seventeen or eighteen years of age. Awards of $3,000, $1,500, $500, and $100 are offered
to students demonstrating talent in the fields of writing, dance, theater, music, and the
visual arts.

Available to: Seventeen- and eighteen-year-olds
Deadline: June 1 or, with late fee, October 1
Apply to: ARTS, above address, or contact high school teachers/counselors

The National Humanities Center
PO Box 12256
Research Triangle Park, NC 27709-2256

Residential Fellowships are awarded annually to scholars of demonstrated achievement and to
promising younger scholars for advanced study in history, languages and literature,
philosophy, and other fields of the humanities. Applicants must hold doctorate or have
equivalent professional accomplishments; younger scholars should be engaged in work
significantly beyond the revision of a doctoral dissertation. Most fellowships are for the
academic year (September through May), though a few may be awarded for a semester.
In addition to scholars from fields normally associated with the humanities, represen-
tatives of the natural and social sciences, the arts, the professions, and public life may
be admitted to the center if their work has humanistic dimensions. Fellowship stipends
are individually determined in accordance with the needs of each fellow and the center's
ability to meet them. Write for further information and application form.

Available to: No restrictions
Deadline: October 15
Apply to: Fellowship Program, above address

National League of American Pen Women
1300 17th Street, NW
Washington, DC 20036

Ⓜ The *NLAPW Scholarship for Mature Women in Letters,* in memory of Dr. Adeline Hoffman,
offers $1,000 biennially to an American woman over the age of thirty-five to "further
creative goals at an age when encouragement can lead to realization of long-term purposes." Applicants may submit a published or unpublished article, short story, editorial,
drama, teleplay, three poems, or first chapter of a novel. NLAPW members are ineligible. There is an $8 handling fee. The next award will be made in 1998. Send an SASE
for complete guidelines.

Available to: Women over the age of thirty-five
Deadline: January 15, 1998
Apply to: Scholarship for Mature Women in Letters, above address

National Marine Manufacturers Association
600 Third Avenue
New York, NY 10016

Ⓙ The *NMMA Directors' Award,* of $1,000, is presented to an individual in the communications
profession who has made an outstanding contribution to recreational boating through

(N) newspaper, magazine, radio, television, film, or book, as a writer, artist, photographer, editor, or broadcaster. Nominations must be submitted by a representative of one of NMMA's member companies or a marine dealer. Write for complete guidelines.

Available to: No restrictions
Deadline: November; inquire for exact date
Apply to: Above address for nomination procedures

The National Poetry Series
PO Box G
Hopewell, NJ 08525

(P) The *National Poetry Series* oversees an annual open competition. Five books of poetry will be selected by five well-known poets and published by the participating publishers. Each winning poet receives a $1,000 cash award. Manuscripts must be accompanied by an entrance fee of $25. Send an SASE for guidelines.

Available to: U.S. citizens only
Deadline: February 15 (no submissions accepted prior to January 1)
Apply to: Above address; include an SASE and a $25 check (entry fee) payable to The National Poetry Series. No entries accepted before January 1

The National Repertory Theatre Foundation
PO Box 286
Hollywood, CA 90078

(D) The *National Play Award* of $5,000 is given biennially for original unpublished full-length plays that have not been produced with a paid Equity cast, and have not won a major award or been previously submitted to NPA. Send an SASE for fact sheet before sending script.

Available to: No restrictions
Deadline: Between January 1 and June 30, 1997
Apply to: National Play Award, above address

National Right to Work Committee
8001 Braddock Road, Suite 500
Springfield, VA 22160

(J) The *William B. Ruggles Journalism Scholarship*, of $2,000, is available yearly to graduate or undergraduate students majoring in journalism or related mass media or mass communications programs. A 500-word essay is required based on the applicant's knowledge of the Right-to-Work principle.

Available to: See above
Deadline: Applications are accepted between January 1 and March 31
Apply to: Public Relations Department, above address

The National Women's Studies Association
7100 Baltimore Avenue, Suite 301
College Park, MD 20740

(N) The *Illinois-NWSA Manuscript Award* offers $1,000 and publication by the University of Illinois Press to the best book-length manuscript on any subject in women's studies. Manuscripts can be on any subject in women's studies that expands understanding of gender systems or women's lives. Interdisciplinary studies and discipline specific studies are welcome. Anthologies, essay collections, fiction, poetry, or unrevised doctoral dissertations are not eligible for the award.

Available to: No restrictions

Deadline: January 31
Apply to: Illinois-NWSA Manuscript Award, above address

The *NWSA Graduate Scholarship in Lesbian Studies* awards $500 to a student who in the fall of 1996 will be doing research or writing a master's thesis or Ph.D. dissertation in Lesbian Studies.

Available to: See above
Deadline: February 15, 1996; inquire for 1997
Apply to: Lesbian Studies Scholarship, above address

The *NWSA Scholarship in Jewish Women's Studies* awards $500 to a graduate student who is enrolled for the fall semester and whose area of research is Jewish Women's Studies.

Available to: See above
Deadline: February 15
Apply to: Jewish Women's Studies Scholarship, above address

The *Pergamon-NWSA Graduate Scholarship in Women's Studies* awards a first place of $1,000 and a second place of $500 to a student who in the fall of 1996 will be doing research for or writing a master's thesis or Ph.D. dissertation in the interdisciplinary field of women's studies. The awards will be made with special preference given to NWSA members and to those whose research projects on women examine color or class.

Available to: See above
Deadline: February 15
Apply to: Pergamon-NWSA Scholarship, above address

National Writers Association
1450 South Havana, Suite 424
Aurora, CO 80012

(F)   The *NWA Novel Writing Contest* offers a first prize of $500, a second prize of $250, and a third prize of $150 for unpublished novels of any genre. Manuscripts may be up to 90,000 words. Send an SASE for the required entry form. There is a $35 entry fee. A critique of the submitted manuscript is available for an additional $1.25/1,000 words; judging sheets are sent if an SASE is enclosed. Write for full guidelines and application form.

Available to: No restrictions
Deadline: April 1
Apply to: NWA Novel Writing Contest, above address

Native Writers Circle of the Americas
Native American Studies
University of Oklahoma
455 West Lindsey, Room 804
Norman, OK 73019

IN   The *Lifetime Achievement Award for Literature,* the *Diane Decorah Memorial Award for Poetry,* and the *Louis Littlecoon Oliver Memorial Award for Short Fiction* are given to Native American writers who are elected by their fellow Native American writers. The awards carry a cash prize which varies yearly according to funding. There is no application process. *By Internal Nomination Only.*

(M)   The *North American Native Authors First Book Award for Poetry and Prose* offers $500 in each genre and publication for a book of poems and prose (short stories, novella, novel, or nonfiction). The winning books will be published by the Greenfield Review Press. The awards are open to Native Americans of American Indian, Aleut, Inuit, or Metis ancestry who have not yet published a book. Writers may be from any part of North America, including Mexico and Central America, but manuscripts must be in English or bilingual format. Write for complete guidelines and further information.

Available to: Native Americans
Deadline: May 1
Apply to: North American Native Authors First Book Awards, The Greenfield Review Literary Center, PO Box 308, Greenfield Center, New York, NY 12633

The Naval Historical Center
Washington Navy Yard
901 M Street, SE
Washington, DC 20374-5060

The *Rear Admiral John D. Hayes Pre-Doctoral Fellowship* offers a stipend of $8,000 to support dissertation research and writing on any aspect of the history of the U.S. Navy.

Available to: U.S. citizens enrolled in a recognized graduate school who will complete all requirements for a Ph.D. except the dissertation by June 30 of the application year and have an approved dissertation topic in the field of U.S. naval history
Deadline: February 28
Apply to: Dr. William S. Dudley, Director, above address

Ⓝ The *United States Navy Prize in Naval History* offers $500 and a certificate for the best scholarly article on U.S. naval history published in a scholarly journal in the previous year.

Available to: No restrictions
Deadline: June 1
Apply to: Dr. William S. Dudley, Director, United States Navy Prize in Naval History, above address

The *Vice Admiral Edwin B. Hooper Research Grant* offers two awards of up to $2,500 each to assist scholars in the research or writing of books or articles by helping to defray the costs of travel, living expenses, and document duplication related to the research project.

Available to: U.S. citizens who have completed a Ph.D. from an accredited university or equivalent attainment as a published author
Deadline: February 28
Apply to: Dr. William S. Dudley, Director, above address

Nebraska Arts Council
3838 Davenport
Omaha, NE 68131-2329

Individual Artist Fellowships in literature are given biennially to Nebraska writers with demonstrated records of professional achievement. Master Awards, of $4,000, and Merit Awards, of $2,000, are available. Writers must be residents of Nebraska for at least two years prior to application and may not be students in an undergraduate or graduate degree program in the fellowship field.

Available to: Nebraska residents
Deadline: Inquire
Apply to: Above address

The Nebraska Review
University of Nebraska at Omaha
College of Fine Arts
Omaha, NE 68182-0324

Ⓕ The *Nebraska Review Fiction Prize and Poetry Prize* offers $500 and publication for the best story of 5,000 words or less, and for the best poem or group of poems (not to exceed five Ⓟ poems or six pages). All entrants receive a one-year subscription to the *Nebraska Review*. There is a $9 entry fee.

Available to: No restrictions

Deadline: November 30
Apply to: Fiction Prize or Poetry Prize, above address

Negative Capability Magazine
62 Ridgelawn Drive East
Mobile, AL 36608

(F)
(P)
The *Leon Driskell Award for Short Fiction* and the *Eve of St. Agnes Award in Poetry* each offer a cash prize of $1,000 and publication in *Negative Capability*. Fiction writers should submit two copies of an unpublished short story of 1,500 to 4,500 words, with the author's name, address, and phone numbers on one copy only, along with a $10 reading fee. Poets may submit as many poems as they like, with a $3 per poem entry fee. Submissions for either award may not have been accepted elsewhere.

Available to: No restrictions
Deadline: January 15
Apply to: Leon Driskell Award for Short Fiction or Eve of St. Agnes Award in Poetry, above address

Nevada State Council on the Arts
602 North Curry Street
Capitol Complex
Carson City, NV 89710

Jackpot Grants of various amounts up to $1,000 are available quarterly to individual professional artists in areas including fiction, nonfiction, and poetry. *Fellowships* of $5,000 each will be offered to two Nevada writers working in any genre in 1996. Write for additional information and application guidelines.

Available to: Resident Nevada professional artists
Deadline: Inquire
Apply to: Artist Services Program Director, above address

New Dramatists
424 West 44th Street
New York, NY 10036

(D)
Membership in New Dramatists, a service organization, is granted to playwrights who have completed at least two original plays, produced or unproduced. Full-lengths are preferred over one-acts. Screenplays and adaptations are not accepted for admission. Programs and services include cold and rehearsed readings, free theater tickets, a national script distribution network, at-cost copying, a loan fund, exchange opportunities, etc. Members may be active for a maximum of seven years. Members pay no dues or fees.

Available to: Playwrights who live in the New York area or who can spend enough time in New York to take advantage of our programs
Deadline: July 15 to September 15
Apply to: Cheri Magid, Literary Manager, above address

(D)
The *L. Arnold Weissberger Playwriting Competition* annually awards $5,000 for an unpublished full-length play that has not been professionally produced. All plays must be nominated by a theatre professional (artistic directors and literary managers of professional non-profit theaters, literary agents, dramaturgs affiliated with university drama departments or professional producing theater companies, or chairpersons of accredited university theater or playwriting programs). Write for nomination and submission procedures.

Available to: No restrictions
Deadline: May 31
Apply to: L. Arnold Weissberger Playwriting Competition, above address

New England Poetry Club
2 Farrar Street
Cambridge, MA 02138

(P) The *Daniel Varoujan Prize*, funded by royalties from the *Anthology of Armenian Poetry*, annually awards $500 for a poem "worthy of the Armenian poet Daniel Varoujan, who was killed by the Turks in 1915." Translations are not eligible. There is a $2 reading fee for non-members of the New England Poetry Club. Send an SASE for complete guidelines.

Available to: No restrictions
Deadline: June 30
Apply to: Above address

The New England Poetry Club offers several other awards, with lesser cash prizes, for individual poems. Inquire for further information.

New England Theatre Conference
c/o Department of Theatre
Northeastern University
306 Huntington Avenue
Boston, MA 02115

(D) The *John Gassner Memorial Playwriting Awards* of $500 and $250 are given to authors of commercially unpublished, unproduced, full-length plays. A staged reading of portions of the prizewinning scripts will be given at the annual NETC convention in November, followed by critique and discussions. There is a $10 handling fee for non-NETC members. Write for application guidelines.

Available to: New England residents and NETC members
Deadline: April 15
Apply to: John Gassner Memorial Playwriting Awards, above address

New Hampshire State Council on the Arts
40 North Main Street
Concord, NH 03301-4974

(M) Approximately ten *Artists Fellowships*, of up to $3,000, are available each year in areas including general writing, fiction, poetry, and playwriting. Write for guidelines and application form.

Available to: New Hampshire residents of at least one year, over eighteen years of age, not enrolled as a full-time student, and not a previous recipient
Deadline: July 1
Apply to: Audrey V. Sylvester, Artist Services Coordinator, above address

The New Jersey Council for the Humanities
28 West State Street, 6th Floor
Trenton, NJ 08608-1602

(N) The *New Jersey Council for the Humanities Book Award* is given annually for the best book in the humanities directed toward a general audience and written by a New Jersey author. For the winning book, $1,000 will be given to the author. In addition, the NJCH will purchase up to 100 copies of the book for placement in certain New Jersey public libraries. Coauthored works are not eligible.

Available to: Writers who have a New Jersey connection either by birth, by residence, or by full-time occupation at the time of submitting the manuscript
Deadline: February 1 (may vary; inquire first)
Apply to: Above address

New Jersey State Council on the Arts
CN 306
Trenton, NJ 08625

Fellowships of up to $12,000 are available each year to New Jersey residents in areas including prose, poetry, and playwriting. Fellowships are awarded strictly on the basis of artistic merit and promise to the very finest New Jersey artists to help them develop and produce.

Available to: New Jersey residents
Deadline: December 15
Apply to: Above address

The *Writers in the Schools* program places dozens of professional writers, playwrights, and poets in short-term residences in New Jersey schools each year. Schools make the application. The council funds pay for a portion of the artists' fees. Writers may apply to become certified to conduct residences.

Available to: New Jersey residents
Deadline: Inquire
Apply to: Writers in the Schools, above address

New Letters Magazine
University of Missouri-Kansas City
University House
5101 Rockhill Road
Kansas City, MO 64110

In addition to the following monetary prizes, winners will be published in the annual awards issue of *New Letters,* an international magazine of arts and letters. Each entry for each prize must be accompanied by a $10 reading fee. Send an SASE for complete guidelines.

(N) The *Dorothy Churchill Cappon Essay Prize* awards $500 plus publication for the best personal essay of 5,000 words or less.

(F) The *New Letters Fiction Prize* awards $750 plus publication for the best short story of 5,000 words or less.

(P) The *New Letters Poetry Prize* awards $750 plus publication for the best group of three to six poems.

Available to: No restrictions
Deadline: May 15
Apply to: New Letters Literary Awards, above address

New Millennium
PO Box 2463
Knoxville, TN 37901

(M) The *New Millennium Awards* biannually offer $500 for fiction, $350 for poetry, and $250 for essay. All winning submissions will be published in *New Millennium Writings, A Journal for the 21st Century.* There are no restrictions as to style, content or length, though stories and essays longer than twenty pages may not be published in their entirety. There is a $10 fee for each contest entry (one story, one essay, or up to three poems). All contestants will receive a copy of the issue in which the winning submissions appear. Send an SASE for complete contest rules.

Available to: No restrictions
Deadline: June 1 for fall issue; December 1 for spring
Apply to: NMW Contest, above address

New Orleans Literary Festival. *See* **Tennessee Williams/New Orleans Literary Festival**

New Rivers Press
420 North 5th Street, Suite 910
Minneapolis, MN 55401

Ⓜ The *Minnesota Voices Project* offers $500 and publication by New Rivers Press to writers from Iowa, Minnesota, North Dakota, South Dakota, and Wisconsin in the categories of poetry, short fiction, novella, and personal essay/memoir. Writers must not have been previously published by a commercial publishing house. Send an SASE for further guidelines and application form.

Available to: Residents of Iowa, Minnesota, North Dakota, South Dakota, and Wisconsin
Deadline: April 1
Apply to: Minnesota Voices Project, above address

New York Foundation for the Arts
155 Avenue of the Americas
New York, NY 10013

Artists' Fellowships provide fellowships to individual New York State creative artists, based on the excellence of their recent work. Applications are accepted for the 1996-97 cycle for fellowships in poetry and nonfiction literature; the 1997-98 cycle will be for fiction and playwriting/screenwriting. The $7,000 fellowship award may be used however the artist sees fit. Recipients are required to provide a mutually agreed upon public service during the grant period.

Ⓕ Applicants for *Fellowships in Fiction* must submit three copies of a portion of a completed manuscript, which may be an excerpt from a novel or collection of short stories. The maximum amount of text is twenty double-spaced pages.

Ⓟ Applicants for *Fellowships in Poetry* must submit three copies of at least two examples of work. The maximum amount of text is ten pages.

Ⓓ Applicants for *Fellowships in Playwriting/Screenwriting* should submit three copies of up to twenty pages of a play or film script in addition to one copy of the entire script.

Ⓝ Applicants for *Fellowships in Nonfiction* should submit three copies of up to twenty double-spaced pages from a collection of essays, creative writing depicting actual events, biography, autobiography, or other nonfiction.

Available to: New York residents (two years minimum), nonstudents
Deadline: Mid-October 1996 for poetry and nonfiction literature; mid-October 1997 for fiction and playwriting/screenwriting; inquire for exact date
Apply to: Artists' Fellowships, above address

New York Mills Arts Retreat
24 North Main Avenue
PO Box 246
New York Mills, MN 56567

Ⓡ One- to four-week residences are offered at the New York Mills Arts Retreat, a former working dairy farm, surrounded by cornfields and cows. Through the Jerome Foundation, each resident artist is offered a stipend ranging from $400 for a one-week residence to $1,500 for four weeks. In exchange, retreat residents are asked to interact with the community for five to six hours per week. This outreach might include teaching in the local schools, conducting a workshop, or pursuing any other creative activity that involves the community. Residents are provided with housing and studio space. Send an SASE for additional information and application.

Available to: No restrictions
Deadline: Applications reviewed in January and June
Apply to: Above address

New York State Archives Partnership Trust
Cultural Education Center, Room 9C49
Albany, NY 12230

The *Larry J. Hackman Research Residency Program* awards funds to pursue research using the holdings of the New York State Archives. The program is intended to support advanced work in New York State history, government or public policy, with preference given to projects that have application to enduring public policy issues, particularly in New York State, and that have a high probability of publication or other public dissemination. Applicants working on doctoral dissertations and those at the postdoctoral level are particularly encouraged to apply, but any proposal for advanced research will be considered. Two awards of $6,000 each will be made for in-depth research, and two smaller awards of $1,500 will be made for shorter research visits. The awards are intended to defray costs of travel, living expenses, and other research-related expenses. Write for application form.

Available to: No restrictions
Deadline: Inquire
Apply to: Jill Rydberg, above address; fax 518-473-7058, or e-mail: jrydberg @mail.nysed.gov

New York State Council on the Arts
Literature Program
915 Broadway, 8th Floor
New York, NY 10010

Writer-in-Residence Awards are offered biennially in odd-numbered years to provide a writer with time to work on his/her own writing and to support the writer in organizing public programming. Each writer designs his or her own community service associated with the residence (such as readings and workshops), and awards are made through the sponsoring organizations. Funding is available at the maximum rate of $2,500 a month for up to three months for the writer's fee, and up to an additional $1,000 for the administrative costs on the part of the sponsoring organization. Only not-for-profit organizations in New York state may apply, but individual writers may write for guidelines.

Available to: Writers working with not-for-profit organizations in New York State
Deadline: March 1, 1997
Apply to: Above address

(T) Support for translators' fees is available biennially in even- numbered years to organizations sponsoring the completion of literary translations into English. Translators must be residents of New York State. Preference is given to work that has already received a commitment from a publisher or a theater, and to translators who have not previously received support through NYSCA in this category. All organizations contemplating an application should consult with the Literature Program staff prior to the application deadline.

Available to: See above
Deadline: March 1, 1996 and 1998
Apply to: Above address

New York State Historical Association
PO Box 800
Cooperstown, NY 13326

(N) The *New York State Historical Association Manuscript Award*, of $1,500 and assistance in publication, is awarded annually to the best unpublished, book-length monograph on some aspect of New York State history, as judged by a special editorial committee.

Available to: No restrictions

Deadline: February 20
Apply to: Wendell Tripp, Director of Publications, above address

New York University
Washington Square & University College of Arts and Sciences
Washington Square
New York, NY 10003

IN   The *Delmore Schwartz Memorial Award in Poetry* is offered at intervals of two or three years
to an outstanding young poet, or an older poet whose work has been neglected, and
ordinarily to someone who has published more than one book. The committee of judges
consists of Theodore Weiss and M. L. Rosenthal, and choices are made on the basis of
their knowledge of the poetic situation and consultation with one another. Awards thus
far have been $1,000 each. *By Internal Nomination Only.*

New York University Press
70 Washington Square South, 2nd Floor
New York, NY 10012-1091

F
P   The *Mamdouha S. Bobst Awards for Emerging Writers* offer publication by NYU Press for two
book-length manuscripts by authors who have no previously published books and to
emerging writers whose talents, in the opinion of the committee, have been insuffi-
ciently recognized. One award will be given each year in the category of fiction, and
one award may also be given in the category of poetry.

Available to: No restrictions
Deadline: Inquire for 1996
Apply to: Mamdouha S. Bobst Awards, above address

The Newberry Library
60 West Walton
Chicago, IL 60610

Short-term Residential Fellowships in the Humanities are available to scholars, including those
at the dissertation stage, who desire a short period of residency to use particular Newberry collections. The fellowships carry a stipend of $800 per month. Write for further
information and application forms.

Available to: No restrictions
Deadline: March 1 for fall fellowships; October 15 for spring
Apply to: Awards Committee, Newberry Short-term Fellowships, above address

The Center for Renaissance Studies at the Newberry Library offers three types of awards:
Consortium Funds are available for faculty members and graduate students of the center's
member institutions to participate in a broad range of interdisciplinary and archival
programs, either at the Newberry Library or the Folger Institute. *Summer Institute Stipends* of $1,500 are available to ten postdoctoral scholars teaching in colleges and uni-
versities in the United States who wish to attend the Center's six-week summer
institute. The *Audrey Lumsden-Kouvel Fellowship*, carrying a stipend of up to $3,000, is
available to postdoctoral scholars wishing to carry on research in residence at the Newberry Library for three months in late medieval or Renaissance studies.

Available to: See above
Deadline: Inquire
Apply to: The Center for Renaissance Studies, above address

The Newcomen Society in the United States
412 Newcomen Road
Exton, PA 19341

N   The *Thomas Newcomen Book Award in Business History* is given in cooperation with the *Business
History Review* to the author of an outstanding book dealing with the history of business

in the United States or Canada. One award of $1,000 is granted triennially. It will be awarded next in 1998 to the author of a book published from 1995 to 1997.

Available to: No restrictions
Deadline: 1998; inquire for exact date
Apply to: Book Review Editor, *Business History Review,* Harvard Business School Publishing, 60 Harvard Way, Boston, MA 02163

The Newspaper Guild
8611 Second Avenue
Silver Spring, MD 20910

(J) The *Heywood Broun Award* is given for outstanding journalistic achievement "in the spirit of Heywood Broun," the newspaper columnist who was the guild's founder. Eligible are nonmanagerial employees of newspapers, news services, news magazines, and radio and television stations in the United States, Canada, and Puerto Rico, whether they are members of the guild or not. One award of $2,000 is given annually.

Available to: See above
Deadline: Late January; inquire for exact date
Apply to: The Broun Award Committee, above address

Nieman Foundation
Harvard University
Walter Lippmann House
One Francis Avenue
Cambridge, MA 02138

(J)
(R) The *Lucius W. Nieman Fellowships for Journalists* offer working journalists a midcareer opportunity to study and broaden their intellectual horizons in residence at Harvard University. Applicants must have at least three years of media experience and obtain his/her employer's consent for a leave of absence for the academic year. Fellows must agree to refrain from professional work during that period, to complete all work in at least two academic courses, one each semester; to remain in residence during term time; and to return at the end of the sabbatical year to the employer who granted the leave of absence. Each year approximately twelve fellowships are awarded to U.S. journalists and ten to twelve to international journalists. U.S. journalists receive tuition and a $25,000 stipend for living expenses. Funding arrangements vary for international journalists as they must obtain funding by competing successfully for restricted grants available to the Nieman Foundation, or by securing their own financial backing from outside sources.

Available to: Working journalists
Deadlines: January 31 for U.S. journalists; March 1 for international journalists
Apply to: Program Officer, above address

Nimrod Magazine
Arts and Humanities Council of Tulsa
2210 South Main
Tulsa, OK 74114

(F)
(P) The *Pablo Neruda Prize for Poetry* and the *Katherine Anne Porter Prize for Fiction,* each offering two first prizes of $1,000, and two second prizes of $500, are sponsored by *Nimrod.* Winners are flown to Tulsa for readings and an awards dinner with the judges. A $15 entry fee is required; applicants receive a copy of *Nimrod.* Send a business-sized SASE for complete contest guidelines.

Available to: Previously unpublished works; no dual submissions
Deadline: Submit material between January 1 and April 15
Apply to: Nimrod Prize Competition, above address

96 Inc.
PO Box 15559
Boston, MA 02115

The *Bruce Rossley Literary Award*, of $1,000, recognizes a Massachusetts writer of merit. The award, which is named for Boston's first commissioner of the arts and humanities, is presented by *96 Inc.*, a literary magazine and resource center in Boston. There are no specific publication requirements for nominating a writer; anyone may nominate a writer for the award by sending a letter of recommendation and support materials. In addition to writing, the writer's accomplishments in the fields of teaching and community service will also be considered.

Available to: Massachusetts residents
Deadline: September 30 (nominations not accepted prior to August 1)
Apply to: Bruce Rossley Literary Award, above address

Norcroft
Box 300105
Minneapolis, MN 55403

(R) Residences of one to four weeks at a remote lodge on the shores of Lake Superior are available to women writers of drama, fiction, and poetry whose work demonstrates an understanding of and commitment to feminist change. Each resident is provided with her own private bedroom and separate individual "writing shed." Housing is free; groceries are provided for residents to do their own cooking. Residences are offered from May through October. Write for application.

Available to: Feminist writers
Deadline: Inquire
Apply to: Above address

North Carolina Arts Council
Department of Cultural Resources
Raleigh, NC 27601-2807

(M)
(R) Fellowships of $8,000 are available to artists in North Carolina in areas including fiction and poetry. A two-month residence at Headlands Center for the Arts in California, and a three-month residence at the La Napoule Foundation in France are also available to writers of fiction, poetry, literary nonfiction, and literary translation. A one-month residence at the MacDowell Colony in New Hampshire is available for writers of fiction, poetry, and literary nonfiction.

Available to: North Carolina residents
Deadline: Inquire
Apply to: Write for guidelines and application to Literature Director, above address

The North Carolina Writers' Network
PO Box 954
Carrboro, NC 27510

(D) The *Paul Green Playwrights Prize*, of $500 and possible production, is given annually for an unpublished/unproduced play of any theme (no musicals). Playwrights should submit two copies and a synopsis of the script. There is a $10 entry fee.

Available to: No restrictions
Deadline: September 30
Apply to: Paul Green Playwrights Prize, NC Writers' Network, 3501 Highway 54 West, Studio C, Chapel Hill, NC 27516

(P) The *Randall Jarrell Poetry Prize*, of $500, is given annually for an unpublished poem composed in any form or genre. The winner will be published in *Parnassus: Poetry in Review*. Two copies of up to three poems should be submitted, not exceeding a total of ten single-spaced pages. There is a $5 entry fee.

Available to: No restrictions
Deadline: November 1
Apply to: Randall Jarrell Poetry Prize, NC Writers' Network, 3501 Highway 54 West, Studio C, Chapel Hill, NC 27516

(F) The *Thomas Wolfe Fiction Prize*, of $500 with possible publication, is given annually for an unpublished work of fiction. Writers may submit two copies of up to twelve pages (novel excerpt or short story). There is a $5 entry fee.

Available to: No restrictions
Deadline: August 31
Apply to: Thomas Wolfe Fiction Prize, NC Writers' Network, 3501 Highway 54 West, Studio C, Chapel Hill, NC 27516

Northeastern University
English Department
406 Holmes Hall
Boston, MA 02115

(P) The *Samuel French Morse Poetry Prize*, awarded annually for the manuscript of a first or second book of poems by a U.S. poet, consists of publication of the manuscript with Northeastern University Press and a cash award of $500. Send an SASE for further information and rules. A $10 reading fee must accompany the manuscript.

Available to: U.S. citizens and residents
Deadline: September 15
Apply to: Professor Guy Rotella, Editor, Morse Poetry Prize, above address

Northern Kentucky University
Department of Theatre
Highland Heights, KY 41099-1007

(D) The *Year-End-Series New Play Festival* biennially awards three prizes of $400 each, plus production and travel expenses to attend late rehearsals and performance, for unproduced musicals, adaptations, and plays. Preference is given to plays with roles that can be handled by actors age eighteen to twenty-five. Write for application.

Available to: No restrictions
Deadline: October 15, 1996; inquire for 1998
Apply to: Y.E.S., Project Director, above address

Northern Michigan University
Forest Roberts Theatre
1401 Presque Isle
Marquette, MI 49855-5364

(D) The *Mildred and Albert Panowski Playwriting Award*, of $2,000, is awarded to the author of the best original, full-length, and previously unproduced, unpublished play submitted to the competition. A fully mounted production of the winning play will be included in the Forest Roberts Theatre season. The winning playwright will be flown to Marquette to act as artist-in-residence at Northern Michigan University during the run of the show, expenses provided. For manuscript preparation guidelines write to Playwriting Award Information, above address.

Available to: No restrictions
Deadline: Mid-November; inquire for exact date
Apply to: Panowski Playwriting Contest, above address

Northwest Writers, Inc.
PO Box 3437
Portland, OR 97208

(M) The *Andres Berger Awards* offer $1,000 prizes in fiction, nonfiction, and poetry to writers living in Oregon, Washington, Idaho, British Columbia, and Alaska. The awards recognize published writing by professional Northwest authors. Among works of comparable merit, preference will be given to those that touch on social concerns. Work submitted must have been published in the five years before the contest deadline. There is a $20 entry fee; an entry is one to six poems, a work of short prose, or an excerpt from one longer work. Send an SASE for complete guidelines and entry form.

Available to: Writers from Oregon, Washington, Idaho, British Columbia, and Alaska
Deadline: January 31
Apply to: Andres Berger Awards, above address

Northwood University
Alden B. Dow Creativity Center
3225 Cook Road
Midland, MI 48640-2398

(R) The *Summer Resident Fellowship Program* is open to individuals in all fields and professions who wish to pursue innovative ideas having the potential for impact in their fields. Awards include round-trip travel to Midland, room and board, and a stipend to be used at the discretion of the awardee. Fellows are expected to be capable of working independently and living cooperatively. No accommodations for spouses/families are available. In considering project ideas, the evaluation board is most concerned with the newness, significance, and quality of the idea.

Available to: No restrictions
Deadline: December 31
Apply to: Above address

NORWAY
Nordmanns-Forbundet
Radhusgata 23b
N-0158 Oslo
Norway

(T) The Nordmanns-Forbundet, in its desire to make Norwegian culture known abroad, awards an annual grant of 15,000 Norwegian crowns to one or more publishing houses introducing Norwegian fiction or poetry in translation (preferably contemporary).

Available to: American publishing houses
Deadline: December 15
Apply to: Nordmanns-Forbundet's Translation Grant, above address

NORWAY
NORLA-Norwegian Literature Abroad
Bygdoy alle 21
N-0262 Oslo
Norway

(T) NORLA offers grants for the translation of Norwegian fiction, poetry, and children's books into any language. Translators must apply for grants through their publisher, and grants will be assessed both on the quality of the book and its translation and the publisher's ability to market the translation satisfactorily. Contact NORLA for additional information and application form.

Available to: No restrictions

Deadline: Inquire
Apply to: Ms. Kristin Brudevoll, above address

Scott O'Dell Award for Historical Fiction
c/o Zena Sutherland
1700 East 56th Street, #3906
Chicago, IL 60637

© The *Scott O'Dell Award for Historical Fiction* offers $5,000 for a distinguished work of historical fiction for children or young adults published in the United States during the calendar year under consideration. The book must be set in the New World (North, Central, or South America).

Available to: U.S. citizens
Deadline: December 31
Apply to: Above address

Off Center Theater
Tampa Bay Performing Arts Center
Box 518
Tampa, FL 33601-0518

Ⓓ The *New Women Playwright's Festival* offers $1,000, full production, and travel and housing to attend rehearsals and performances for a play by and about women with casts at least fifty percent female. Submissions should preferably be unproduced comedies depicting "strong, intelligent, contemporary women with keen senses of humor, sharp wit and fascinating insights." Write for guidelines.

Available to: Women playwrights
Deadline: September 15
Apply to: Wendy Leigh, Artistic Director, above address

Oglebay Institute
c/o Stifel Fine Arts Center
1330 National Road
Wheeling, WV 26003

Ⓓ The *Towngate Theatre Playwriting Competition* is an annual contest that includes a cash prize of $300 and a limited-run production of the play. An author may submit more than one play, and coauthored plays are accepted. The author's travel expenses up to $200 may be reimbursed, if funding permits, if he or she attends the production of the play. Scripts of a serious and thoughtful nature which may not have wide appeal are encouraged.

Available to: Playwrights whose nonmusical plays (submitted) have not been previously produced
Deadline: January 1
Apply to: Kate Crosbie, Director of Performing Arts, Towngate Theatre Playwriting Competition, above address

Ohio Arts Council
727 East Main Street
Columbus, OH 43205-1796

Ⓜ Fellowships of $5,000 and $10,000 are given annually to Ohio poets, fiction writers, nonfiction writers, playwrights, and critics. Write for complete guidelines and application form.

Available to: Ohio residents, nonstudents 18 years and older
Deadline: September 1
Apply to: Ken Emerick, Coordinator, Individual Artists Fellowship Program, above address

Ohio State University Press
180 Pressey Hall
1070 Carmack Road
Columbus, OH 43210

(P) The *Journal/Ohio State University Press Award in Poetry* selects one full-length manuscript each year for a $1,000 cash prize plus publication of the winning manuscript by the Ohio State University Press in its Poetry Series, with usual royalties. Entries must be at least forty-eight pages, and must be submitted during the month of September. A $15 reading and handling fee must accompany each manuscript. Everyone submitting a manuscript receives a one-year subscription to the *Journal.*

Available to: No restrictions
Deadline: Submissions accepted in the month of September only
Apply to: David Citino, Poetry Series Editor, above address

Ohioana Library Association
65 South Front Street, Suite 1105
Columbus, OH 43215

The *Walter Rumsey Marvin Grant* of $1,000 is given biennially to an unpublished Ohio writer under the age of thirty. Up to six pieces of prose may be submitted.

Available to: Those born in Ohio or who have lived in Ohio for a minimum of five years
Deadline: January 31 in even-numbered years
Apply to: Walter Rumsey Marvin Grant, above address

(C) The *Ohioana Award for Children's Literature/Alice Wood Memorial Award* of $1,000 is given to an author whose body of work has made, and continues to make, a significant contribution to literature for children or young adults.

Available to: Those born in Ohio or who have lived in Ohio for a minimum of five years
Deadline: December 31
Apply to: The Alice Wood Memorial Award, above address

(P) The *Ohioana Poetry Award/Helen and Laura Krout Memorial* of $1,000 is given to an individual whose body of work has made, and continues to make, a significant contribution to the poetry of Ohio, and through whose work as a writer, teacher, administrator, or in community service, interest in poetry has developed.

Available to: Poets born in Ohio or who have lived in Ohio for a minimum of five years
Deadline: December 31
Apply to: Ohioana Poetry Award, above address

The Eugene O'Neill Theater Center
234 West 44th Street, Suite 901
New York, NY 10036

(D) The *National Playwrights Conference* offers staged readings at the Eugene O'Neill Theater Center in Waterford, Connecticut, of nine to twelve original stage plays, as well as development and reading of two or three original scripts for the New Drama for Media Project. The authors of the selected plays receive a stipend, transportation to and from the conference, plus room and board. Attendance for the duration of the conference, held in the month of July, is required.

Available to: U.S. citizens or permanent residents
Deadline: December 1
Apply to: National Playwrights Conference, above address; request guidelines with an SASE in September

Oregon Arts Commission
775 Summer Street NE
Salem, OR 97310

Ⓜ *Individual Artists Fellowships*, of $3,000, are available to Oregon residents in areas including fiction, nonfiction, poetry, and playwriting. Write for application.

Available to: Oregon residents
Deadline: September 1
Apply to: Individual Artists Fellowship Program, above address

Organization of American Historians
112 North Bryan Street
Bloomington, IN 47408-4199

The organization sponsors or cosponsors several awards and prizes given in recognition of scholarly and professional achievements in the field of American History.

Ⓝ The *ABC-Clio America: History and Life Award*, of $750, is given biennially to recognize and encourage scholarship in American history in the journal literature advancing new perspectives on accepted interpretations or previously unconsidered topics.

Available to: No restrictions
Deadline: November 15 of even-numbered years
Apply to: ABC-Clio America: History and Life Award, above address

The *Erik Barnouw Award*, of $500, is given annually to an outstanding television or film program dealing with American history, the study of American history, and/or the promotion of history as a lifetime habit.

Available to: No restrictions
Deadline: December 1
Apply to: Erik Barnouw Award, above address

Ⓝ The *Ray Allen Billington Prize* of $1,000 is made biennially to an author of a book in American frontier history.

Available to: No restrictions
Deadline: October 1 of even-numbered years
Apply to: Ray Allen Billington Prize, above address

Ⓝ The *Binkley-Stephenson Award*, of $500, is given for the best scholarly article published in the *Journal of American History* during the preceding calendar year.

Available to: Contributors to the *Journal of American History*
Deadline: December 31
Apply to: *Journal of American History*, above address

Ⓝ The *Avery O. Craven Award*, of $500, is given annually for the most original book on the coming of the Civil War, the Civil War years, or the era of Reconstruction, with the exception of works of purely military history. The exception recognizes and reflects the Quaker convictions of Craven.

Available to: No restrictions
Deadline: October 1
Apply to: Avery O. Craven Award, above address

Ⓝ The *Merle Curti Award*, of $1,000, is given alternately to a book in American intellectual history (in odd-numbered years) and to one in social history (in even-numbered years), published during the preceding two years.

Available to: No restrictions
Deadline: October 1
Apply to: Merle Curti Award, above address

The *Huggins-Quarles Awards* are given annually to minority graduate students in American history at the dissertation research stage of their Ph.D. programs. Amounts vary but do not exceed $1,000.

Available to: Minority doctorate students
Deadline: January 8, 1996; inquire for 1997
Apply to: Huggins-Quarles Awards, above address

(N) The *Richard W. Leopold Prize* gives $1,500 biennially for the best book written by a historian connected with federal, state, or municipal governments, in the areas of foreign policy, military affairs broadly construed, the historical activities of the federal government, or biography in one of the foregoing areas.

Available to: Applicants must have been employed in a government position for at least five years
Deadline: September 1 of odd-numbered years
Apply to: Richard W. Leopold Prize, above address

The *Lerner-Scott Prize* offers $1,000 and a certificate annually for the best doctoral dissertation in U.S. women's history completed during the previous academic year (July 1 to June 30).

Available to: Doctoral candidates
Deadline: November 1
Apply to: Lerner-Scott Prize, above address

(N) The *Louis Pelzer Memorial Award* is given for the best essay (up to 7,000 words), about any topic or period of U.S. history written by a graduate student in any field. Publication of the essay in the *Journal of American History,* a medal, and a prize of $500 are awarded annually.

Available to: Graduate students
Deadline: November 30
Apply to: Louis Pelzer Memorial Award, *Journal of American History,* 1125 East Atwater, Indiana University, Bloomington, IN 47401

(N) The *James A. Rawley Prize* of $750 is given annually for a book dealing with the history of race relations in the United States.

Available to: No restrictions
Deadline: October 1
Apply to: James A. Rawley Prize, above address

(N) The *Elliott Rudwick Prize,* of $2,000, and a certificate is awarded biennially for a book on the experience of racial and ethnic minorities in the United States.

Available to: No restrictions
Deadline: September 1 of even-numbered years
Apply to: Elliott Rudwick Prize, above address

(N) The *Frederick Jackson Turner Award,* of $1,000, is given each year for an author's first book on a significant phase of American history. Write for specific rules and details of competition.

Available to: No restrictions
Deadline: September 1
Apply to: Frederick Jackson Turner Award, above address

Overseas Press Club of America
320 East 42nd Street
New York, NY 10017

The Overseas Press Club annually offers eighteen awards for newspaper, magazine, wire service, radio, television, cartoon, book, and photographic reporting and/or interpretation from abroad that has been published or broadcast in the United States during the calendar year. Each award offers a $1,000 cash prize, and each submission must be accompanied by a $100 entry fee. The following are awards for print journalists:

Ⓙ The *Hal Boyle Award*, sponsored by AT&T, is given for the best daily newspaper or wire service reporting from abroad.

Ⓙ The *Bob Considine Award*, sponsored by King Features Syndicate, is given for the best daily newspaper or wire service interpretation on foreign affairs.

Ⓙ The *Ed Cunningham Memorial Award*, sponsored by Mead Data Central, is given for the best magazine reporting from abroad.

Ⓙ The *Morton Frank Award* is given for the best business reporting from abroad in magazines.

Ⓙ The *Malcolm Forbes Award*, sponsored by *Forbes Magazine*, is given for the best business reporting from abroad in newspapers or wire services.

Ⓙ The *Cornelius Ryan Award* is given for the best nonfiction book on foreign affairs.

Ⓙ The *Madeline Dane Ross Award* is given for international reporting, in any medium, showing a concern for the human condition.

Ⓙ The *Eric and Amy Burger Award* is given for the best reporting, in any medium, dealing with human rights.

Ⓙ The *Whitman Bassow Award*, sponsored by AT&T, is given for the best reporting, in any medium, on environmental issues.

Available to: No restrictions
Deadline: January 30
Apply to: Sonia Fry, Manager, above address

Owl Creek Press
1620 North 45 Street
Seattle, WA 98103

Ⓟ The *Green Lake Chapbook Prize* offers $500 and publication by Owl Creek Press for an unpublished poetry manuscript of forty pages or less. Writers should include an acknowledgements page, a short bio, an SASE, and a $10 entry fee. Send an SASE for complete guidelines.

Available to: No restrictions
Deadline: August 15
Apply to: Green Lake Chapbook Prize, above address

Ⓟ The *Owl Creek Poetry Prize* offers $750 and publication by Owl Creek Press for an unpublished poetry manuscript over fifty pages. Writers should include an acknowledgements page, a short bio, an SASE, and a $10 entry fee. Send an SASE for complete guidelines.

Available to: No restrictions
Deadline: February 15
Apply to: Owl Creek Poetry Prize, above address

Paris Review
541 East 72nd Street
New York, NY 10021

Ⓕ The *Aga Khan Prize for Fiction* is awarded annually by the editors of the *Paris Review* for the best previously unpublished short story (1,000 to 10,000 words). Translations are acceptable and should be accompanied by a copy of the original text. The winner receives

$1,000 in addition to publication of the piece in the *Review*. One submission per envelope. An SASE is required for a response or the return of a manuscript.

Available to: No restrictions
Apply to: Aga Khan Prize for Fiction, at above address

(P) The *Bernard F. Conners Prize for Poetry* is awarded annually for the best previously unpublished long poem (over 200 lines). The winner receives $1,000 plus publication. One submission per envelope. An SASE is required for a response or the return of a manuscript.

Available to: No restrictions
Apply to: Bernard F. Conners Prize for Poetry, above address

Passaic County Community College
Poetry Center
One College Boulevard
Paterson, NJ 07509-1179

(P) The *Allen Ginsberg Poetry Award* offers a first prize of $300 for an original, unpublished poem. Applicants may submit up to three poems, not exceeding ten pages. Send an SASE for guidelines.

Available to: No restrictions
Deadline: March 31
Apply to: Allen Ginsberg Poetry Awards, above address

(P) The *Paterson Poetry Prize* offers $1,000 for a book of poetry published in the preceding year. The prize will be split evenly between the publisher and the poet, who will be asked to participate in an awards ceremony and to give a reading at the Poetry Center. Books must be at least forty-eight pages in length, with a minimum press run of 500 copies. Publishers should submit three copies of eligible books. Send an SASE for the required application form.

Available to: No restrictions
Deadline: February 1
Apply to: Paterson Poetry Prize, above address

(F) The *Paterson Fiction Prize* awards $500 for a novel or collection of short fiction which, in the opinion of the judges, is the strongest work of fiction published in the preceding year. The winning writer will be required to participate in an awards ceremony and to give a public reading as part of the Meet-the-Authors Series at the college. Publishers should send three copies of each book along with an application form.

Available to: No restrictions
Deadline: April 1, 1996; inquire for 1997
Apply to: Maria Mazziotti Gillan, Director, above address

(C) The *Paterson Prize for Books for Young People* offers a $500 award in each of three categories: pre-K through Grade 3, Grades 4-6, and Grades 7-12. In each category one book will be selected which, in the opinion of the judges, is the most outstanding book for young people published in the preceding year. Publishers should submit three copies of each book along with an application form.

Available to: No restrictions
Deadline: March 15, 1996; inquire for 1997
Apply to: Maria Mazziotti Gillan, Director, above address

Alicia Patterson Foundation Fellowship Program
1730 Pennsylvania Avenue, NW, Suite 850
Washington, DC 20006

(J) One-year grants of $30,000 are given to print journalists to pursue independent projects of significant interest. Candidates must be U.S. citizens with at least five years of professional print journalism experience. Recipients examine their chosen subjects—areas of significant foreign or domestic interest—and write four major articles for the *APF Reporter*, which is circulated to editors and other interested persons throughout the United States. All articles appearing in the *Reporter* may be reprinted freely with proper credit. Fellowships are not awarded for academic study.

Available to: U.S. citizens
Deadline: October 1
Apply to: Above address, after mid-June

Pavement Saw Press
7 James Street
Scotia, NY 12302

(P) The *Pavement Saw Press Chapbook Contest* offers $500 and publication for a poetry chapbook of no more than thirty-two pages. Poets should submit the manuscript and a cover letter with name, address, phone number, poem titles, publication credits, and a brief bio. There is a $6 entry fee.

Available to: No restrictions
Deadline: December 15
Apply to: Chapbook Contest, above address

PEN American Center
568 Broadway
New York, NY 10012-3225

(F) The *Hemingway Foundation/PEN Award for First Fiction*, of $7,500, is given annually to recognize distinguished first books of fiction by American writers. Only works published in the United States by an established publishing house during the current calendar year will be considered. Genre fiction will not be included unless the commercial character of the work is deemed secondary to its overall literary purpose and quality.

Available to: U.S. citizens or permanent residents
Deadline: December 16
Apply to: No application form; send three copies of eligible titles to Hemingway Foundation Award, above address

The *Gregory Kolovakos Award*, of $2,000, is awarded biennially to an American literary translator, editor, or critic whose work honors the richness of Hispanic literature and expands its English-language audience. The award's primary purpose is to recognize work from Spanish, but distinguished contributions from other languages of the Hispanic world will also be considered. Candidates will be considered not only for individual works but for collections of criticism or distinguished careers as translators or editors. Candidates may not nominate themselves. A letter of nomination must be received from the candidate's editor or colleague, accompanied by a copy of the candidate's vita. As the award is intended to recognize a sustained contribution over time to Latin American literatures in English translation, nominating letters should not focus exclusively on a single work published by the candidate, but should persuasively document the candidate's qualifications with particular attention given to the depth and vision of his or her work.

Available to: No restrictions
Deadline: November 1 of odd-numbered years
Apply to: Gregory Kolovakos Award, above address

(N) The *PEN/Martha Albrand Award for Nonfiction*, of $1,000, is given annually for a first-published book of general nonfiction by an American writer, distinguished by qualities of literary and stylistic excellence. The award includes a one-month residence at the Vermont Studio Center. Eligible books must have been published in the calendar year under consideration. There is no restriction on content, but non-literary subjects (such as how-to guides, inspirational tracts, and craft and exercise manuals) will not be considered. There is no application form; three copies of each title should be submitted.

Available to: American citizens or permanent residents
Deadline: December 16
Apply to: PEN/Martha Albrand Award for Nonfiction, above address

(T) The *PEN Award for Poetry in Translation*, of $1,000, is given for a booklength translation of poetry from any language into English published in the United States during the current calendar year. Translators may be of any nationality; U.S. residency or citizenship is not required. Submission of a book of translated poetry to this award does not preclude simultaneous submission to the PEN/Book-of-the-Month Club Translation Prize. There is no application form; two copies of eligible books should be submitted.

Available to: No restrictions
Deadline: December 16
Apply to: PEN Award for Poetry in Translation, above address

(T) The *PEN/Book-of-the-Month Club Translation Prize*, sponsored by the Book-of-the-Month Club, is awarded for the best booklength translation into English from any language published in the United States during the current calendar year. Technical, scientific, or reference works are not eligible. One prize of $3,000 is awarded annually.

Available to: No restrictions
Deadline: December 16
Apply to: No application form; send three copies of eligible books to above address

(N) The *PEN/Jerard Fund Award*, of $4,000, is awarded biennially to a booklength work-in-progress of general nonfiction, distinguished by high literary quality, by a woman writer at an early stage in her career. There are no restrictions upon the content of the work, but the emphasis is on the quality of the writing and the literary character of the subject. Manuscripts such as how-to manuals, cookery or craft books, and vocational guides will not be considered. Applicant should submit two copies of no more than fifty pages of her work-in-progress accompanied by a list of her publications.

Available to: Women who have published at least one magazine article in a national publication or in a major literary magazine, and who have not published more than one book of any kind
Deadline: January 1, 1997
Apply to: PEN/Jerard Fund, above address

(C) The *PEN/Norma Klein Award*, of $3,000, is given biennially to recognize an emerging voice of literary merit among American writers of children's fiction. Candidates are new authors whose books (for elementary school to young adult readers) demonstrate the adventuresome, innovative spirit that characterizes the best children's literature and Norma Klein's own work (but need not resemble her novels stylistically). Candidates may not nominate themselves. Nominations are welcomed from authors and editors of children's books, and should include a list of the candidate's publications.

Available to: No restrictions
Deadline: December 16, 1996
Apply to: PEN/Norma Klein Award, above address

(N) The *PEN/Spielvogel-Diamonstein Award for the Art of the Essay*, of $5,000, is given for a distinguished book of previously uncollected essays on any subject by an American writer published in the calendar year under consideration. Individual essays included in books submitted may have previously appeared in magazines, journals, or anthologies, but must not have been collectively published before in book form. There are no restrictions on the subject matter of the essays; books are judged solely on the basis of literary character and distinction of writing, and equal consideration is given to the work of both renowned essayists and more recently established writers. Essays may deal either with a range of subjects or may explore one specific theme, but the book, on the whole, should be a series of individual essays, not conceived as a single booklength work of nonfiction. There is no application form; four copies of each title should be submitted.

Available to: American citizens or permanent residents
Deadline: December 16
Apply to: PEN/Spielvogel-Diamonstein Award, above address

(P) The *PEN/Voelcker Award for Poetry*, of $5,000, is given biennially, in even-numbered years, to an American poet whose distinguished and growing body of work to date represents a notable and accomplished presence in American literature. Candidates can be nominated only by members of PEN. All letters of nomination should describe the scope and literary caliber of the candidate's work, summarize the candidate's publications, and articulate the degree of accomplishment the nominated poet has attained and the esteem in which his or her work is held within the American literary community.

Available to: American poets
Deadline: January 1, 1998
Apply to: PEN/Voelcker Award for Poetry, above address

The *PEN Writers Fund* helps established writers through a financial emergency. Grants and loans—maximum amount of $1,000—are given periodically. The *PEN Fund for Writers and Editors with AIDS* is administered under the PEN Writers Fund and gives grants ranging from $500 to $1,000. Applications are reviewed every four to six weeks.

Available to: U.S. residents
Deadline: None
Apply to: Writers Fund, above address

(T) The *Renato Poggioli Translation Award*, of $3,000, is given annually to encourage a beginning promising translator who is working on his or her first book-length translation from the Italian into English. Letters of application should be accompanied by a curriculum vitae including the candidate's Italian studies, a statement of purpose, and a sample (or samples) of the translation-in-progress with the original Italian text, not exceeding fifty pages. It is preferable, though not necessary, that the candidate spend the grant period in Italy.

Available to: No restrictions
Deadline: December 31
Apply to: Renato Poggioli Award, above address

PEN Center USA West
672 South Lafayette Park Place, Suite 41
Los Angeles, CA 90057

Nine *PEN West Literary Awards*, of at least $500 each, are available annually in the categories of fiction, nonfiction, poetry, journalism, children's literature, drama, translation, screenplay, and teleplay, published or produced in the current calendar year. Winners are honored at the Literary Festival in Los Angeles held each year. To enter, publishers, agents, or authors should send four copies of each title (for screenplay and teleplay awards, submit author's name and titles only).

Available to: Writers living west of the Mississippi River
Deadline: December 31
Apply to: PEN West Literary Awards, above address

PEN New England. *See* **The Boston Globe**

PEN/Faulkner Award for Fiction
c/o Folger Shakespeare Library
201 East Capitol Street, SE
Washington, DC 20003

(F) The *PEN/Faulkner Award for Fiction*, of $15,000, is awarded annually to recognize the most distinguished work of fiction published by an American writer. Four additional nominees each receive $5,000. All publishers of book-length works of fiction (novels or short story collections), as well as the authors themselves and their agents, are invited to submit four copies of all eligible titles published in the United States in the calendar year preceding that of the award. No juvenile titles.

Available to: U.S. citizens
Deadline: December 31
Apply to: Janice Delaney, above address

Peninsula Community Foundation
1700 South El Camino Real, No. 300
San Mateo, CA 94402-3049

Ⓜ The *Individual Artists Program* provides a small number of grants to artists, including poets, playwrights, and fiction writers who are residents of San Mateo and northern Santa Clara counties, California. Grants up to $500 match writer's expenditures for specific projects. These are one-time grants, not renewable.

Available to: San Mateo and northern Santa Clara county residents only, at least nineteen years of age and working in the field of application
Deadline: Inquire
Apply to: Individual Artists Program Committee, above address

Pennsylvania Council on the Arts
216 Finance Building
Harrisburg, PA 17120

The Pennsylvania Council on the Arts offers fellowships to Pennsylvania writers who demonstrate excellence in work reflecting continued, serious, and exceptional aesthetic investigation. Fellowships of $5,000 are available in alternate years for fiction and poetry. Applicant must have an established career as a writer. Write for application and guidelines.

Available to: Pennsylvania residents; no students
Deadline: August 1, 1996 for fiction; August 1, 1997 for poetry
Apply to: Above address

Penumbra Theatre Company
270 North Kent Street
St. Paul, MN 55102-1794

Ⓓ The *Cornerstone Dramaturgy and Development Project* is intended to nurture the development of new and emerging playwrights who address the African American and/or Pan-African experience. One playwright a year is offered a mainstage production with a possible three- to four-week residency; one playwright is offered a four-week workshop-residence culminating in a staged reading; and three playwrights are offered staged readings. Financial assistance varies according to the needs of the each project and playwright. Write for additional information.

Available to: No restrictions
Deadline: Ongoing
Apply to: Cornerstone Dramaturgy and Development Project, above address

Pew Fellowships in the Arts
University of the Arts
250 South Broad Street, Suite 400
Philadelphia, PA 19102

Ⓜ The *Pew Fellowships in the Arts* offer annual grants of $50,000 to artists working in a wide variety of disciplines, including poetry, scriptworks, fiction, and literary nonfiction. Applicants are required to be residents of Philadelphia, Montgomery, Delaware, Chester, or Bucks County, Pennsylvania.

Available to: Currently restricted to residents of specified counties in Pennsylvania

Deadline: Inquire
Apply to: Above address

Phi Beta Kappa
1811 Q Street, NW
Washington, DC 20009

Ⓝ The *Ralph Waldo Emerson Award,* of $2,500, is given annually for an outstanding interpretation of the intellectual and cultural condition of man published in the United States. Studies in history, religion, philosophy, sociology, anthropology, political science, and related fields are eligible. Submissions must be made by publishers.

> Available to: U.S. citizens or residents
> Deadline: April 30 for books published from May 1 of the preceding year to the deadline date
> Apply to: Above address

Ⓝ The *Christian Gauss Award* is given for an outstanding book of literary scholarship or criticism published in the United States. One award of $2,500 given annually. Submissions must be made by publishers.

> Available to: U.S. citizens or residents
> Deadline: April 30 for books published from May 1 of the preceding year to the deadline date
> Apply to: Above address

Ⓝ The *Phi Beta Kappa Award in Science,* of $2,500, is given annually for an outstanding book on science or interpretation of science written by a scientist and published in the United States. Submissions must be made by publishers.

> Available to: U.S. citizens or residents
> Deadline: April 30 for books published from May 1 of the preceding year to the deadline date
> Apply to: Above address

The *Mary Isabel Sibley Fellowship* is given in odd-numbered years for advanced study, research, or writing projects dealing with Greek language, literature, history, or archaeology, or, in even-numbered years, on any aspect of French language or literature. The fellowship carries a stipend of $10,000 for a period of one year and is awarded annually.

> Available to: Unmarried women between the ages of twenty-five and thirty-five who hold the doctorate or have fulfilled all the requirements for the doctorate except dissertation
> Deadline: January 15
> Apply to: Mary Isabel Sibley Fellowship Committee, above address

Philadelphia Festival Theater for New Plays at Annenberg Center
3680 Walnut Street
Philadelphia, PA 19104

Ⓓ The *Dennis McIntyre Playwriting Award* is given to a full-length, unproduced play by an emerging playwright of conscience whose script examines society's problems with honest scrutiny. The award includes a cash stipend and either a full production with travel expenses and four weeks' room and board for the author to attend rehearsals, or a staged reading with travel expenses and housing to attend the reading. Inquire for guidelines.

> Available to: No restrictions
> Deadline: Inquire
> Apply to: The Dennis McIntyre Playwriting Award, above address

Phillips Exeter Academy
Exeter, NH 03833

The *George Bennett Fellowship* is awarded annually to a person contemplating or embarking on a career as a writer who has underway a manuscript which he or she needs time and freedom from material considerations to complete. The Fellow's only official duties are to be in residence while the Academy is in session and to write, but he or she is expected also to be available to students interested in writing. The primary basis for selection is the manuscript submitted (preferably the manuscript in progress). The grant consists of a stipend of $5,000 plus room and board for the writer and the writer's family during the academic year. Send an SASE for application form and information. The committee favors writers who have not yet published a booklength work with a major publisher.

Available to: See above
Deadline: December 1
Apply to: Above address

Phoenix Theatre
749 North Park Street
Indianapolis, IN 46202

(D) The *Festival of Emerging American Theatre (FEAT) Playwriting Competition* offers an annual award of $750 for full-length plays and $325 for one-acts. Two full-production slots will be filled, each with a full-length play or a bill of one-acts. Plays must be suitable for a 150-seat proscenium and/or a 75-seat black box; availability of the playwright for rehearsals will be a consideration. Submit script with a synopsis and bio, and a $5 entry fee.

Available to: No restrictions
Deadline: February 15
Apply to: FEAT Competition, above address

Pig Iron Press
PO Box 237
Youngstown, OH 44501

(F)
(P) The *Kenneth Patchen Competition* offers a $100 cash prize, publication, and royalties for a full-length manuscript of poetry and fiction (novel or short story collection) in alternate years. The 1996 competition will be for fiction; poetry will be considered in 1997. Of the 1,000 paperback copies printed, the winning author will receive fifty. There is a $10 reading fee. Send an SASE for complete guidelines.

Available to: No restrictions
Deadline: October 31
Apply to: Kenneth Patchen Competition, above address

Pilgrim Project
Religion and Public Life
156 Fifth Avenue, Suite 400
New York, NY 10010

(D) The Pilgrim Project offers grants to playwrights ranging from $1,000 to $7,000, with an average award of $3,350. Grants are intended to defray the cost of readings, workshop productions or full productions of plays that "deal with questions of moral significance." Applications are reviewed year-round, on an ongoing basis. Write for further information.

Available to: No restrictions
Deadline: Ongoing
Apply to: Above address

Pioneer Drama Service
Box 4267
Englewood, CO 80155-4267

(D)   The *Shubert Fendrich Memorial Playwriting Contest* offers publication with a $1,000 advance on royalties (ten percent book royalty, fifty percent performance royalty) for produced, unpublished work of not more than ninety minutes' duration. Full-length plays, one-acts, translations, adaptations, and plays for young audiences are all eligible; the subject matter and language should be appropriate for schools and community theaters. Work with a preponderance of female roles and minimal set requirements are preferred. All entries will be considered for publication. Send an SASE for guidelines.

Available to: No restrictions
Deadline: March 1
Apply to: Shubert Fendrich Memorial Playwriting Contest, above address

Pirate's Alley Faulkner Society
632 Pirate's Alley
New Orleans, LA 70116

(F)   The *William Faulkner Prizes for Fiction* offer $7,500 for a novel ($2,500 of which is designated as an advance against royalties to encourage a publisher to print the winning book); $2,500 for a novella ($1,000 as an advance against royalties); and $1,500 for an individual short story ($250 as an advance against royalties or writer's fees as an incentive for publication). Novels should be 50,000 words or more; novellas should be less than 50,000 words; short stories should be less than 15,000 words. There is a $35 entry fee for the novel competition, a $30 fee for the novella, and a $25 fee for the individual short story. The society also sponsors a $1,000 award for an individual short story by a Louisiana high school student ($750 for the winning student and $250 for the sponsoring teacher). There is a $10 entry fee for this competition. Winners of the competition must make a presentation at the society's annual meeting in September. Send an SASE for an application, guidelines, and further information.

Available to: U.S. citizens; the high school award is limited to Louisiana residents
Deadline: April 1
Apply to: Faulkner Prizes for Fiction, above address

Playboy Foundation
680 North Lake Shore Drive
Chicago, IL 60611

The *Hugh M. Hefner First Amendment Awards*, of $5,000 each, are given to recognize the efforts of individuals working to protect and enhance First Amendment freedoms. Eligibility is not restricted by profession; however, winners have traditionally come from the areas of print and broadcast journalism, government, education, publishing, law, and entertainment (motion pictures, television, and theater).

Available to: No restrictions
Deadline: May 1
Apply to: Hugh M. Hefner First Amendment Awards, above address

Playboy Magazine
680 North Lake Shore Drive
Chicago, IL 60611

(F)   The *Playboy College Fiction Contest* awards a first prize of $3,000 and publication in *Playboy* to a work of fiction, twenty-five pages or less, by a college student of any age (M.F.A. graduate students are eligible). Second prize is $500 and a one-year subscription to *Playboy*. Enclose a 3-by-5-inch card listing name, age, college affiliation, permanent home address, and phone number with manuscript submission.

Available to: College students
Deadline: January 1
Apply to: Playboy College Fiction Contest, above address

The Players
16 Gramercy Park South
New York, NY 10003

(D) The *Playwrights First Plays-in-Progress Award* offers $1,000 and a possible reading for selected plays. When appropriate, chosen playwrights will be directed to literary managers, artistic directors, agents and/or producers with the aim of advancing the play and play-wright toward production. No translations or adaptations are accepted.

Available to: No restrictions
Deadline: October 15
Apply to: Playwrights First, Department PN, above address

Playhouse on the Square
51 South Cooper Street
Memphis, TN 38104

(D) The *Playhouse on the Square New Play Competition* annually awards $500 and production to an unproduced work with a small cast. Full-length plays and musicals are eligible.

Available to: No restrictions, though Southern playwrights preferred
Deadline: April 1
Apply to: New Play Competition, above address

The Playwrights' Center
2301 Franklin Avenue East
Minneapolis, MN 55406

(D) The *Jerome Playwright-in-Residence Fellowships* offer five playwright-in-residence positions with an accompanying stipend of $7,000 annually to promising playwrights who have not had more than two different plays professionally produced. Playwrights have access to public readings and workshops. The recipients are required to participate in Center activities during the year-long residence. Send an SASE after July for an application.

Available to: Citizens or permanent U.S. residents
Deadline: September 15
Apply to: Jerome Fellowship, above address

(D) The *McKnight Fellowship* offers two $10,000 stipends, with one-month residences to play-wrights with a minimum of two different plays professionally produced. Additional funds of up to $2,000 per fellow are available for workshops and staged readings of fellow's scripts. Send an SASE after November 15 for an application.

Available to: U.S. citizens
Deadline: January 15
Apply to: McKnight Fellowship, above address

(D) *PlayLabs*, held in July/August, is a two-week developmental workshop for new plays which provides playwrights with the opportunity to work with their choice of national profes-sional directors, dramaturgs, and a professional company of local actors. Each play receives a public reading. Included is an honorarium, travel expenses, and room and board. Eligible scripts must be unproduced and unpublished. Send an SASE after Oc-tober 16 for an application.

Available to: U.S. citizens
Deadline: December 15
Apply to: PlayLabs, above address

The Playwrights' Center of San Francisco
Box 460466
San Francisco, CA 94146-0466

(D) *Dramarama*, an annual playwriting competition, offers a staged reading of up to eight scripts at the Playwrights' Center fall festival. A $500 prize will be awarded to the best play on the basis of the readings. Plays may be unproduced full-length or one-acts. There is a $25 submission fee. Send an SASE for complete guidelines.

Available to: No restrictions
Deadline: March 15
Apply to: Dramarama, above address

Playwrights Preview Productions
17 East 47th Street
New York, NY 10017

(D) The *Emerging Playwright Award* offers $500, production, and travel to attend rehearsals for full-length plays and one-acts that have not been produced in New York. Submissions by minority playwrights and plays with ethnically diverse casts are encouraged. Write for guidelines.

Available to: No restrictions
Deadline: Ongoing
Apply to: Emerging Playwright Award, above address

Playwrights' Theater of Denton
Box 732
Denton, TX 76202-0732

(D) The *Playwriting Competition* awards $1,000 and possible production for full-length plays and one-acts. There is a $15 reading fee. Write for guidelines.

Available to: No restrictions
Deadline: December 15
Apply to: Playwriting Competition, above address

Ploughshares
Emerson College
100 Beacon Street
Boston, MA 02116

[IN] The *John C. Zacharis First Book Award* offers $1,500 for the best debut book of poetry or short fiction published by a *Ploughshares* writer. Writers are nominated by the advisory editors of *Ploughshares*. There is no application process or deadline. *By Internal Nomination Only.*

The Plum Review
PO Box 1347
Philadelphia, PA 19105

(F)
(P)
The *Plum Review Poetry Contest* and the *Plum Review Fiction Contest* each offer $500 and publication in the *Review*. Poets may submit up to three poems of any length, style, or subject matter, along with a $5 reading fee. Fiction writers may submit a story of any length, style, or subject matter, along with a $10 reading fee. Send an SASE for contest rules and entry form.

Available to: No restrictions
Deadline: February 28 for poetry; November 30 for fiction
Apply to: Poetry Contest or Fiction Contest, above address

The Poetry Center
San Francisco State University
1600 Holloway Avenue
San Francisco, CA 94132

(P) The Poetry Center's *Book Award* offers a $500 cash prize and an invitation to read in the Poetry Center reading series to the author of an outstanding book of poems published in the current year. The award is for a volume by an individual poet; anthologies and translations are not acceptable. A $10 reading fee must accompany the submitted book.

Available to: No restrictions
Deadline: December 31
Apply to: Book Award, above address

Poetry Magazine
60 West Walton Street
Chicago, IL 60610

(P) Eight *Poetry Magazine Awards*, ranging from $100 to $1,000, are given annually to poetry published in the magazine. Applications are not accepted. All verse published in the magazine during the preceding year is automatically considered.

Available to: Poets whose work has appeared in *Poetry* during the previous year

[IN] The *Ruth Lilly Poetry Prize*, of $75,000, is given annually to a U.S. citizen in recognition of outstanding poetic achievement. Applications and nominations are not accepted. *By Internal Nomination Only*.

Poetry Society of America
15 Gramercy Park
New York, NY 10003

In addition to the awards listed below, other awards, some of which are open only to PSA members, are given annually. For competition guidelines, entry forms, and details of all PSA awards, send an SASE to the Society at the above address.

(P) The *George Bogin Memorial Award*, of $500, is given for a selection of four or five poems that reflect "the encounter of the ordinary and extraordinary, uses language in an original way, and takes a stand against oppression in any of its forms." There is a $5 entry fee for non-members.

Available to: U.S. citizens
Deadline: December 22
Apply to: George Bogin Memorial Award, above address

(P) The *Alice Fay Di Castagnola Award*, of $1,000, is given for a manuscript-in-progress of poetry, prose, or verse drama by a PSA member.

Available to: PSA members
Deadline: December 22
Apply to: Alice Fay Di Castagnola Award, above address

(P) The *Norma Farber First Book Award*, of $500, is given annually for a first book (not a chapbook) of original poetry by an American published during the calendar year. Submissions must be made by publishers only. There is a $10 entry fee per book.

Available to: U.S. citizens
Deadline: December 22
Apply to: Norma Farber Book Award, above address

(P) The *Lyric Poetry Award*, of $500, is given for a lyric poem by a PSA member of no more than fifty lines.

Available to: PSA members
Deadline: December 22
Apply to: Lyric Poetry Award, above address

(P) The *Lucille Medwick Memorial Award*, of $500, is given for an original poem in any form, by a PSA member, on freedom or a humanitarian theme.

Available to: PSA members only
Deadline: December 22
Apply to: Lucille Medwick Memorial Award, above address

[IN] The *Shelley Memorial Award*, of between $2,000 and $6,000, is given annually to a living American poet selected with reference to his or her genius and need. *By Internal Nomination Only.*

(P) The *William Carlos Williams Award* is a purchase-prize between $500 and $1,000 for a book of poetry published by a small, nonprofit, or university press. Submissions must made by publishers only and must be original works by a single author who is a permanent resident of the United States. Translations are not eligible. There is a $10 entry fee per book.

Available to: U.S. permanent residents
Deadline: December 22
Apply to: William Carlos Williams Award, above address

(P) The *Robert H. Winner Memorial Award*, of $2,500, is given to a poet over forty years of age who may have not yet published a book or who has had no more than one book published. Poets may submit a brief but cohesive manuscript of up to ten poems or twenty pages. There is a $5 entry fee for non-members.

Available to: Poets over forty
Deadline: December 22
Apply to: Robert H. Winner Award, above address

Poets & Writers
72 Spring Street
New York, NY 10012

The Poets & Writers *Readings/Workshops Program* provides matching fee money to pay poets, fiction writers, and literary performance artists for giving readings and writing workshops in a variety of public settings. Organizations that are eligible to apply for writers' fee payments include libraries, Ys, community centers, small presses, colleges and universities, correctional facilities, bookstores, religious organizations, and any community-based group interested in presenting literary events.

Available to: No restrictions
Deadline: Ongoing
Apply to: Readings/Workshops Program, above address, for Illinois, Indiana, Iowa, Michigan, Minnesota, New York, North Dakota, Ohio, South Dakota, and Wisconsin; for California, apply to Readings/Workshops Programs, Poets & Writers, Inc., 2140 Shattuck Avenue, Suite 601, Berkeley, CA 94704

(F)
(P) The *Writers Exchange Program* is designed to encourage a sharing of works and resources among emerging writers nationwide. Each year two writers from a designated state (a poet and a fiction writer) will be chosen. Each will receive a $500 honorarium and will give readings and meet with the literary community in two states outside the writer's home. Winning writers must be available for a one-week tour on a schedule determined by Poets & Writers. All related travel and lodging expenses and a per diem stipend are included. Inquire for complete guidelines and application form.

Available to: Emerging writers from states designated by Poets & Writers
Deadline: November 15
Apply to: Writers Exchange Program, above address

The Pope Foundation
211 West 56th Street
New York, NY 10019

(J) The Pope Foundation *Journalism Awards* offer three honorariums of $15,000 each to midcareer journalists (with a minimum of ten years journalistic background), to be used as working fellowships. Send an SASE for application and guidelines.

Available to: Midcareer journalists
Deadline: November 15
Apply to: Catherine Pope, Journalism Awards Program Director, above address

Potato Eyes Foundation
PO Box 76
Troy, ME 04987

(P) The *William and Kingman Page Chapbook Award* offers $500, publication by Nightshade Press, and 50 copies for a poetry chapbook. Poets may submit manuscripts of no more than thirty-one typewritten pages of unpublished poetry, with no more than forty-three lines per page. Include a cover sheet with title of the collection only, a separate acknowledgements sheet with the poet's name and address, an SASE, and a $10 reading fee.

Available to: No restrictions
Deadline: November 1
Apply to: William and Kingman Page Chapbook Award, above address

Prairie Schooner
201 Andrews Hall
University of Nebraska
Lincoln, NE 68588-0334

The following awards are given to writers whose work has been published in *Prairie Schooner* during the preceding calendar year.

The *Virginia Faulkner Award for Excellence in Writing,* of $1,000, is given annually for the best writing of any kind. The *Lawrence Foundation Award,* of $1,000, is given annually for the best short story. The *Bernice Slote Award,* of $500, is given annually for the best work by a beginning writer. The *Strousse Award,* of $500, is given annually for the best poem or group of poems.

Available to: *Prairie Schooner* contributors

Princess Grace Foundation—USA
725 Park Avenue
New York, NY 10021

(D) The *Princess Grace Awards: Playwright Fellowship* is awarded annually to a young, American playwright. The fellowship consists of a $7,500 grant and a ten-week residence, including travel expenses, at New Dramatists in New York City. The award is based primarily on the artistic quality of the submitted play and the potential of the fellowship to assist in the writer's growth. Write for guidelines.

Available to: U.S. citizens or permanent residents
Deadline: March 31
Apply to: Playwright Fellowship, above address

Princeton University
The Council of the Humanities
122 East Pyne
Princeton, NJ 08544-5264

The *Alfred Hodder Fellowship*, of $42,000, is given to a writer or scholar with "much more than ordinary intellectual and literary gifts" for the pursuit of independent work in the humanities. The selected fellow is usually someone outside academia, in the early stages of his or her career. The fellow spends an academic year in residence at Princeton working independently and may choose to present a lecture to students and faculty in the humanities. Candidates for Ph.D. degrees are not eligible. Write for application guidelines and further information.

Available to: No restrictions
Deadline: November 15
Apply to: Hodder Fellowship, above address

Princeton University Press
41 Williams Street
Princeton, NJ 08540-5237

(T) The *Lockert Library of Poetry in Translation* series publishes translations of both classic and modern works from many languages and cultures. Usually, two volumes are added to the Lockert Library series annually. There is no cash grant or award.

Available to: No restrictions
Deadline: None
Apply to: Literary Editor, Lockert Library of Poetry in Translation, above address

The Publishing Triangle
PO Box 114
Prince Street Station
New York, NY 10012

[IN] The *Bill Whitehead Award*, of $1,000, is given for a lifetime achievement in gay and lesbian literature. There is no application process. *By Internal Nomination Only.*

[IN] The *Ferro-Grumley Award*, of $1,000, is given for literary excellence in lesbian and gay-themed writing. There is no application process. *By Internal Nomination Only.*

Puffin Foundation Ltd.
20 East Oakdene Avenue
Teaneck, NJ 07666

The Puffin Foundation offers grants to artists and performers, including writers, who are committed to "continuing the dialogue between art and the lives of ordinary people. In particular, the foundation intends to foster and encourage younger artists and those projects which might find funding difficult because of the projects' genre and/or social philosophy." Average grants range from $500 to $2,000. Write for further information and application.

Available to: No restrictions
Deadline: December 31
Apply to: Above address

Pulliam Journalism Fellowships
The Indianapolis News
PO Box 145
Indianapolis, IN 46206-0145

(J) The *Pulliam Journalism Fellowships* provide an extensive crash course in daily newspaper
     journalism for twenty recent college graduates. Each Fellow joins the staff of the *Indi-
     anapolis News*, the *Indianapolis Star*, the *Phoenix Gazette*, or the *Arizona Republic*. Some
     may join the newsroom staffs as general assignment reporters; others may work as
     editorial writers or feature writers. Each fellow will receive a cash grant of $4,500, one-
     third of which will be paid before the fellowship begins. The remainder of the stipend
     will be disbursed during the course of the fellowship. Each fellow is responsible for
     providing his or her own housing, and each must provide transportation to Indianapolis
     or Phoenix. The fellowship runs from early June to mid-August. Candidates must have
     received their undergraduate degrees between August of the year preceding the appli-
     cation and June of the current year. Write for further information and application ma-
     terials.

     Available to: Recent newspaper journalism majors of liberal arts majors with part-time
          or full-time newspaper experience
     Deadline: March 1
     Apply to: Pulliam Journalism Fellowships, above address

Purdue University Press
1532 South Campus Courts-E
West Lafayette, IN 47907-1532

(P) The *Verna Emery Poetry Competition* offers publication of an unpublished collection of original
     poems, sixty to ninety pages in length. Multiple submissions are acceptable as long as
     the press is informed. There is a $10 reading fee. Write for guidelines and further
     information.

     Available to: No restrictions
     Deadline: January 15
     Apply to: Verna Emery Poetry Competition, above address

Pushcart Press
Box 380
Wainscott, NY 11975

(F)
     The *Editors' Book Award* offers $1,000 and hardcover publication to any booklength manu-
     script, either fiction or nonfiction, submitted to, but not yet accepted by, a commercial
(N) publisher. Manuscripts must be nominated by an editor at an American or Canadian
     publishing company.

     Available to: No restrictions
     Deadline: September 15
     Apply to: By editors' nomination only

Quality Paperback Book Club
1271 Avenue of the Americas
New York, NY 10017

[IN] The *New Voices Award* and the *New Visions Award* offer $5,000 each to the most distinctive
     and promising work of fiction and nonfiction, respectively, offered by the Quality Pa-
     perback Book Club each year. A panel of QPBC editors chooses the winner from work
     already selected as Book Club offerings. All publishers' submissions to the QPBC will
     be considered for the awards. There is no application process.

Quarterly Review of Literature Poetry Book Series
26 Haslet Avenue
Princeton, NJ 08540

(P) The *Quarterly Review of Literature Poetry Book Awards* are presented annually to four or five winners for a previously unpublished manuscript of poetry. The award consists of $1,000 and 100 books and publication in the *QRL* Series. Applicants should submit a book of miscellaneous poems, a poetic play, a long poem, or poetry translation of sixty to 100 pages. Manuscripts in English are also invited from outside the United States. Send an SASE for complete information. To encourage support, a $20 subscription to *QRL*, is requested with submission.

Available to: No restrictions
Deadlines: Submissions accepted only in the months of May and October
Apply to: QRL Awards, above address

Radcliffe College
The Mary Ingraham Bunting Institute
34 Concord Avenue
Cambridge, MA 02138

The *Bunting Fellowship Program* supports women of exceptional promise and demonstrated accomplishment who wish to pursue independent study in academic or professional fields, in creative writing, or in the arts. Appointments are full-time for the year September 1 through August 1 and require residence in the Boston area during the term of appointment. The fellowship stipend for the year is $30,000 with additional privileges. Applicants should have received their doctorate at least two years prior to the date of fellowship appointment. Academic applicants without doctorates but with equivalent professional experience will be considered. Applicants in creative writing, the visual arts, or music are expected to be at an equivalent stage in their careers. Please note that for the 1996-97 fellowship year, creative writers and other artists were awarded appointments only through an internal nomination process. That process is currently under review. Contact the institute for up-to-date application procedures.

Available to: As stated above
Deadline: October 15
Apply to: Bunting Fellowship Program, above address

Ragdale Foundation
1260 North Green Bay Road
Lake Forest, IL 60045

(R) Ragdale provides an opportunity for writers, artists, and composers to work, undisturbed, on their own projects. Comfortable living and working space is provided in beautiful buildings adjoining a large nature preserve. Studios are available for visual artists and composers. Maximum stay is two months. Those accepted for residences are asked to pay $15 per day. Some full and partial waivers are available based on financial need.

Available to: No restrictions
Deadline: Inquire
Apply to: Michael Wilkerson, above address

(R) The *Frances Shaw Fellowship for Older Women Writers* offers a two-month residence to a woman whose serious writing career began after the age of fifty-five. Send an SASE to above address for information.

Available to: See above
Deadline: February 1
Apply to: Above address

Rhode Island State Council on the Arts
95 Cedar Street, Suite 103
Providence, RI 02903-1034

(M) Literature fellowships are given to encourage the creative development of professional Rhode
Island artists by enabling them to set aside time to pursue their work and achieve specific
career goals. One fellowship of $5,000 and one runner-up prize of $1,000 are awarded
to a poet, fiction-writer, or dramatist.

Available to: Rhode Island residents, eighteen years of age or older who are not full-
time undergraduate or graduate students
Deadline: April 1
Apply to: Fellowships, above address

Mary Roberts Rinehart Fund
MSN 3E4
English Department
George Mason University
4400 University Drive
Fairfax, VA 22030-4444

(M) The *Mary Roberts Rinehart Fund* awards two grants to unpublished creative writers who need
financial assistance not otherwise available to complete work definitely projected.
Amount of grants depends upon the fund's ability to generate income (recent grants
have been around $950). Grants are given in two of four categories—fiction and poetry,
drama and nonfiction—on an alternate basis each year. From December 1, 1995, to
November 30, 1996, the fund will accept submissions in drama and nonfiction; from
December 1, 1996, to November 30, 1997, submissions will be accepted in fiction and
poetry. Candidates must be nominated by established writers or editors. Query for
details.

Available to: Unpublished writers
Deadline: November 30
Apply to: Above address

Rites and Reason Theatre
Brown University
Box 1148
Providence, RI 02912

(D) The *George Houston Bass Play-Rites Festival and Memorial Award* is given annually to a one-act
or full-length play that explores and analyzes "the cultural diversity of the New World."
Each finalist receives $250 and travel and housing for the rehearsal/production period.
From the finalists, one play will receive the Memorial Award, consisting of a $1,000
developmental contract and workshop production in Rites and Reason's subsequent
season. Playwrights must work with assigned dramaturgs on re-writes. Write for complete guidelines.

Available to: No restrictions
Deadline: March 1
Apply to: George Houston Bass Play-Rites Festival and Memorial Award, above address

River City
Department of English
University of Memphis
Memphis, TN 38152

(F) Three *River City Writing Awards in Fiction* are given annually for unpublished short stories
of up to 7,500 words. First prize is $2,000 and publication, second prize is $500, and
third prize is $300. There is a $12 entry fee which, upon request, will be applied toward
a new or continuing subscription to *River City*. No manuscripts will be returned.

Available to: No restrictions
Deadline: Inquire
Apply to: Paul Naylor, Editor, River City Writing Awards, above address

The Rockefeller Foundation
Bellagio Study and Conference Center
420 Fifth Avenue
New York, NY 10018-2702

Ⓡ Four-week residences in the Italian Alps from February 1 to December 15 for artists and
scholars. Room is available for spouses. Residents must pay their own travel cost. Only
applicants with several book publications will be seriously considered.

Available to: No restrictions
Deadline: One year prior to requested dates
Apply to: Susan Garfield, Manager, above address

Rome Arts and Community Center
308 West Bloomfield Street
Rome, NY 13440

Ⓟ The *Milton Dorfman Poetry Prize,* of $500, is awarded annually for original, previously un-
published poems. There is no limit to the numbers of submissions, but a reading fee
of $3 per poem is required. The winning poem will be published and read by the contest
judge at the center's open house. Write for further information.

Available to: No restrictions
Deadline: November 1
Apply to: Milton Dorfman Poetry Prize, above address

St. Martin's Press
175 Fifth Avenue
New York, NY 10010

Ⓕ The *Best First Private Eye Novel Contest,* cosponsored by Private Eye Writers of America,
annually awards $10,000 (as an advance against royalties) and publication. Send a #10
SASE for information before submitting manuscript. Authors must not be published
previously in the mystery genre and must have no novels in the genre under contract
for publication.

Available to: No restrictions
Deadline: Inquire
Apply to: Private Eye Contest, Thomas Dunne Books, above address

Ⓕ The *Malice Domestic Best First Novel Contest* for traditional mystery novels annually awards
$10,000 (as an advance against royalties) and publication. Send a #10 SASE for infor-
mation before submitting manuscript. Authors must not be published previously in the
mystery genre and must have no novels in the genre under contract for publication.

Available to: No restrictions
Deadline: Inquire
Apply to: Malice Domestic Contest, Thomas Dunne Books, above address

St. Mary's University of Minnesota
700 Terrace Heights
Campus Box 78
Winona, MN 55987-1399

Ⓓ The *Gilmore Creek Playwriting Competition* biennially offers $2,500, plus production, and a
stipend to cover travel, room and board for a two- to three-week residence for full-
length work that has not been produced professionally. The winning playwright is

expected to be involved in the rehearsal and artistic process of the production, and contribute to the academic life of the university. Write for guidelines and application form.

Available to: No restrictions
Deadline: January 15, 1997
Apply to: Gilmore Creek Playwriting Competition, above address

Salmon Run Press
PO Box 231081
Anchorage, AK 99523-1081

(P) The *Salmon Run Poetry Book Award* offers $500 and publication for a poetry manuscript of forty-eight to ninety-six pages. The winning book will be published in an edition of 500 or 1,000 copies, and will be advertised nationally. There is a $10 reading fee. Send an SASE for guidelines.

Available to: No restrictions
Deadline: December 30
Apply to: Poetry Book Award, above address

Salt Hill Journal
Syracuse University
Department of English
401 Hall of Languages
Syracuse, NY 13244-1170

(P) The *Salt Hill Journal Poetry Prize* offers a $500 first prize and publication in *Salt Hill Journal,* Syracuse University's literary magazine, for an unpublished poem. A $100 second prize and three honorable mentions will also be given. All entries will be considered for publication in the journal. Poets may submit three poems of any length, style, or subject matter. There is a reading fee of $5.

Available to: No restrictions
Deadline: Spring; inquire for exact date
Apply to: Michael Paul Thomas, Editor, above address

Sarabande Books
2234 Dundee Road, Suite 200
Louisville, KY 40205

(F) The *Mary McCarthy Prize in Short Fiction* awards $2,000 and publication by Sarabande Books for a collection of short stories or novellas. Winners will also receive a standard royalty contract. Send an SASE for complete contest guidelines and entry form.

Available to: Residing citizens of the United States
Deadline: Submissions accepted from January 1 to February 15
Apply to: Mary McCarthy Prize in Short Fiction, above address

(P) The *Kathryn A. Morton Prize in Poetry* awards $2,000 and publication by Sarabande Books for a full-length volume of poetry. Winners will also receive a standard royalty contract. Send an SASE for complete contest guidelines and entry form.

Available to: Residing citizens of the United States
Deadline: Submissions accepted from January 1 to February 15
Apply to: Kathryn A. Morton Prize in Poetry, above address

Scholastic
555 Broadway
New York, NY 10012

The *Scholastic Writing Awards* provide junior and senior high school students in grades seven through twelve with cash prizes from $100 to $5,000. In addition, several scholarship grants and special equipment prizes are available.

Available to: Students in grades 7 through 12
Deadline: Write for rules book between September and December
Apply to: Scholastic Writing Awards, above address

Scripps Howard Foundation
312 Walnut Street
Cincinnati, OH 45202

Ⓙ The *Environmental Reporting/Edward J. Meeman Awards*, totaling $4,000, are given in recognition of outstanding environmental reporting published in daily newspapers during the preceding calendar year. This award is given to encourage journalists to help educate the public and public officials to better environmental understanding and support for environmental protection. Work published in magazines or periodicals is not eligible.

Available to: Any daily newspaper journalist in the United States and its territories
Deadline: January 31
Apply to: Meeman Environmental Journalism Awards, above address

Ⓙ The *Ernie Pyle Writing Award*, of $2,500, is given annually to an individual whose newspaper writing "most exemplifies the style and craftsmanship of the late Ernie Pyle. . . writing everyday copy about everyday people with everyday dreams." Warmth, human interest, and the ability for storytelling rank high in the judging of the award. Submitted material must have been published in a newspaper in the preceding calendar year; work published in magazines or periodicals is not eligible.

Available to: Any daily newspaper journalist in the United States and its territories
Deadline: January 17
Apply to: Ernie Pyle Writing Award, above address

Ⓙ The *Editorial Writing/Walker Stone Award* is given to honor outstanding achievement by an individual in the field of editorial writing. Submitted material must have been published in a newspaper in the preceding calendar year; work published in magazines or periodicals is not eligible. A prize of $2,000 is awarded annually.

Available to: Any daily newspaper journalist in the United States and its territories
Deadline: January 24
Apply to: Walker Stone Editorial Award, above address

Seattle Arts Commission
312 First Avenue North
Seattle, WA 98109

The *Seattle Artist Program* offers awards of $2,000 and $7,500 to Seattle artists in a variety of disciplines, including poetry, prose/fiction, scriptwriting, screenwriting, and critical writing/creative nonfiction. Write for further information.

Available to: Seattle artists
Deadline: July; inquire for exact date
Apply to: Above address

Seattle Post-Intelligencer
101 Elliot Avenue, West
Seattle, WA 98119

Ⓙ The *Bobbi McCallum Memorial Scholarship*, of $1,000, is given to provide financial assistance to women college students from Washington State interested in pursuing a career in print journalism. Selection is based on need, academic achievement, and motivation to pursue a career on a newspaper. Application must include five samples of work, published or unpublished.

Available to: Women journalism majors entering their junior or senior year at any college or university in the state of Washington
Deadline: March 1
Apply to: Janet Grimley, Assistant Managing Editor, above address

Seventeen Magazine
850 Third Avenue
New York, NY 10022

(F)   The *Seventeen Magazine Fiction Contest* is open to anyone at least thirteen but under twenty-one years of age. Each entry should be a previously unpublished short story not exceeding 4,000 words and should include the writer's birth date, address, and signature. A first, second, and third prize are offered, as well as five honorable mentions. There is also the possibility of publication in *Seventeen*.

Available to: No restrictions
Deadline: Inquire in writing, or see November issue
Apply to: Fiction Contest, above address

The Sewanee Review
The University of the South
735 University Avenue
Sewanee, TN 37383-1000

[IN]   The *Aiken Taylor Award for Modern American Poetry* of $10,000 is awarded annually to a writer who has had a substantial and distinguished career. *By Internal Nomination Only.*

Shenandoah
Washington and Lee University
Box 722
Lexington, VA 24450

The following awards are given to work published in *Shenandoah* during the calendar year.

The *James Boatwright III Prize for Poetry* annually awards $500 to the author of the best poetry. The *Thomas H. Carter Prize for the Essay* annually awards $500 to the author of the best essay. The *Jeanne Charpiot Goodheart Prize for Fiction* annually awards $1,000 to the author of the best story.

Available to: No restrictions
Deadline: None
Apply to: Above address

Shenandoah International Playwrights Retreat
Pennyroyal Farm
Route 5, Box 167-F
Staunton, VA 24401

(D)
(R)   Ten to twelve playwrights and screenwriters are offered a five week retreat in the Shenandoah Valley of Virginia. Starting in 1996, this August/September retreat will feature international writers from specific regions of the world, who work alongside American writers. All collaborate with a multi-cultural company of professional theater artists in the translation, development and adaptation of new plays and screenplays. The culminating event of each retreat is a Festival of New Works for a New World, hosted by established professional theatres in cities in the United States and, possibly, abroad. In 1996, the focus is the Middle East Project; in 1997 the Hong Kong Project. All writers receive fellowships that provide round-trip transportation, room and board, and the services of the professional company.

Available to: No restrictions
Deadline: February 1
Apply to: Above address

Ⓓ Virginia playwrights will also be considered for *Virginia TheaterWorks*, a statewide conference/workshop program. Selected playwrights will work in collaboration with the Commonwealth's leading theaters and theater artists in regional and statewide conferences.

Available to: Virginia playwrights
Deadline: March 1
Apply to: Above address

Reva Shiner Full-Length Play Contest
308 South Washington Street
Bloomington, IN 47401

Ⓓ The *Reva Shiner Full-Length Play Contest* offers $500, a staged reading, and production for an unpublished, unproduced full-length play suitable for production in a seventy-five-seat theater, with simple sets. There is a $5 reading fee. Write for guidelines.

Available to: No restrictions
Deadline: January 15
Apply to: Above address

The Joan Shorenstein Center on the Press, Politics, and Public Policy
John F. Kennedy School of Government
Harvard University
Cambridge, MA 02128

Ⓝ The *Goldsmith Awards Book Prize* offers $5,000 to the author(s) of the best English-language book that aims at improving the quality of government or politics through an examination of the press and government or the intersection of press and politics in the formation of public policy. Publication must have occurred within twelve months preceding the submission deadline. Edited volumes will not be accepted. Write for guidelines and application form.

Available to: No restrictions
Deadline: November 1
Apply to: Goldsmith Awards Book Prize, above address

Ⓙ The *Goldsmith Prize for Investigative Reporting* annually awards $25,000 to the journalist or journalists whose investigative reporting in a story or series of related stories best promotes more effective and ethical conduct of government, the making of public policy, or the practice of politics. While the subject can address issues of foreign policy, a submission qualifies only if it has an impact on U.S. public policy. Publication must have occurred within twelve months preceding the submission deadline. Print and broadcast submissions are accepted. Write for guidelines and application form.

Available to: Journalists with U.S. news organizations
Deadline: November 1
Apply to: Goldsmith Prize for Investigative Reporting

The *Goldsmith Research Awards* offer grants of varying amounts, rarely exceeding $5,000, to stimulate and assist research by scholars, graduate students and journalists in the field of press/politics. Applications are accepted throughout the year and award recipients will be notified quarterly. Write for guidelines and application form.

Available to: No restrictions

Deadline: Ongoing
Apply to: Goldsmith Research Awards, above address

Siena College
Department of Creative Arts, Theatre Program
515 Loudon Road
Loudonville, NY 12211-1462

Ⓓ The *Siena College International Playwrights' Competition* biennially awards $2,000, full production, and up to $1,000 for travel, housing, and board during a four- to six-week production residence for full-length, unpublished, unproduced, nonmusical plays. Scripts with roles for college-age performers, small casts, and simple sets are encouraged. Write for guidelines before submitting manuscript; guidelines are available after November 1 of odd-numbered years.

Available to: No restrictions
Deadline: February 1 to June 30 (in even-numbered years)
Apply to: Siena College International Playwrights' Competition, above address

Sierra Repertory Theatre
Box 3030
Sonora, CA 95370

Ⓓ The *Marvin Taylor Playwriting Award* offers $500 and production to a full-length play that has received no more than two productions or staged readings, and has no more than two sets and fifteen cast members.

Available to: No restrictions
Deadline: August 31
Apply to: Marvin Taylor Playwriting Award, above address

Slipstream Annual Poetry Chapbook Contest
Box 2071
New Market Station
Niagara Falls, NY 14301

Ⓟ The *Slipstream Annual Poetry Chapbook Contest* awards $500 and publication of a chapbook for winning manuscript. Winner also receives fifty copies of the winning chapbook. All entrants receive one copy as well as a one-issue subscription to *Slipstream*. Send up to forty pages of poetry, an SASE with sufficient postage for return of your manuscript, and a $10 reading fee.

Available to: No restrictions
Deadline: December 1
Apply to: Above address

The Smithsonian Institution
Office of Fellowships
955 L'Enfant Plaza, Suite 7000
Washington, DC 20560

Fellowships are offered by the Smithsonian Institution to provide graduate students, predoctoral students, and postdoctoral and senior investigators with opportunities to conduct research in association with members of the Smithsonian professional research staff, and to utilize the resources of the institution. Graduate student fellows are appointed for ten weeks with a stipend of $300 per week. Predoctoral, postdoctoral and senior fellows are appointed for three to twelve months with a stipend of $14,000 per year for predoctoral fellows and $25,000 per year for postdoctoral and senior fellows. In addition to the stipend, a travel allowance and an allowance for research-related expenses, up to $2,000, are possible. Write for additional information and application form.

Available to: No restrictions
Deadline: Mid-January; inquire for exact date
Apply to: Above address

Snake Nation Press
110 No. 2 West Force Street
Valdosta, GA 31601

(P) The *Violet Reed Haas Poetry Prize* offers $500 and publication by Snake Nation Press for a fifty- to seventy-five-page manuscript of poems. There is a $10 entry fee, which includes a copy of the winning book. Write for further information.

Available to: No restrictions
Deadline: January 15
Apply to: Violet Reed Haas Poetry Prize, above address

Social Science Research Council
605 Third Avenue
New York, NY 10158

The Social Science Research Council offers *Dissertation Fellowships, Postdoctoral Fellowships,* and *Advanced Research Grants* in Africa, China, Eastern Europe, Japan, Korea, Latin America and the Caribbean, the Near and Middle East, South Asia, Southeast Asia, the Soviet Union (and its successor states), and Western Europe. Stipends vary according to geographic region and type of grants. Write for complete information.

Available to: Restrictions vary according to program; inquire
Deadline: Varies according to program; inquire
Apply to: Above address

The *Louis Dupress Prize for Research on Central Asia,* of $2,500, is awarded for the most promising dissertation involving field research in Central Asia, a region broadly defined to include Afghanistan, Azerbaijan, Kirghizia, Mongolia, Tajikistan, Turkmenistan, Uzbekistan, and culturally-related contiguous areas of China, Iran, Kazakhstan, and Pakistan.

Available to: Dissertation Fellowship recipients
Deadline: Inquire
Apply to: Above address

The *Ibn Khaldun Prize,* of $1,000, is awarded for outstanding papers on topics relating to the contemporary Middle East and North Africa, or on historical topics in that region since the beginning of Islam. Theoretically informed and/or comparative studies incorporating the Middle East and other regions of the world are encouraged.

Available to: Graduate students
Deadline: July 15
Apply to: Joint Committee on the Near and Middle East, Graduate Student Paper Competition, above address

Society of American Historians
Professor Mark Carnes
Butler Library, Box 2
Columbia University
New York, NY 10027

(F) The *James Fenimore Cooper Prize for Historical Fiction,* of $2,500, is awarded every two years for a work of literary fiction which significantly advances the development of the his-

154

torical imagination. The winner will be chosen for its literary quality and historical scholarship. To be eligible, books must be copyrighted either in 1995 or 1996.

Available to: No restrictions
Deadline: January 15, 1997
Apply to: Above address for submission procedures

The *Allan Nevins Prize,* for the best-written Ph.D. dissertation on a significant theme in the field of American history, is open to graduates of any Ph.D.-granting department in the United States. One award of $1,000 is made each year. The winning manuscript is normally published by one of the distinguished houses which currently supports the Prize. Manuscripts must be submitted by the chairman of the department awarding the degree or by the sponsor of the dissertation.

Available to: No restrictions
Deadline: January; inquire for exact date
Apply to: Above address

Ⓝ The *Francis Parkman Prize* is awarded for the book in American history or biography that best combines sound scholarship and literary excellence. One award of $2,500, a certificate, and an engraved bronze medal is given annually.

Available to: No restrictions
Deadline: January 15 (earlier submission is preferable)
Apply to: By publisher's nomination

Society of Children's Book Writers
22736 Vanowen Street, Suite 106
West Hills, CA 91307

Ⓒ Four work-in-progress grants, one for a contemporary novel for young people, one for a work whose author has never had a book published, one for a general work-in-progress, and one for a nonfiction research project will be awarded annually. Each grant is $1,000, and each category offers a runner-up award of $500. Applications and guidelines are available beginning October 1 each year.

Available to: Full and Associate members of the Society of Children's Book Writers
Deadline: April 1, 1996; inquire for 1997
Apply to: Above address

Ⓒ The *Barbara Karlin Grant* has been established to recognize and encourage the work of aspiring picture-book writers. One grant of $1,000 and a runner-up grant of $500 will be awarded annually.

Available to: Full and Associate members of the Society of Children's Book Writers who have never had a picture book published
Deadline: Applications accepted from April 1 to May 15
Apply to: Barbara Karlin Grant, above address

Society for Historians of American Foreign Relations
Temple University
Department of History
Philadelphia, PA

Ⓝ The *Stuart L. Bernath Book Prize* is given to a young author for a first book dealing with any aspect of the history of American foreign relations. One award of $2,000 is available annually for books published during the preceding year.

Available to: No restrictions
Deadline: Inquire
Apply to: Professor Richard Immerman, Committee Chair, above address

Also available are the *Stuart L. Bernath Lecture Prize* of $500 and the *Stuart L. Bernath Scholarly Article Prize* of $300. For further information, apply to above address.

Society for the History of Technology
Auburn University
Department of History
Auburn, AL 36849-5207

The *Dexter Prize,* of $2,000, is offered annually to the author of an outstanding book in the history of technology published during any of the three years preceding the award. Although there is no formal application procedure, publishers or authors may call attention to their books by writing to the secretary of the society; three copies of the book must accompany letters of nomination.

Available to: No restrictions
Deadline: April 15
Apply to: Professor Lindy Biggs, Secretary, above address

The Society of Midland Authors
PO Box 10419
Chicago, IL 60610-0419

Ⓜ The Society of Midland Authors *Literary Competition* offers awards in six categories for books published and plays produced during the calendar year. The categories are: adult fiction and nonfiction, juvenile fiction and nonfiction, biography, and poetry. Authors must currently reside in a midland state—Illinois, Indiana, Iowa, Kansas, Michigan, Minnesota, Missouri, Nebraska, North Dakota, Ohio, South Dakota, or Wisconsin. The award consists of a cash prize of $300 or more and a plaque to be presented at the society's annual dinner. Send an SASE for information on submission procedures.

Available to: See above
Deadline: January 15
Apply to: Above address

Society for the Study of Social Problems
University of Tennessee
906 McClung Tower
Knoxville, TN 37996-0490

The *C. Wright Mills Award* is an annual prize of $500 for a book that best exemplifies social science scholarship, published during the calendar year preceding that in which the award is made.

Available to: No restrictions
Deadline: January; inquire for exact date
Apply to: Tom Hood, Executive Director, above address

Society for Theatrical Artists' Guidance and Enhancement (STAGE)
PO Box 214820
4633 Insurance
Dallas, TX 75221

Ⓓ The *Stages Festival of New Plays* offers productions of previously unproduced one-act plays of no more than twenty minutes' duration. Winning playwrights receive an honorarium and full production. Write for guidelines.

Available to: No restrictions
Deadline: April 15, 1996; March 31 for 1997
Apply to: Marilyn Pyeatt, Executive Producer, above address

Sons of the Republic of Texas
5942 Abrams Road, Suite 222
Dallas, TX 75231

The *Presidio La Bahia Award* is given for writing that promotes research into and preservation of the Spanish Colonial influence on Texas culture. A total of $2,000 is available annually as an award or awards (depending upon the number and quality of entries) with a minimum first prize of $1,200. Entries must be submitted in quadruplicate and cannot be returned.

Available to: No restrictions
Deadline: September 30
Apply to: Above address for information

Ⓜ The *Summerfield G. Roberts Award*, of $2,500, is given annually for the best book or manuscript of biography, essay, fiction, nonfiction, novel, poetry, or short story that describes or represents the Republic of Texas, 1836-46. The manuscript must be written or published during the calendar year for which the award is given. Entries must be submitted in quintuplicate and cannot be returned.

Available to: U.S. citizens
Deadline: January 15
Apply to: Above address for information

Source Theatre Company
1835 14th Street, NW
Washington, DC 20009

Ⓓ The *Source Theatre Company National Playwriting Competition* annually offers a $250 prize for a professionally unproduced play. The work receives a showcase production as part of Source's Annual Washington Theatre Festival in July. The festival also features the *Ten-minute Play Competition* for short scripts, and *Musical Sources*, a workshop for musical theater projects.

Available to: No restrictions
Deadline: January 15
Apply to: Keith Parker, Literary Manager, above address

The South Carolina Academy of Authors
c/o College of Charleston
SPO 2700
Charleston, SC 29424

Ⓜ Nine fellowship awards—three each in the categories of poetry, fiction, and drama—are offered annually to South Carolina writers who have not published more than one book. The awards in each category consist of a first prize of $500, a second prize of $300, and a third prize of $200. There is a $5 fee per entry. Send an SASE for complete guidelines.

Available to: South Carolina residents
Deadline: Inquire
Apply to: Above address

South Carolina Arts Commission
1800 Gervais Street
Columbia, SC 29201

Ⓜ The *Individual Artist Fellowships in Literature* are given to poets, playwrights, fiction or creative nonfiction writers of exceptional promise or proven professional ability, to set aside time and/or purchase materials or in other ways to advance their careers as creative writers. Two fellowships, one for prose and one for poetry, of $7,500 are awarded annually. Full-time undergraduate students are not eligible.

157

Available to: South Carolina writers only
Deadline: September 15
Apply to: Fellowships Program, above address

Ⓜ *Individual Project Grants*, of up to $7,500 in matching funds, are offered to writers with specific writing projects (that is, to complete a manuscript, travel to conferences, or conduct research).

Available to: South Carolina writers only
Deadline: December 15
Apply to: Project Grants, above address

Ⓕ The *South Carolina Fiction Project*, cosponsored by the South Carolina Arts Commission and the Charleston *Post and Courier*, sponsors a short, short story competition. Stories are selected by a panel of professional writers, with $500 payment to the writer and first publication rights to the *Post and Courier*. Up to twelve stories are selected annually; one is published each month in the *Post and Courier*.

Available to: South Carolina writers only
Deadline: March 15
Apply to: South Carolina Fiction Project, above address

The *Writers Forum* brings professional, published writers to South Carolina to conduct readings and informal discussions, usually on college campuses but also open to the public. Fees are negotiated, and travel and per diem are provided. Please note that *Writers Forum* guests are usually chosen by recommendation of participating sponsors; however, established writers may apply.

Apply to: Director of Literary Arts, above address

South Coast Repertory
Box 2197
Costa Mesa, CA 92628

Ⓓ The *California Playwrights Competition* offers two biannual awards, of $3,000 and $2,000, for full-length plays that have not been professionally produced or optioned. Winning plays may be produced or given a workshop/reading in South Coast Repertory's spring California play festival, with negotiable royalty. South Coast Repertory has first refusal for production of winning plays. Two scripts per playwright may be submitted; scripts submitted to previous competitions are ineligible. No children's plays, translations, or large-scale musicals are eligible.

Available to: Playwrights whose principal residence is California
Deadline: Inquire
Apply to: Project Director, California Playwrights Competition, above address

Ⓓ The *Hispanic Playwrights Project* selects three full-length plays by Hispanic-American playwrights for a two-week workshop at South Coast Repertory, at which the playwrights will work with directors and casts of professional actors. New, unproduced plays are preferred, but previously produced plays that would benefit from further development may also be considered. Musicals are not accepted, nor are plays written fully in Spanish. Manuscripts submitted should include a synopsis and a biography of the playwright.

Available to: Hispanic-American playwrights
Deadline: March 29
Apply to: Jose Cruz Gonzalez, Hispanic Playwrights Project, above address

South Dakota Arts Council
800 Governors Drive
Pierre, SD 57501-2294

Ⓜ Approximately thirty-six *Touring Arts Programs* (approximately one-half fee paid to presenter) are available each year in areas including general writing, fiction, and nonfiction.

Available to: Any practicing artist who wishes to tour South Dakota cities
Deadline: February 1
Apply to: Write for guidelines and application to Colin Olsen, Arts Coordinator, above
address

Forty to fifty grants of approximately $800 per week are available each year for Artists-in-Schools in areas including general writing, fiction, and nonfiction.

Available to: Any practicing, professional artist who wishes to work in residences
throughout South Dakota, at all grade levels
Deadline: September 15
Apply to: Write for guidelines and application to Colin Olsen, Arts Coordinator, above
address

(M) *Artist Fellowship Grants,* of $5,000, and *Artist Career Development Grants,* of $1,000, are available each year to South Dakota residents of at least two years in areas including general writing, fiction, and nonfiction.

Available to: South Dakota artists
Deadline: February 1
Apply to: Write for guidelines and application to Dennis Holub, Executive Director,
above address

Southeastern Theatre Conference
Box 9868
Greensboro, NC 27429-0868

(D) The *Southeastern Theatre Conference New Play Project* offers $1,000; a staged reading at the SETC Annual Convention; travel, room and board to attend the convention; and submission of the winning work by SETC to the O'Neill Center for favored consideration at the National Playwrights Conference, for an unproduced, full-length play or bill of two related one-acts by a resident of the states in the SETC region. Write for complete guidelines prior to submitting.

Available to: Residents of Alabama, Florida, Georgia, Kentucky, Mississippi, North Carolina, South Carolina, Tennessee, Virginia, or West Virginia
Deadline: June 1; no submissions accepted prior to March 1
Apply to: New Play Project, above address

Southern Appalachian Repertory Theatre
Box 620
Mars Hill, NC 28754-0620

(D) The *Southern Appalachian Playwrights' Conference* selects up to five playwrights to participate in their annual three-day conference in January at which one work by each writer is given an informal reading and is critiqued by a panel of theatre professionals. One work is selected each year for production in the theatre's summer season. Playwrights receive room and board, and the writer of the work selected for production receives a $500 honorarium. Send an SASE for guidelines.

Available to: No restrictions
Deadline: October 1
Apply to: Southern Appalachian Playwrights' Conference, above address

Southern Environmental Law Center
201 West Main Street, Suite 14
Charlottesville, VA 22902-5065

(F)
(N) The *Phillip D. Reed Memorial Award for Outstanding Southern Environmental Writing,* of $1,000, is given for a work of either fiction or nonfiction that relates to the southern environment and has been published during the calendar year preceding the award deadline. Sub-

missions may be made by any member of the reading public or by the author. Write for further information regarding guidelines.

Available to: No restrictions
Deadline: February 15
Apply to: Tina Wolk, above address

Southern Historical Association
Department of History
University of Georgia
Athens, GA 30602

Each of the Southern Historical Association's cash awards is presented in odd-numbered years for books published during the preceding year.

(N) The *Frank Lawrence and Harriet Chappell Owsley Award* is given for a distinguished book in Southern history. The *H. L. Mitchell Award* is given for a distinguished book concerning the history of the Southern working class, including but not limited to industrial laborers and/or small farmers and agricultural laborers. The *Francis Butler Simpkins Award* is given for the best first book by an author in the field of Southern history. The *Charles S. Sydnor Prize* is given for a distinguished book in Southern history.

Available to: U.S. citizens
Deadline: Inquire, for each of the above
Apply to: Above address

Southern Illinois University at Carbondale
English Department
Carbondale, IL 62901-4503

(F)
(P) The *Charles Johnson Awards for Fiction and Poetry* offer $500 in each genre to ethnic minority college students and college students "whose work freshly explores the experience/ identity of a minority or marginalized culture." Eligible writers may submit one short story of twenty-five pages or less, or three to five poems of six pages or less. Manuscripts cannot be returned. Send an SASE for more information.

Available to: See above
Deadline: Late January; inquire for exact date
Apply to: Ricardo Cortez Cruz, above address

Southern Oregon State College
Extended Campus Programs
1250 Siskiyou
Ashland, OR 97250

(R) The *Walden Residency Program* offers residences of six weeks for writers of drama, fiction, poetry, and creative nonfiction.

Available to: Residents of Oregon
Deadline: Inquire
Apply to: Celeste Stevens, above address

The Southern Poetry Review
University of North Carolina at Charlotte
Department of English
Charlotte, NC 28223

(P) The *Guy Owen Poetry Prize,* of $500, is given annually for the best poem selected by an outside judge. A maximum of three to five poems may be submitted with an $8 entry fee during the month of April. In exchange for the entry fee, each applicant will receive a one-year subscription to the *Southern Poetry Review.*

Available to: No restrictions
Deadline: May 1
Apply to: Guy Owen Poetry Prize, above address

The Southern Review
Louisiana State University
43 Allen Hall
Baton Rouge, LA 70803

(F)   The *Southern Review/Louisiana State University Short Fiction Award* offers $500 to the best first
collection of short stories by a U.S. writer published in the United States in the preceding
year. Publishers or authors may send two copies of qualifying books for consideration.

Available to: U.S. citizens
Deadline: January 31
Apply to: Above address

Southwest Review
307 Fondren Library West
Box 374
Southern Methodist University
Dallas, TX 75275

(F)
(N)   The *John H. McGinnis Memorial Awards,* of $1,000, are given annually to the best essay and
story appearing in the *Southwest Review* during the preceding year.

(P)   The *Elizabeth Matchett Stover Memorial Award,* of $150, is awarded annually to the author of
the best poem or group of poems published in the magazine during the preceding year.

Available to: *Southwest Review* contributors
Apply to: Above address

The Sow's Ear Poetry Review
19535 Pleasant View Drive
Abingdon, VA 24211-6827

(P)   The *Sow's Ear Chapbook Competition* offers a first prize of $500, publication, 50 copies, and
distribution to subscribers; a second prize of $100; and a third prize of $100 for the best
collection of poems, twenty-two to twenty-six pages in length. Simultaneous submissions accepted. There is a $10 entry fee. Send an SASE for guidelines.

Available to: No restrictions
Deadline: Submissions accepted in March and April only
Apply to: Chapbook Competition, above address

(P)   The *Sow's Ear Poetry Competition* offers a first prize of $500, a second prize of $100 and a
third prize of $50 for the for the best unpublished poems. Winners as well as approx-
imately fifteen to twenty finalists are published. No simultaneous submissions. There
is a reading fee of $2 per poem; entering five poems entitles you to a subscription to
Sow's Ear.

Available to: No restrictions
Deadline: Submissions accepted in September and October only
Apply to: Poetry Competition, above address

SPAIN
Cultural Office
Embassy of Spain
2735 Pennsylvania Avenue, NW
Washington, DC 20037

Several organizations and foundations in Spain offer sizable literary prizes to authors of all
nationalities for unpublished work (fiction, poetry, and nonfiction) written in Castilian.
Information may be obtained on all the prizes from the Consulate General of Spain.

Available to: Authors of all nationalities writing in Castilian
Deadline: Inquire
Apply to: Above address

Spoon River Poetry Review
4240 Department of English
Illinois State University
Normal, IL 61790-4240

(P) The *Editor's Prize* awards $500 and publication in the *Spoon River Poetry Review* for an un-
published poem. All submissions to the contest will be considered for publication in
the review. Poets may submit up to three poems, of no more than ten pages total, in
duplicate, with the poet's name on one copy only. There is a reading fee of $15, which
includes a one-year subscription to the review. Send an SASE for complete guidelines.

Available to: No restrictions
Deadline: May 1
Apply to: Editor's Prize, above address

Stanford University
Building 120, Room 426
Stanford, CA 94305-2050

(J) The *John S. Knight Fellowships* are offered each year to twelve U.S. journalists who have
demonstrated uncommon excellence in their work and who have the potential of reach-
ing the top ranks in their specialties. The fellowships are awarded for an academic year,
from mid-September to mid-June. Fellows receive a stipend of $37,500, plus a book
allowance. The fellowship program pays university tuition for all fellows. Applicants
must have at least seven years of full-time professional experience. Write for additional
information and application.

Available to: Professional journalists
Deadline: February 1
Apply to: John S. Knight Fellowships, above address, or fax 415-725-6154

Stanford University
Creative Writing Center
Department of English
Stanford, CA 94305-2087

(F)
(P) Ten *Wallace E. Stegner Fellowships* are offered to five promising fiction-writers and five poets
who can benefit from residence at the university and from the instruction and criticism
of the staff of the writing program. The two-year fellowships provide a stipend of
$13,000 each year, plus the required tuition (about $5,000). Previous publication is not
essential.

Available to: No restrictions
Deadline: January 1
Apply to: Program Coordinator, Wallace E. Stegner Fellowships, above address

The State Historical Society of Wisconsin
816 State Street
Madison, WI 53706-1488

The *Amy Louise Hunter Fellowship,* of $2,500, is awarded in even-numbered years for research on topics related to the history of women and public policy, broadly construed, with preference given to Wisconsin topics and/or for research using the collections of the State Historical Society of Wisconsin. Write for further information and guidelines.

Available to: No restrictions
Deadline: May 1, 1996, and 1998
Apply to: Dr. Michael E. Stevens, State Historian, above address

The *Alice E. Smith Fellowship,* of $2,000, is awarded to a woman doing research in American history, with preference given to applicants doing graduate research in the history of Wisconsin or the Middle West. Write for further information and guidelines.

Available to: Women historians
Deadline: July 15
Apply to: Dr. Michael E. Stevens, State Historian, above address

STORY
1507 Dana Avenue
Cincinnati, OH 45207

(F) *STORY* magazine annually offers two fiction contests, a *Short Short Story Competition* in the fall, and a theme short story contest in the spring. Each competition offers a first prize of $1,000, a second prize of $500, and a third prize of $250. Winners may also receive prizes from the corporate sponsor for that given year (recent sponsors have included Parker Pen and Smith Corona). Submissions for the *Short Short Story Competition* must be original, unpublished manuscripts of 1,500 words or less. The theme for the 1996 spring competition is "Naked Fiction." Submissions should be original, unpublished manuscripts of no more than 5,000 words. All winning entries will be considered for publication in *STORY*. There is a $10 entry fee for each submission. Send an SASE for complete rules and entry form.

Available to: No restrictions
Deadline: October 31 for Short Short Story Competition; May 1 for "Naked Fiction";
   Inquire for theme for 1997
Apply to: Above address, or by fax 513-531-1843

Story Line Press
Three Oaks Farm
Brownsville, OR 97327

(P) The *Nicholas Roerich Poetry Prize* awards $1,000, publication with Story Line Press, and a reading upon publication at the Nicholas Roerich Museum in New York to the author of a first book-length poetry manuscript. Manuscripts should be accompanied by SASE, $15 reading fee, and a brief biography. One runner-up receives a full scholarship to the Wesleyan Writers' Conference.

Available to: Poets who have not previously published a book-length volume of poetry; authors of chapbooks under thirty-two pages are eligible
Deadline: October 15
Apply to: Nicholas Roerich Poetry Prize, above address

Sunset Center
Box 5066
Carmel, CA 93921

(D) The *Festival of Firsts Playwriting Competition* offers up to $1,000 and possible production for previously unproduced full-length plays. No musicals or operas. Send an SASE for registration guidelines. Entries are not accepted before June 15.

Available to: No restrictions
Deadline: June 15 to August 31
Apply to: Brian Donoghue, Director, above address

Syracuse University
Department of English
401 Hall of Languages
Syracuse, NY 13244-1170

The Syracuse University Department of English offers five one-year fellowships to applicants for the M.F.A. degree in Creative Writing: the *Cornelia Carhart Ward Fellowship* (fiction), the *Mead Fellowship* (poetry), and three *Creative Writing Fellowships*. In 1995/96 the *Cornelia Carhart Ward Fellowship* carried a stipend of $9,970; the *Mead Fellowship* carried a stipend of $11,300; *Creative Writing Fellowships* each carried a stipend of $7,092. All fellowships include remitted tuition for a full-time load of twenty-four credit hours for the academic year.

Available to: Creative Writing applicants
Deadline: January 1
Apply to: Michael Martone, Director, Creative Writing Program, above address

Syracuse University Press
1600 Jamesville Avenue
Syracuse, NY 13244-5160

(N) The *John Ben Snow Prize*, of $1,500, is given annually for a nonfiction manuscript dealing with some aspect of New York State that makes the most distinguished contribution to the study of the upstate area. The prize includes publication by Syracuse University Press and is given as an advance against royalties. No substantial portion of the manuscript submitted may have been previously published. Unrevised theses and dissertations are not eligible; dissertations available in Xerographic and microfilm forms are considered to be published. Authors are urged to send a query letter before submitting manuscripts.

Available to: No restrictions
Deadline: December 31
Apply to: Director, Syracuse University Press, above address

Mark Taper Forum
Center Theatre Group
135 North Grand Avenue
Los Angeles, CA 90012

(D) Playwrights are encouraged to submit original, full-length scripts to be considered for production in the Mark Taper Forum's year-round season. There are no restrictions as to format or subject matter. Scripts submitted are automatically considered for *Taper Too*, *New Work Festival* workshops and readings. Playwrights should first query, describing the play in whatever terms they deem appropriate and should include sample pages of dialogue. On this basis, the Taper will request the entire manuscript of those plays that would seem to have a reasonable chance of being produced.

Available to: No restrictions
Deadline: None
Apply to: Oliver Mayer, Associate Literary Manager, above address

Tennessee Arts Commission
404 James Robertson Parkway, Suite 160
Nashville, TN 37243-0780

(M) The Tennessee Arts Commission offers a writing fellowship, of approximately $2,500, on a rotating basis to writers of poetry, fiction, nonfiction, playwriting, and belles lettres. The 1997 award will be given for poetry.

Available to: Tennessee residents only
Deadline: Inquire
Apply to: Above address

Tennessee Writers Alliance
PO Box 120396
Nashville, TN 37212

(F)
(P)
The *Tennessee Writers Alliance Literary Awards* offer a first prize of $500, a second prize of $250, and a third prize of $100 for works of short fiction in odd-numbered years and for poems in even-numbered years. The entry fee is $5 for members of the Alliance and $10 for nonmembers.

Available to: U.S. poets and writers
Deadline: August 1
Apply to: Literary Awards, above address

Texas Center for Writers
University of Texas at Austin
PCL 3.102, Mail Code 55401
Austin, TX 78713

The *James A. Michener Fellowships*, of $12,000 per year, plus remission of tuition, are offered to all candidates accepted for the University of Texas M.F.A. program. The M.F.A. offered is designed for students who have already produced work in at least two fields of writing. Applicants must submit a portfolio that includes two manuscripts: one in the proposed primary field and one in the secondary. Write for complete application procedures.

Available to: No restrictions
Deadline: January 15
Apply to: Above address

Texas Institute of Letters
Texas Christian University Press
PO Box 30783
Fort Worth, TX 76129

The Texas Institute of Letters gives various annual literary awards in March for books by Texan authors or on Texan subjects. Query the Institute with an SASE for more details and list of judges.

(F)
The *Brazos Bookstore Award for the Best Short Story*, of $500, is given for the best short story.

(N)
The *Carr P. Collins Award*, of $5,000, is given to an outstanding book of nonfiction.

(T)
The *Soeurette Diehl Fraser Award*, of $1,000, is given for the best translation of a book into English.

The *Friends of the Dallas Public Library Award*, of $1,000, is given to the author of a book that constitutes the most important contribution to knowledge.

(J)
(N)
The *O. Henry Award*, of $500, is given for the best nonfiction writing appearing in a magazine, journal, Sunday newspaper supplement, or other periodical.

(F)
The *Jesse H. Jones Award* of $6,000 is given for the best book of fiction.

(P)
The *Natalie Ornish Poetry Award in Memory of Wayne Gard*, of $1,000, is given for the best published book of poetry.

The *Lon Tinkle Award*, of $1,000, is given to a writer associated with Texas who has been voted by the Institute's membership to have shown continuing excellence in letters.

(F)   The *Steven Turner Award* of $1,000 is given for the best first book of fiction.

(N)   The *Stanley Walker Award*, of $500, is given for the best nonfiction writing appearing in a newspaper—an individual article or a series on a single subject—with emphasis on literary merit.

Available to: Texan authors or books on a Texan subject
Deadline: First working day in January
Apply to: Judy Alter, Secretary-Treasurer, above address

The Thanks Be to Grandmother Winifred Foundation
PO Box 1449
Wainscott, NY 11975

Grants of up to $5,000 are offered to women of at least fifty-four years of age "to develop and implement projects, programs or policies that empower and enrich one or more aspects of the cultural, economic, educational, ethnic, mental, physical, professional, racial, sexual, social, and spiritual well-being of women." Write for additional information and application.

Available to: Women fifty-four and over
Deadline: March 21 and September 21
Apply to: Above address

Theater Association of Pennsylvania (TAP)
1919 North Front Street, 3rd Floor
Harrisburg, PA 17102-2284

(D)   The *Biennial Playwriting Contest* offers a cash prize, a staged reading, and possible production at a university in Pennsylvania for an original unproduced, unpublished full-length play by a Pennsylvania playwright. There is a $35 entry fee for nonmembers which includes membership in TAP. Write for guidelines and application form.

Available to: TAP members
Deadline: May 1996 and 1998; inquire for exact date
Apply to: Al Franklin, Executive Director, above address

Theater at Lime Kiln
14 South Randolph Street
Lexington, VA 24450

(D)   The *Theater at Lime Kiln Regional Playwriting Contest* offers a $1,000 first prize, a $500 second prize, and the possibility of a staged reading and/or production for unproduced, unpublished full-length plays, one-acts, and musicals relating to the Appalachian region. Write for complete guidelines.

Available to: No restrictions
Deadline: Submissions accepted from August 1 to September 30
Apply to: Regional Playwriting Contest, above address

Theatre Americana
Box 245
Altadena, CA 91003-0245

(D)   The *David James Ellis Memorial Award*, of $500, is given annually to the author of the best original new play of the four plays produced each fiscal year by the Theatre Americana. Unpublished, original plays of two or three acts, preferably on "the American scene" will be considered. No musicals or children's plays. Send an SASE for more information.

Available to: No restrictions, but American writers preferred
Deadline: January 31
Apply to: Playreading Chairman, above address

Theatre Communications Group
355 Lexington Avenue, 4th Floor
New York, NY 10017

Ⓓ The TCG *Observership Program* enables artistic directors, managing directors and other resident artistic or management personnel of TCG constituent theaters to travel for purposes that will broaden their exposure to the field and aid in their professional growth. A maximum of $2,000 in transportation and per diem funds will be awarded for each observership. Write for complete information and application guidelines.

Available to: Key artistic or administrative personnel holding salaried positions with TCG constituent theaters
Deadline: Inquire
Apply to: Observership Program, above address

Ⓓ The *TCG/Metropolitan Life Foundation Extended Collaboration Grants* are designed to enable writers to work collaboratively with other artists for a period beyond the sponsoring theater's normal preproduction and rehearsal schedule. Grants of $3,000 to $6,000 each are awarded to support playwrights, in collaboration with directors, designers, composers, actors or other artists, to develop projects proposed by the sponsoring theater. Grants will be issued to the theater in two equal installments: half at the commencement of the collaboration and half upon receipt of the final reports from the theater and the playwright.

Available to: Artistic directors of TCG Constituent theaters must apply on behalf of the artists
Deadline: Inquire
Apply to: Extended Collaboration Grants, above address

Theatre Memphis
PO Box 240117
Memphis, TN 38124-0117

Ⓓ Theatre Memphis seeks full-length plays for its triennial *New Play Competition*. The next round will be in 1996. No musicals or one-acts are considered. The winning submission will receive $1,500 and an option to produce. Should the judges deem two scripts to be of equal merit, the prize money would be split between the two winning playwrights, and Theatre Memphis would consider both plays for production. Write for details.

Available to: No restrictions
Deadline: July 1, 1996
Apply to: New Play Competition, above address

The James Thurber Residency Program
The Thurber House
77 Jefferson Avenue
Columbus, OH 42315

Ⓡ The *James Thurber Residency Program* selects journalists, novelists, poets, and playwrights to spend a season living, writing, and teaching at the Thurber House in Columbus, Ohio. Each writer will receive a stipend and housing in James Thurber's boyhood home. The majority of the writer's time will be reserved for the writer's own work, but each will have limited responsibilities as follows: The *James Thurber Journalist-in-Residence* will teach a class in the Ohio State University School of Journalism and will act as a staff writing coach for reporters at the *Columbus Dispatch*. Candidates should have experience in reporting, feature writing, reviewing, or other areas of journalism, as well as significant publications; experience as a teacher or writing coach is helpful. The stipend is $5,000 per quarter, available for one or two quarters. The *James Thurber Playwright-in-Residence* will have one play considered for mounting, public reading, or production by the Ohio State University Press Department of Theatre, and will teach one class in playwriting within the department. Candidates should have had at least one play published and/or produced by a significant company and show some aptitude for the teaching aspects of the position. The stipend is $5,000. The *James Thurber Writer-in-Residence* will teach a class in the Creative Writing Program at Ohio State University and will offer one public reading and a short workshop for writers in the community. Candidates should have published at least one book with a major publisher, in any area of fiction, nonfiction, or poetry, and should possess some teaching experience. The stipend is $5,000.

Available to: No restrictions other than those stated above
Deadline: January 1
Apply to: For application, send an SASE to Michael J. Rosen, Literary Director, above address

Towson State University
Towson, MD 21204-7097

Ⓜ The *Towson State University Prize for Literature,* of $1,000, is offered annually for a single book or book-length manuscript of fiction, poetry, drama, or creative nonfiction by a Maryland writer. The prize, supported by a grant from the Alice & Franklin Cooley Endowment, is given on the basis of aesthetic excellence. If published, the book must have appeared within three years prior to the year of its nomination. If unpublished, the book must have been accepted by a publisher. Nomination forms required.

Available to: Maryland residents under the age of forty
Deadline: May 1
Apply to: Dean, College of Liberal Arts, above address

TriQuarterly
Northwestern University
2020 Ridge Avenue
Evanston, IL 60208-4302

Ⓕ The *Terrence Des Pres Prize for Poetry* and the *William Goyen Prize for Fiction* consist of a cash award of $1,000 and publication by TriQuarterly Books/Northwestern University Press.
Ⓟ The prizes are awarded in alternate years to distinguished new books of poetry and fiction. Interested authors should send queries to the editors, with sample chapters of prose (for works of fiction) or up to ten pages (for poetic works). Winners will be selected through the normal editorial process at TriQuarterly Books. We cannot consider submission of full books without first receiving a query. Queries should be sent between October 1 and April 30. Queries received outside that period may require additional time before being answered. New writers are especially encouraged to apply.

Available to: No restrictions
Deadline: See above
Apply to: Above address

Harry S. Truman Library Institute
Harry S. Truman Library
U.S. Highway 24 and Delaware
Independence, MO 64050-1798

The institute offers several awards and research grants to scholars and graduate students to encourage study of the history of the Truman administration and the public career of Harry S. Truman and to promote the use of the Truman Library as a national center for historical scholarship. Prospective applicants should write to the Committee on Research and Education at the above address for current information.

(N) The *Harry S. Truman Book Award*, of $1,000, is awarded biennially in even-numbered years to the best book written within the previous two years devoted to the career of Harry S. Truman or the economic, political, and social development of the United States during the Truman presidency.

> Available to: No restrictions
> Deadline: January 20 in even-numbered years
> Apply to: Secretary of the Institute, above address

Trustus Theatre
Box 11721
Columbia, SC 29211

(D) The *South Carolina Playwrights' Festival* awards $500 plus full production and travel and accommodations for a full-length play. A second-place prize of $250 and a staged reading is also awarded. Casts of winning plays must be limited to eight, and a single set is preferred. Send an SASE for guidelines and an application form.

> Available to: South Carolina natives, current or former residents, or those who have attended South Carolina schools
> Deadline: December 31
> Apply to: South Carolina Playwrights' Festival, above address

Tulsa Library Trust
400 Civic Center
Tulsa, OK 74103

[IN] The *Peggy V. Helmerich Distinguished Author Award*, of $20,000, is given to a nationally acclaimed writer for a body of work. There is no application process. *By Internal Nomination Only.*

Ucross Foundation
U.S. Highway 14-16E
Clearmont, WY 82834

(R) The Ucross Foundation, located at the base of the Big Horn Mountains, offers residences of two weeks to two months to writers and other creative artists (the average length of stay is six weeks). There is no charge for room, board, or studio space.

> Available to: No restrictions
> Deadlines: March 1 for the Fall session; October 1 for the Spring session
> Apply to: Residency Program, above address

Ukiah Players Theatre
1041 Low Gap Road
Ukiah, CA 95482

(D) The *New American Comedy Festival* offers two awards biennially for an unproduced, unpublished, full-length comedy, preferably with a small cast and simple set. Each winner receives $500 and is brought to Ukiah, California, where he or she is given lodging and a small per diem for the two-week workshop. Winning plays are given a staged reading at the Ukiah Playhouse for two weekends; open forums with the playwrights are held after the performances on the first weekend. Write for guidelines and an application form.

> Available to: No restrictions
> Deadline: December 31
> Apply to: New American Comedy Festival, above address

Unicorn Theatre
3820 Main Street
Kansas City, MO 64111

Ⓓ The *National Playwrights' Award* gives an annual $1,000 first prize and production for a previously unproduced work (no musicals, one-acts, or historical plays) to an American playwright. Each entry should contain a cover letter, synopsis, sample dialogue/scene, and an SASE.

> Available to: No restrictions
> Deadline: Inquire
> Apply to: Lisa Church, Literary Manager, above address

Unitarian Universalist Association
25 Beacon Street
Boston, MA 02108

Ⓜ The *Melcher Book Award* consists of $1,000 and a citation, given to a book of fiction, nonfiction, drama, or poetry published in the year preceding the award, that has made a significant contribution to religious liberalism. Books must be nominated by the Melcher Book Award Committee or the publisher.

> Available to: No restrictions
> Deadline: January 1
> Apply to: Melcher Book Award, above address

United Daughters of the Confederacy
328 North Boulevard
Richmond, VA 23220-4057

Ⓝ The *Mrs. Simon Baruch University Award* is offered as a grant-in-aid for publication of an unpublished book or monograph dealing with Southern history in or near the period of the Confederacy. One award of $2,000 and one of $500 are given biennially.

> Available to: Graduate students or those who have received a master's, doctoral, or other advanced degree within the last fifteen years
> Deadline: May 1 in even-numbered years
> Apply to: Chairman of the Committee on Mrs. Simon Baruch University Award, above address

UNITED KINGDOM
British Comparative Literature Association
St. John's College
Oxford OX1 3JP
England

Ⓣ The BCLA awards a first prize of £350 and a second prize of £150 for the best literary translation from any language into English. Literary translation includes poetry, fiction, or literary prose, from any period. Write for complete rules and entry form.

> Available to: No restrictions
> Deadline: December 15
> Apply to: Dr. Nicholas Crowe, above address

Ⓣ The BCLA also awards several special prizes for literary translations from Swedish and Persian, and for translations of works on Jewish themes from Hebrew, Yiddish, and other languages. Winning translations from each of the above languages receive a £350 first prize and a £150 second prize.

> Available to: No restrictions
> Deadline: December 15
> Apply to: Dr. Nicholas Crowe, above address

UNITED KINGDOM
Forward Publishing
c/o Colman Getty Public Relations
Carrington House
126-130 Regent Street
London W1R 5FE
England

(P) The *Forward Poetry Prizes* are awarded annually for the best poetry published in the United Kingdom or the Republic of Ireland. A £10,000 prize is given for the best collection of poetry published in the preceding year; £5,000 is given for the best first collection of poetry; and £1,000 is given for the best individual poem to appear in a newspaper, periodical or magazine. The winning individual poem and selected poems from the winning collections will be published in *The Forward Book of Poetry*, an anthology of the year's best poetry. Entries must be submitted by editors of books or periodicals published in the U.K. or the Republic of Ireland; editors may nominate five poems or collections of poetry in each of the three categories. For the 1996 prize, collections of poetry must have publication dates between October 1, 1995 and September 30, 1996; individual poems must have been published between June 1, 1995 and April 30 1996. Entries from writers will not be accepted. Write for complete guidelines.

Available to: No restrictions
Deadline: May 10, 1996; inquire for 1997
Apply to: Forward Poetry Prize Administrator, above address

UNITED KINGDOM
The International Retreat for Writers at Hawthornden Castle
Lasswade
Midlothian EH18 1EG
Scotland

(R) The retreat offers residences of four weeks for five published creative writers (novelists, poets, playwrights, etc.) at a time. Residences include room and board and are scheduled in the spring, summer and fall. Write for application and further information.

Available to: Published writers
Deadline: September 15 for the coming year
Apply to: Above address

UNITED KINGDOM
Royal Society of Literature of the United Kingdom
One Hyde Park Gardens
London W2 2LT
England

The *Heinemann Award for Literature* is given "primarily to reward those classes of literature which are less remunerative; namely, poetry, criticism, biography, history, etc.," and "to encourage the production of works of real merit." Submitted works must have been written originally in English. The amount of the award in 1996, for books published in 1994, will be £5,000. Nominations may be made only by publishers.

Available to: No restrictions
Deadline: October 31
Apply to: Above address

(F) The *Winifred Holtby Memorial Award*, consisting of a cash prize, is given for the best regional novel of the year written in English by a writer of British or Irish nationality, or a citizen of the commonwealth. If in any year it is considered that no regional novel is of sufficient merit the prize may be awarded to an author of a literary work of non-fiction or poetry, concerning a regional subject.

Available to: See above

Deadline: October 31
Apply to: Winifred Holtby Prize, above address

UNITED KINGDOM
The Scottish Arts Council
12 Manor Place
Edinburgh EH3 7DD
Scotland

(IN) The *Neil Gunn International Fellowship* is a Scottish award to honor international achievement in the field of novel writing. Named after the distinguished Scottish novelist, Neil Gunn, the fellowship is awarded every two years. The next award will be given in 1996. *By Internal Nomination Only.*

UNITED KINGDOM
Stand Magazine
179 Wingrove Road
Newcastle-upon-Tyne NE4 9DA
England

(F)
(P) *Stand Magazine's Short Story Competition* and *Poetry Competition* offer a first and second prizes of £1,250 and £500 each to, respectively, the best short stories and poems submitted. Send an SASE to the U.S. address below for entry form and guidelines.

Available to: No restrictions
Deadline: Short story submissions accepted from October 1, 1996, to March 31, 1997; poetry from January 1 to March 31
Apply to: Daniel Schenker and Amanda Kay, Route #2, Box 122-B, Lacey's Spring, AL 35754

UNITED KINGDOM
The Translators Association
84 Drayton Gardens
London SW10 9SB
England

(T) The *John Florio Prize* is awarded "for the best translation from the Italian published in the United Kingdom by a British publisher of Italian twentieth-century works of literary merit and general interest," published in the year of the award or the year preceding it. One prize of approximately £1,000 is awarded biennially.

Available to: No restrictions
Deadline: December 31
Apply to: John Florio Prize, above address

(T) The *Scott Moncrieff Prize* is awarded "for the best translation from the French published in the United Kingdom by a British publisher of French twentieth-century works of literary merit and general interest," published in the year of the award. One prize of approximately £1,000 is given annually.

Available to: No restrictions
Deadline: December 31
Apply to: Scott Moncrieff Prize, above address

(T) The *Portuguese Translation Prize* offers £3,000 for the best translation into English of a Portuguese work, published in the United Kingdom in the five years preceding the award. The author of the original work must be Portuguese. Unpublished translations may be submitted also but must be full-length works.

Available to: No restrictions

172

Deadline: Inquire
Apply to: Kate Pool, above address

(T) The *Schlegel-Tieck Prize* is awarded "for the best translation from the German published in the United Kingdom by a British publisher of German twentieth-century works of literary merit and general interest," published in the year of the award. One prize of approximately £2,000 is given annually.

Available to: No restrictions
Deadline: December 31
Apply to: Schlegel-Tieck Prize, above address

(T) The *Bernard Shaw Prize* offers £1,000 every three years for the best English translation of a Swedish work of literary merit in any genre. The translation must have been first published in the United Kingdom by a British publisher in the three years preceding the contest. Books must be submitted by the publisher. The next award is in 1997. For further information contact Kate Pool, above address.

(T) The *Vondel Translation Prize* offers £2,000 for translations into English of Dutch and Flemish works of literary merit and general interest. The translation must have been first published in the United Kingdom or the United States. Three copies of the original work and three of the translation should be submitted by the publishers to Kate Pool. The first Vondel Prize was awarded in 1996; guidelines and a deadline for the next round of submissions has not yet been set. Contact Kate Pool at the above address for current information.

UNITED KINGDOM
University of Cambridge
Corpus Christi College
Cambridge CB2 1RH
England

Research scholarships are available annually in all literary subjects to students of any nationality not eligible for United Kingdom state grants who hold a first-class honours degree or the equivalent. Excellent English is essential. Students must register for a postgraduate research degree (Ph.D.) at the University of Cambridge. Duration of the award is three years, subject to satisfactory progress. The value of the awards in 1995-96 was £5,614 per annum. Scholarships are normally awarded in collaboration with the Cambridge Overseas Trust and Cambridge Commonwealth Trust.

Available to: See above
Deadline: March 30
Apply to: Tutor for Advanced Students, above address

UNITED KINGDOM
University of Edinburgh
South Bridge
Edinburgh EH8 9YL
Scotland

(F)
(N) The *James Tait Black Memorial Prizes*, of £3,000 each, are awarded annually to the best novel and the best biographical work published during the previous calendar year. These two awards are judged by the Professor of English Literature at the University. Books must originate with a British publisher, and books by previous winners will not be considered. Works may be submitted only by publishers. Winners announced in December.

Available to: No restrictions
Deadline: September 30
Apply to: Above address

UNITED KINGDOM
University of London
Senate House
Malet Street
London WC1E 7HU
England

Ⓝ The *Norman Hepburn Baynes Prize,* of £3,000, is awarded biennially for an essay on some aspect of the history, including the art, religion, and thought, of the Mediterranean lands within the period 400 B.C. and A.D. 1453. The essay may take the form of one or more completed chapters of an intended thesis.

> Available to: All persons who have taken a degree at the University of London or persons who are pursuing a course at the university for a higher degree
> Deadline: March 1
> Apply to: Above address

United Methodist Communications
PO Box 320
Nashville, TN 37202

Ⓙ The $2,500 *Leonard M. Perryman Communications Scholarship for Ethnic Minority Students* is offered yearly in recognition of Perryman, a journalist for the United Methodist Church for nearly thirty years. The scholarship is intended to aid ethnic minority students (junior or senior) who intend to pursue a career in religious communication and are attending an accredited institution of higher education. The scholarship enables the recipient to continue his/her studies in media including audiovisual, electronic, and print journalism, and to promote a level of excellence in communication on the under-graduate level by an ethnic minority student.

> Available to: U.S. minority undergraduate students
> Deadline: February 15
> Apply to: Scholarship Committee, above address, for application and guidelines

Ⓙ The *Stoody-West Fellowship in Religious Journalism,* of $6,000, is offered annually in recognition of the professional competence and inspired service of Dr. Ralph Stoody and Dr. Arthur West. The grant will assist a Christian engaged in religious journalism, or one planning to enter this field, in taking graduate study at an accredited school or department of journalism of his/her choice. Religious journalism may include audiovisual, electronic, and print journalism.

> Available to: Christian journalists with an undergraduate degree
> Deadline: February 15
> Apply to: The Scholarship Committee, above address, for application and guidelines

United States Institute of Peace
1550 M Street, NW, Suite 700G
Washington, DC 20005-1708

Ⓡ The *Jennings Randolph Program for International Peace* offers fellowships to outstanding profes-sionals and scholars who wish to "undertake research and other kinds of communication that will improve understanding and skills on the part of policymakers and the public regarding important problems of international peace and conflict management." Fellows work in residence at the U.S. Institute of Peace in Washington; they receive a stipend (amount keyed to the recipient's earned income in the twelve months preceding the fellowship), health benefits if needed, and support for appropriate project costs. The program works closely with the institute's press toward the objective of publishing the products of fellows' research. Write for further information and application form.

> Available to: No restrictions
> Deadline: Inquire
> Apply to: Jennings Randolph Program for International Peace, above address

United States Naval Institute
118 Maryland Avenue
Annapolis, MD 21402-5035

(N) The *Vincent Astor Memorial Leadership Essay Contest* annually awards prizes for essays of up to 3,500 words that address topics of leadership in the sea services. Offered are a first prize of $1,500, second prize of $1,000, and two third prizes of $500. Winning essays will be published in *Proceedings* magazine. Send an SASE for rules.

   Available to: Junior Officers and Officer Trainees of the U.S. Navy, Marine Corps, and Coast Guard
   Deadline: February 15
   Apply to: Vincent Astor Memorial Leadership Essay Contest, *Proceedings*, above address

(N) The *Arleigh Burke Essay Contest* annually awards prizes for original, unpublished essays of up to 3,500 words that address "the advancement of professional, literary, and scientific knowledge in the naval and maritime services, and the advancement of the knowledge of sea power." First prize is $3,000, first honorable mention is $2,000, and second honorable mention is $1,000. Winning essays will be published in *Proceedings* magazine. Send an SASE for rules.

   Available to: U.S. citizens
   Deadline: December 1
   Apply to: Arleigh Burke Essay Contest, above address

(N) The *Colin L. Powell Joint Warfighting Essay Contest* annually awards prizes for essays of up to 3,000 words about "combat readiness in a joint context (key issues involving two or more services). Essays may be heavy in uni-service detail, but must have joint application in terms of tactics, strategy, weaponry, combat training, force structure, doctrine, operations, organization for combat, or interoperability of hardware, software and procedures." First prize is $2,500, second prize is $2,000, and third prize is $1,000. Winning entries will be published in *Proceedings* magazine. Send an SASE for rules.

   Available to: U.S. citizens
   Deadline: April 1
   Apply to: Colin L. Powell Joint Warfighting Essay Contest, above address

(N) The *Marine Corps Essay Contest* annually awards prizes for essays which discuss current issues and new directions for the Marine Corps. First prize is $1,000, second prize is $750, and third prize is $500. Winning essays are published in *Proceedings* magazine. Send an SASE for rules.

   Available to: U.S. citizens
   Deadline: May 1
   Apply to: Marine Corps Essay Contest, above address

(N) The *Coast Guard Essay Contest* annually awards prizes for essays which discuss current issues and new directions for the Coast Guard. First prize is $1,000, second prize is $750, and third prize is $500. Winning essays are published in *Proceedings* magazine. Send an SASE for rules.

   Available to: U.S. citizens
   Deadline: May 1
   Apply to: Coast Guard Essay Contest, above address

(N) The *International Navies Essay Contest* annually awards prizes for essays on "strategic, geographic, and cultural influences on individual or regional navies, their commitments and capabilities, and relationships with other navies." First prize is $1,000, second prize is $750, and third prize is $500. Winning essays are published in *Proceedings* magazine. Send an SASE for rules.

   Available to: U.S. citizens
   Deadline: May 1
   Apply to: International Navies Essay Contest, above address

United States Trotting Association
United States Harness Writers' Association
750 Michigan Avenue
Columbus, OH 43215

(J) The *John Hervey Awards for Writing Excellence* and the *Broadcasters Awards* are available to writers of stories and productions with harness racing as a focus. Not limited to USHWA members. Awards of $500 first place, $250 second place, and $100 third place are given in each of four categories: newspaper, magazine, radio, and television.

Available to: No restrictions
Deadline: December, with March announcement
Apply to: John Pawlak, Hervey/Broadcasters Awards Administrator, above address

University of Akron Press
374B Bierce Library
Akron, OH 44325-1703

(P) The *Akron Poetry Prize* awards $500 and publication by the University of Akron Press for a collection of poems, from sixty to 100 pages. Other manuscripts may also be considered for publication in the series. There is a $15 entry fee. Send an SASE for contest rules.

Available to: No restrictions
Deadline: Manuscripts accepted from May 15 to June 30
Apply to: The Akron Poetry Prize, above address

University of Alabama in Huntsville
Department of English
Huntsville, AL 35899

(F) The *H. E. Francis Award*, cosponsored by the University of Alabama in Huntsville and the Ruth Hindman Foundation, offers $1,000 and publication in *Hometown Press* to the best unpublished short story, not exceeding 5,000 words. Two honorable mentions will also receive publication. There is a $15 submission fee. Inquire for complete guidelines.

Available to: No restrictions
Deadline: December 1
Apply to: Above address

University of Alaska, Anchorage
Department of Theatre
3211 Providence Drive
Anchorage, AK 99508-8120

(D) The *Alaska Native Plays Contest* annually awards a $500 prize for full-length plays, one-acts, or adaptations dealing with Native American characters, themes, and/or events. Excerpts from the winning entries will be produced at the Valdez Playwright's Conference in August 1997. Send an SASE for complete guidelines.

Available to: No restrictions
Deadline: March 20, 1996; inquire for 1997
Apply to: Alaska Native Plays Contest, above address

University of Arizona
Poetry Center
1216 North Cherry Avenue
Tucson, AZ 85719

(R) The Poetry Center provides a writer with a one-month summer residence (from mid-July to mid-August) at the guest cottage of a historic adobe located two houses from the collections of the center. Applicants should submit no more than ten pages of poetry or twenty pages of fiction or literary nonfiction.

Available to: Writers who have not published more than one full-length work
Deadline: Submissions accepted from February 15 to March 15
Apply to: Residency Program, above address

University of Arkansas Press
201 Ozark Avenue
Fayetteville, AR 72701

(P) The *Arkansas Poetry Award* offers publication by the University of Arkansas Press for the best original manuscript of poetry by a living U.S. poet whose work has not been published or accepted for publication in book form. Send fifty to eighty typed pages with no more than one poem per page, a $15 reading fee, and an SASE.

Available to: U.S. citizens
Deadline: May 1
Apply to: Arkansas Poetry Award, above address

University of California at Irvine
Department of Spanish and Portuguese
School of Humanities
Irvine, CA 92717

(M) The *Chicano/Latino Literary Contest* offers a $1,000 first prize plus publication by the University of California Press for a book-length manuscript in the genre specified for that year by a Chicano or Latino writer. The award will be given for short stories in 1996, poetry in 1997, drama in 1998, and the novel in 1999. A second prize of $500 and a third prize of $250 are also offered. Submissions may be in either English or Spanish. Send an SASE for guidelines and further information.

Available to: U.S. citizens or permanent residents
Deadline: April 30
Apply to: Chicano/Latino Literary Contest, above address

University of California, Los Angeles
William Andrews Clark Memorial Library
2520 Cimarron Street
Los Angeles, CA 90018

The Clark Library offers a limited number of resident fellowships, funded by the Ahmanson Foundation, to scholars who hold the Ph.D. or equivalent and have entered a career of advanced research. Fellowships may be requested for periods of from one week to three months during the academic year or the summer for research in any field appropriate to the Clark's collections. The stipend is $1,500 per month.

Available to: Ph.D. scholars doing research in a field relative to the Clark's holdings
Deadline: March 15
Apply to: The Fellowship Coordinator, above address

University of Chicago
Harriet Monroe Poetry Award
Division of Humanities
1050 East 59th Street
Chicago, IL 60637

[IN] The *Harriet Monroe Poetry Award*, of $1,000, is awarded periodically to U. S. poets of notable achievement and special promise to advance and encourage poetry. The president of the university regularly designates poets from different sections of the United States as a committee for the award, which gives preference to poets of "progressive rather than academic tendencies." *By Internal Nomination Only.*

University of Georgia Press
330 Research Drive, Suite B-100
Athens, GA 30602-4901

(F) The *Flannery O'Connor Award for Short Fiction* offers $1,000 plus publication under a standard book contract for volumes of original short fiction. Two winners are selected annually. Stories that have been previously published in magazines or in anthologies may be included. Stories that have been published in a book-length collection written solely by the author may not be included. Published and unpublished writers welcome. Include a $10 handling fee. Manuscripts will not be returned. No submissions accepted before June 1. Send an SASE for complete guidelines.

Available to: English-language writers
Deadline: Between June 1 and July 31
Apply to: The Flannery O'Connor Award for Short Fiction, above address

University of Hawaii at Manoa
Department of Theatre and Dance/Kumu Kahua
1770 East-West Road
Honolulu, HI 96822

(D) The *Kumu Kahua Playwriting Contest* annually awards $500 for a full-length play and $200 for a one-act set in Hawaii and dealing with some aspect of the Hawaiian experience. The contest also awards $250 for a full-length play and $100 for a one-act not dealing with Hawaii but written by a Hawaiian resident. Reading and/or production possible for winning submissions. Write for guidelines before entering.

Available to: No restrictions for the first category; Hawaiian residence for the second
Deadline: January 1
Apply to: Kumu Kahua Playwriting Contest, above address

University of Iowa Press
University of Iowa
100 Kuhl House
Iowa City, IA 52242-1000

(P) Two *Iowa Poetry Prizes,* of $1,000 each plus publication by the University of Iowa Press, are given annually for unpublished poetry manuscripts by poets who have already published at least one full-length book of poems with a print run of at least 500 copies.

Available to: No restrictions other than those listed above
Deadline: February 1 to March 31
Apply to: Iowa Poetry Prizes, above address

(F) The *Iowa Short Fiction Award* and the *John Simmons Short Fiction Award* are offered for a book-length collection of short fiction by a writer who has not published a prose book previously. Publication of two prize-winning books by the University of Iowa Press is available annually.

Available to: No restrictions
Deadline: August 1 to September 30
Apply to: Iowa Short Fiction Award or John Simmons Short Fiction Award, University of Iowa, Department of English, Iowa City, IA 52242

University of Massachusetts Press
PO Box 429
Amherst, MA 01004

(P) The *Juniper Prize* is granted annually for an original manuscript of poems, alternately to a poet's first book (in odd-numbered years) and to his or her subsequent books (in even-numbered years). In the "first books" category, manuscripts will be accepted from writers whose poems may have appeared in literary journals and/or anthologies but have not been published in book form. In the "subsequent books" category, manuscripts will be considered only from authors who have had at least one full-length book or chapbook of poetry published or accepted for publication. In both cases, the winning manuscript will be published by the University of Massachusetts Press and will be awarded $1,000. There is an entry fee of $10. For additional information write to the Juniper Prize at the above address.

Available to: No restrictions except University of Massachusetts employees and students, and previous recipients of the Juniper Prize
Deadline: September 30
Apply to: Juniper Prize, University of Massachusetts Press, c/o Mail Room, University of Massachusetts, Amherst, MA 01003

University of Miami
Iberian Studies
North-South Center
PO Box 248123
Coral Gables, FL 33124

Ⓜ The *Letras de Oro Spanish Literary Prizes* were created to recognize the present and future importance of Hispanic culture in the United States. Prizes are awarded annually for creative excellence in the Spanish language in the following five categories: novel, short story, poetry, drama, and essay. In each category there is a first prize of $2,500 and publication of the work.

Available to: All U.S. citizens
Deadline: October 12
Apply to: Above address for competition rules

University of Michigan
Mike and Mary Wallace House
620 Oxford Road
Ann Arbor, MI 48104-2635

Ⓙ The *Mike Wallace Fellowship in Investigative Reporting*, the *Burton R. Benjamin Fellowship in Broadcast Journalism*, the *Knight Fellowships in Specialty Reporting*, the *Sports Reporting Fellowship*, the *Public Service Journalism Fellowships*, the *Daniel B. Burke Fellowship*, and the *Time-Warner Fellowship* are available to full-time employees (free-lance included) of any print or broadcast medium who have had at least five years' experience. Each fellowship carries a $20,000 stipend plus tuition.

Available to: See above
Deadline: February 1
Apply to: Michigan Journalism Fellows, above address for information

Ⓙ The *Livingston Awards for Young Journalists* offer three $10,000 prizes for the best local, national, and international reporting in any print or broadcast medium. Entrants must be under the age of thirty-five.

Available to: Journalists under thirty-five
Deadline: Early February; inquire for exact date
Apply to: Livingston Awards, above address

University of Michigan Press
PO Box 1104
Ann Arbor, MI 48106-1104

ⒾⓃ The *University of Michigan Press Book Award*, of $1,000, is given annually for a work, written or edited by a member of the University of Michigan teaching and research staff, including emeritus members, which has added the greatest distinction to the Press's list. *By Internal Nomination Only.*

University of Minnesota
109 Walter Library
117 Pleasant Street, SE
Minneapolis, MN 55455

Ⓒ The *Ezra Jack Keats/Kerlan Collection Memorial Fellowship* provides $1,500, transportation, and a per diem to a "talented writer and/or illustrator of children's books who wishes to use the Kerlan Collection for the furtherance of his or her artistic development. Special consideration will be given to someone who would find it difficult to finance the visit to the Kerlan Collection."

Available to: No restrictions
Deadline: First business day in May
Apply to: Ezra Jack Keats/Kerlan Collection Memorial Fellowship Committee, above address

University of Mississippi
Festival of Southern Theatre
Department of Theatre
University, MS 38677

Ⓓ The Festival of Southern Theatre and the University of Mississippi sponsor an annual *Southern Playwriting Competition*. Each of up to three winning playwrights receive $1,500 and production.

Available to: Southern writers or other playwrights whose work treats a Southern theme
Deadline: December 1
Apply to: Above address

University of Missouri
School of Journalism
Neff Hall
Columbia, MO 65205

Ⓙ The *Missouri Lifestyle Journalism Awards* (formerly known as the J C Penney—Missouri Newspaper Awards) are available to writers, editors, and reporters for daily and weekly newspapers. Winners are chosen in the following categories: single-story and series reporting; consumer affairs reporting; fashion and design reporting; multicultural reporting; arts/entertainment; food/nutrition; health/fitness; and lifestyle pages or sections. Fifteen $1,000 awards are given annually.

Available to: Newspaper writers, editors, and reporters
Deadline: December 15
Apply to: Director, Missouri Lifestyle Journalism Awards, above address

Ⓙ The *Maria Caleel Awards* honor outstanding writing on the social impact of interpersonal violence. Emphasis is placed on reporting that explains the underlying causes and constructive responses to interpersonal violence. Awards are given in three categories: newspapers with a circulation over 100,000, newspapers with a circulation under 100,000, and magazines. One $3,500 prize is given annually in each category. The contest is managed by the University of Missouri and the Science Journalism Center; the awards are sponsored by Chicago Osteopathic Health Systems.

Available to: Newspaper and magazine writers, for stories published between July 1995 and July 9, 1996
Deadline: July 10, 1996; inquire for 1997
Apply to: Maria Caleel Awards, Rob Logan, above address

University of Nebraska-Kearney Theatre
Kearney, NE 68849-5260

(D)   The *Great Platte River Playwrights' Festival* offers a $500 first prize plus full production and travel and housing to attend rehearsals for an unproduced, unpublished, full-length play. A second prize of $300 and a third prize of $200 are also offered. Submissions of works-in-progress for possible development are encouraged. Write for further information.

Available to: No restrictions
Deadline: April 1
Apply to: Great Platte River Playwrights' Festival, above address

University of Nevada
Department of Theatre Arts
4505 Maryland Parkway
Box 455036
Las Vegas, NV 89154-5036

(D)   The *Morton R. Sarett Memorial Award* biennially offers $3,000 and production for an original, innovative, full-length play in English which has not been previously produced. The winning playwright will also be provided with travel and housing to attend rehearsals. Send an SASE for guidelines and an application form.

Available to: No restrictions
Deadline: December 1997; inquire for exact date
Apply to: Morton R. Sarett Memorial Award, above address

University of New Hampshire
Department of Theater and Dance
Paul Creative Arts Center
30 College Road
Durham, NH 03824-3538

(D)   The *Anna Zornio Memorial Children's Theatre Playwriting Award* offers $1,000 plus production every four years for an unpublished play or musical for young audiences that has not been produced professionally. Plays should be not more than one hour long, preferably with a single or unit set. The next award will be given in 1997. Write for rules and guidelines.

Available to: U.S. or Canadian resident
Deadline: Spring 1997; query for exact date
Apply to: Anna Zornio Playwriting Award, above address

University of North Texas Press
PO Box 13856
Denton, TX 76203

(P)   The *Vassar Miller Prize in Poetry* consists of $500 and publication by the University of North Texas Press of an original, book-length poetry manuscript of fifty to eighty pages. There is a $16 handling fee, payable to UNT Press. Send an SASE for guidelines.

Available to: No restrictions
Deadline: November 30
Apply to: Scott Cairns, Series Editor, Vassar Miller Prize in Poetry, c/o English Department, Old Dominion University, Norfolk, VA 23529

University of Notre Dame Press
Notre Dame, IN 46556

(P)   The *Ernest Sandeen Prize in Poetry* and the *Richard Sullivan Prize in Fiction* each award $500 and publication of a booklength manuscript of, respectively, a volume of poems and a

(F) volume of short fiction. Entrants must have previously published at least one book of poetry or short fiction. The *Sandeen Prize* is offered in odd-numbered years, the *Sullivan Prize* in even-numbered years.

Available to: No restrictions
Deadline: August 31, 1996 (Sullivan Prize); August 31, 1997 (Sandeen Prize)
Apply to: The Sandeen/Sullivan Prizes, Director of Creative Writing, Department of English, University of Notre Dame, Notre Dame, IN 46556

University of Pittsburgh Press
127 North Bellefield Avenue
Pittsburgh, PA 15260

(F) The *Drue Heinz Literature Prize*, awarded annually, consists of a cash award of $10,000 and publication of a collection of short fiction by the University of Pittsburgh Press under a standard royalty contract.

Available to: Writers who have published a book-length collection of fiction or a minimum of three short stories or novellas in commercial magazines or literary journals of national distribution
Deadline: Manuscripts must be postmarked during July and August; contestants should send an SASE for current guidelines before sending manuscripts
Apply to: Drue Heinz Literature Prize, above address

(P) The *Agnes Lynch Starrett Prize*, given annually, consists of a cash award of $2,500 and publication of a first book of poetry by the University of Pittsburgh Press under a standard royalty contract. There is a $15 reading fee.

Available to: Anyone who has not previously published a full length book of poetry
Deadline: Submit manuscripts during March and April only; contestants must send an SASE for current guidelines before sending manuscripts
Apply to: Agnes Lynch Starrett Poetry Prize, above address

University of Rochester
Susan B. Anthony Center
Lattimore Hall, Room 538
Rochester, NY 14627-0434

(F) The *Janet Heidinger Kafka Prize* is awarded annually to a female citizen of the United States who has written the best book-length published work of prose fiction (novel, short story collection, experimental writing). Works submitted must have been published within the previous twelve months; collections of short stories must have been assembled for the first time, or at least one-third of the material must be previously unpublished. Entries may be submitted by publishers only. The prize consists of a cash award which may vary due to funding (in 1994 the prize was $1,000). Write for submission guidelines.

Available to: U.S. female citizens
Deadline: February 28
Apply to: Janet Heidinger Kafka Prize, above address

University of Southern California
The Professional Writing Program
WPH 404
Los Angeles, CA 90089-4034

(P) The *Ann Stanford Poetry Prize* offers a first prize of $750, a second prize of $250, and a third prize of $100 to previously unpublished poems. Poets may submit up to five poems with a $10 reading fee. Winning entries are published in the *Southern California Anthology*. Send an SASE for contest rules. All entrants will receive a free issue of the anthology.

Available to: No restrictions

Deadline: April 15
Apply to: Ann Stanford Poetry Prize, above address

University of Texas. *See* **Dobie-Paisano Project**

University of Toledo
Department of Theatre, Film and Dance
Toledo, OH 43606-3390

(D) The *Midwestern Playwrights Festival* offers a first prize of $1,000, a staged reading in the fall, and production at the Toledo Repertoire Theatre in the spring for full-length plays that have not been professionally produced. The first-prize winner also receives a stipend for travel and room and board for the reading and for a two-week residence during production. Only playwrights from Illinois, Indiana, Michigan, or Ohio may apply, and submitted work must be unpublished and not produced professionally. Write for complete guidelines.

Available to: Playwrights from Illinois, Indiana, Michigan, or Ohio
Deadline: May 1
Apply to: John S. Kuhn, Playwriting Festival Coordinator, above address

University of Virginia
Department of English
Charlottesville, VA 22903

At least six *Henry Hoyns Fellowships* which cover approximately the cost of tuition are available to incoming students enrolled as candidates for the M.F.A. in creative writing. Write for further information and application guidelines.

Available to: No restrictions
Deadline: February 1
Apply to: Creative Writing Program, 219 Bryan Hall, above address

University of Wisconsin Press
114 North Murray Street
Madison, WI 53715

(P) The *Brittingham Prize in Poetry* and the *Felix Pollak Prize in Poetry,* each consisting of a cash award of $1,000 and publication by the University of Wisconsin Press, are awarded annually to the two best book-length manuscripts of original poetry, fifty to eighty pages in length. A $15 nonrefundable reading fee must accompany manuscript. Send an SASE for submission guidelines.

Available to: No restrictions
Deadline: Manuscripts must be received between September 1 and October 1
Apply to: Ronald Wallace, Series Editor, above address

The Unterberg Poetry Center of the 92nd Street Y
1395 Lexington Avenue
New York, NY 10128

(P) The *"Discovery"/The Nation Poetry Contest: Joan Leiman Jacobson Poetry Prizes* are offered to four poets who have not yet published a book of poems (chapbooks and self-published books included). Each award consists of a $300 cash prize, a reading at the Poetry Center of the 92nd Street Y in New York City, and publication in the *Nation.* Submit four stapled, identical sets of a ten-page manuscript, with each set containing the same poems in the same order. All poems must be original and in English (no translations), and the entire manuscript should not exceed 500 lines. All pages must be numbered. Personal identification must only appear in a single, separate cover letter, not on the poems. The cover letter must include your name, address, and day and evening telephone numbers.

Biographical information is not necessary. For full guidelines, send SASE to the above address.

Available to: See above
Deadline: February 9, 1996; inquire for 1997
Apply to: *"Discovery"/The Nation*, above address

Utah Arts Council
617 East South Temple Street
Salt Lake City, UT 84102

(M) The *Utah Original Writing Competition* offers a $5,000 prize that will go directly to a publisher to assist in the publication and promotion of a book by a Utah writer. The winner is selected from among four book-length categories which alternate yearly: novel, collection of short fiction or poetry, biography/autobiography or general nonfiction, and juvenile books or books for young adults. The council also offers prizes of up to $1,000 for novels, book-length collections of poems, individual poems, and short stories by Utah residents. Write for further information and guidelines.

Available to: Utah residents
Deadline: June 15
Apply to: Literary Competition Division, above address

Vermont Council on the Arts
136 State Street, Drawer 33
Montpelier, VT 05633-6001

(M) The *Fellowship Grants Program* awards fellowships of $3,500 to poets, fiction writers, essayists, and playwrights to finance working time.

Available to: Vermont residents only
Deadline: March 1 (disciplines vary by year)
Apply to: Fellowship Grants, above address

Vermont Studio Center
PO Box 613NW
Johnson, VT 05656

(R) The Vermont Studio Center offers two- to twelve-week residences year-round for writers. Fellowships of one-quarter to one-half the residence fee are available. Inquire for further information and/or application.

Available to: Emerging and midcareer writers
Deadline: Applications accepted all year; reviewed monthly
Apply to: Write to the above address for information

Very Special Arts
1300 Connecticut Avenue, NW, Suite 700
Washington, DC 20004

(D) The *Young Playwrights Program* seeks scripts by students between the ages of twelve and eighteen, with or without disabilities, that address some aspect of disability. Winning plays will be produced with a professional director and cast at the John F. Kennedy Center for the Performing Arts, and winning playwrights and chaperones will travel to Washington, D.C., to participate in rehearsals and be honored guests at the premiere of the production. Write for application packet.

Available to: Students ages twelve to eighteen
Deadline: April 15
Apply to: Very Special Arts, Young Playwrights Program, Education Office, the John F. Kennedy Center for the Performing Arts, Washington, D.C. 20566

Veterans of Foreign Wars and Its Ladies Auxiliary National Headquarters
Voice of Democracy Program
406 West 34th Street
Kansas City, MO 64111

(N) The annual *Voice of Democracy Audio Essay Competition* awards fifty-two national scholarships, totaling over $100,000, to high school students grades 10 through 12 for tape-recorded essays, three to five minutes long, on an announced theme. For more information, check with high school counselor or contact your local VFW Post.

Available to: High school students
Deadline: November 15
Apply to: High school counselor or local VFW Post

Villa Montalvo Artist Residency Program
PO Box 158
Saratoga, CA 95071

(R) Some financial aid in the form of fellowships is available to artists, composers, and writers for one- to three-month residences at the 1912 Villa Montalvo in the foothills of the Santa Cruz mountains. Send SASE for guidelines.

Available to: No restrictions
Deadlines: September 1 and March 1
Apply to: Lori A. Wood, Artist Residency Program Manager, above address

(P) The *Villa Montalvo Biennial Poetry Competition* awards $1,000 and a one-month residence at Villa Montalvo for unpublished, original poems by a resident of California, Nevada, Oregon, or Washington. A $500 second prize is offered, as well as a $300 third prize. Send an SASE for complete guidelines.

Available to: Residents of California, Nevada, Oregon, or Washington
Deadline: Inquire for 1997
Apply to: Villa Montalvo Biennial Poetry Competition, above address

The Vineyard Playhouse Company
PO Box 2452
Vineyard Haven, MA 02568-2452

(D) The *New England New Play Competition* offers staged readings and the possibility of production of a full-length, nonmusical, unpublished, previously unproduced play written by a resident of New England. Four finalists are selected, each of whom is provided with travel and housing to attend rehearsals and reading. The grand-prize winner also receives $500. Each finalist is considered for a full stage production at The Vineyard Playhouse.

Available to: Playwrights residing in New England
Deadline: June 1
Apply to: New England New Play Competition, above address

Virginia Center for the Creative Arts
Mount San Angelo
Sweet Briar, VA 24595

(R) Applications are accepted from professional writers and other artists of demonstrated promise for residences from two weeks to three months at Mount San Angelo. Standard daily fee of $30 provides private studio, room, and three meals. Financial assistance is available for qualified applicants with demonstrated need.

Available to: No restrictions

Deadline: January 15 (May–August residences); May 15 (September–December); September 15 (January–April)
Apply to: William Smart, Director, above address

Virginia Commonwealth University
Department of English
PO Box 842005
Richmond, VA 23284-2005

(F) The *Hurston/Wright Award* offers a first-place prize of $1,000 and publication in the *New Virginia Review* for fiction written by African American students enrolled full-time as undergraduate or graduate students in any college or university in the United States. A second-place prize of $500 is also offered. Writers may submit an unpublished short story or an excerpt from a novel. Send an SASE for guidelines.

Available to: African American college students
Deadline: December; inquire for exact date
Apply to: The Hurston/Wright Award, above address

Virginia Quarterly Review
One West Range
Charlottesville, VA 22903

(F)
(P) The *Emily Clark Balch Awards,* each $500, are given annually to the best short story and best poem published in the *Virginia Quarterly Review* during the calendar year. The editors will not consider unsolicited stories and poems for the prizes, but only those which have been accepted and published.

Available to: U.S. citizens
Apply to: Emily Clark Balch Awards, above address

Visiting Writers Program
Knapp Hall
State University of New York at Farmingdale
Farmingdale, NY 11735

(P) The *Paumanok Poetry Award* offers $1,000 plus expenses for a reading as part of the SUNY Farmingdale Visiting Writers Program series. Two runners-up receive $500 plus expenses for a reading in the series. To enter the competition, send five to seven poems (published or unpublished), a one-paragraph biography, a $15 reading fee and an SASE. Write for further information.

Available to: No restrictions
Deadline: September 15
Apply to: Above address

Ludwig Vogelstein Foundation
P.O. Box 277
Hancock, ME 04640

Ludwig Vogelstein Foundation is a small foundation giving fewer than fifty grants to individuals in the arts and humanities, with an average grant of $2,500. No student aid is offered. Write for complete instructions and deadlines in June, enclosing a #10 SASE.

Available to: Artists and writers
Deadline: Inquire
Apply to: Above address

Wagner College
Department of Humanities
Howard Avenue and Campus Road
Staten Island, NY 10301

(D)   The *Stanley Drama Award* is given for an original full-length play or musical which has not
been professionally produced or published. Consideration will also be given to two or
three one-act plays that are thematically connected. One award of $2,000 is given an-
nually, with occasional production when it is feasible. Nomination must be made by a
theater professional (teacher of drama or creative writing, critic, agent, director, or
another playwright or composer), who must have seen or read the play in question.
Previous winners may not reapply.

   Available to: No restrictions
   Deadline: September 1
   Apply to: Stanley Drama Award, above address

Lila Wallace-Reader's Digest Fund
Two Park Avenue, 23rd Floor
New York, NY 10016

   The *Lila Wallace-Reader's Digest Writers' Awards* are given annually to enable writers of demonstrated talent and exceptional promise to devote significant time to their writing for
up to three years and, during the period of the award, to encourage them to develop
meaningful interactions with a broader public through affiliation with a community
agency. Writers receive $35,000, with the possibility of two annual renewals; their af-
filiated organizations receive a modest grant to defray the direct costs they incur in
managing the affiliation. There is no application process. *By Internal Nomination Only.*

Edward Lewis Wallant Book Award
c/o Dr. and Mrs. Irving Waltman
3 Brighton Road
West Hartford, CT 06117

(F)   The *Edward Lewis Wallant Book Award* is presented annually to an American writer for a novel
or collection of short stories of significance to the American Jew. Work must have been
published during the calendar year. A $300 prize and citation are awarded.

   Available to: American writers who work in English
   Deadline: December 31
   Apply to: Dr. and Mrs. Irving Waltman, above address

Washington Independent Writers (WIW)
220 Woodward Building
733 15th Street, NW
Washington, DC 20005

(C)   The *Joan G. Sugarman Children's Book Award,* of $1,000, is given to a published work of fiction
or nonfiction geared to children ages one through fifteen. Query for guidelines.

   Available to: Residents of Washington, D.C., Maryland, or Virginia
   Deadline: January 31
   Apply to: Book Award, above address

The Washington Prize for Fiction
1301 South Scott Street, No. 424
Arlington, VA 22204-4656

(F)   The *Washington Prize for Fiction*, consisting of three prizes of $5,000, $2,500, and $1,000, are
awarded annually to American and Canadian fiction writers for a previously unpub-

lished manuscript of at least 65,000 words. Submissions may be novels, several novellas, or a short story collection. There are no content or thematic restrictions. There is a $30 entry fee for each submission.

Available to: No restrictions
Deadline: November 30
Apply to: Larry Kaltman, Director, above address

Washington State Arts Commission. *See* **Artist Trust**

The Frank Waters Foundation
PO Box 1127
Taos, NM 87571

(F) The *Frank Waters Southwest Writing Award*, cosponsored by the Frank Waters Foundation and the Martin Foundation for the Creative Arts, offers $2,000 plus publication by the University of New Mexico Press for a novel whose focus is "the non-urban West." Only writers from Arizona, Colorado, Nevada, New Mexico, Texas, or Utah may apply. Two honorable mentions receive $2,000 each. There is a reader's fee of $25. Write for complete rules.

Available to: Writers from New Mexico, Arizona, Nevada, Utah, Colorado, or Texas
Deadline: August 31
Apply to: Mag Dimond, Waters Writing Award, PO Box 1357, Ranchos de Taos, NM 87529

Wesleyan Writers Conference
Wesleyan University
Middletown, CT 06459-0094

(M) The Wesleyan Writers Conference awards full and partial scholarships to writers interested in attending the conference, held annually during the last week in June. Among these awards are the *Joan and John Jakobson Scholarships*, open to writers of fiction, nonfiction, and poetry, and the *Jon Davidoff Scholarships for Journalists*. Teaching fellowships, including the *Barach Fellowship*, are also awarded. Fellowship candidates should have completed a book-length manuscript. Write for further information and guidelines.

Available to: No restrictions
Deadline: April 12, 1996; inquire for 1997
Apply to: Fellowship and Scholarship Committee, above address

The West Coast Ensemble
Box 38728
Los Angeles, CA 90038

(D) The *Full-Length Play Competition* awards $500 and production (and royalty on any performance beyond an eight-week run) for unproduced, unpublished, full-length plays. The play must not have been produced previously in Southern California; playwrights looking for a second production of a play produced elsewhere are welcome to submit.

(D) The *Musical Stairs Competition* selects five finalist musicals for presentation in a workshop, staged-reading format with the winner receiving a fully-staged production and a prize of $500. Write for complete information.

Available to: No restrictions
Deadline: December 31 for full-length plays; June 30 for musicals
Apply to: Above address

West Virginia Commission on the Arts
The Cultural Center
1900 Kanawha Boulevard East
Charleston, WV 25305-0300

(M) Eight *Literature Fellowships*, of $3,500 each, will be awarded to West Virginia poets, playwrights, fiction and nonfiction writers every two to three years. The next round of literature fellowships will be in 1997. Write for further information.

    Available to: West Virginia residents
    Deadline: June 1, 1997
    Apply to: Above address

Western History Association
University of New Mexico
Department of History
Albuquerque, NM 87131

(N) The *Athearn Book Award* is offered in even-numbered years for a published book on the twentieth century which has a copyright date no more than two years old. The association awards $500 to the author and $500 to the publishing house.

    Available to: No restrictions
    Deadline: June 1, 1996 and June 1, 1998
    Apply to: Above address for list of award committee members

(N) The *Caughey Western History Association Award* annually offers $2,500 to the author of the most outstanding book on the history of the American West. Presses should submit nominations for books published in the previous calendar year.

    Available to: No restrictions
    Deadline: June 1
    Apply to: Above address for list of award committee members

The *Sara Jackson Award* offers $500 annually to support graduate student research in the field of western history. Preference will be given to African American or other minority students. Write for additional application information.

    Available to: Graduate students
    Deadline: July 1
    Apply to: Above address for list of award committee members

(N) The *W. Turrentine Jackson Prize* biennially awards $1,000 to a beginning professional historian for a first book on any aspect of the American West. Presses should send nominations to the committee for books published in 1995 and 1996 for the 1997 prize.

    Available to: No restrictions
    Deadline: June 30, 1997
    Apply to: Above address for list of award committee members

The *Rundell Graduate Student Award* annually offers $1,000 to a doctoral candidate who has completed comprehensive Ph.D. examinations and is in the process of researching a dissertation topic. Write for additional application information.

    Available to: Doctoral candidates
    Deadline: June 1
    Apply to: Above address

The Western History Association offers several other awards with lesser monetary stipends for articles and research work on western history. Contact the Association for further information.

Western States Arts Federation
236 Montezuma Avenue
Santa Fe, NM 87501

(M) The *Western States Book Awards* honor outstanding writers and publishers of fiction, creative nonfiction, and poetry. This series of awards features cash prizes of $5,000 for authors of manuscripts and $5,000 for respective publishers. To be eligible for the awards, works must be written by an author who is a resident of one of the federation's member states: Alaska, Arizona, California, Colorado, Idaho, Montana, Nevada, New Mexico, Oregon, Utah, Washington, and Wyoming. Work must have been already accepted for publication by a publisher in one of the member states. Contact the federation for an entry form and complete awards criteria.

>   Available to: See above
>   Deadline: Inquire
>   Apply to: Above address

Whetstone
Barrington Area Arts Council
PO Box 1266
Barrington, IL 60011

(M) The *Whetstone Prize* is given for the best poem, fiction, or creative nonfiction accepted for publication in *Whetstone*, an annual literary journal published by the Barrington Area Arts Council. Winning writers receive a cash prize which varies yearly due to funding (the 1994 prize was $500). Send an SASE for additional information guidelines.

>   Available to: No restrictions
>   Deadline: Submissions accepted year round
>   Apply to: Whetstone Prize, above address

White Pine Press
10 Village Square
Fredonia, NY 14063

(P) The *White Pine Press Poetry Prize* offers $500 and publication by White Pine Press for a book-length collection of poems by a U.S. author. Poets may submit an original typed manuscript of forty-eight to ninety-six pages; poems may have been published in periodicals or in limited-edition chapbooks. There is a $15 reading fee.

>   Available to: U.S. citizens
>   Deadline: Submissions accepted from September 15 to December 1
>   Apply to: Poetry Prize Contest, above address

White-Willis Theatre
5266 Gate Lake Road
Fort Lauderdale, FL 33319

(D) The *New Playwrights Contest* awards $500 and production at the White-Willis Theatre for full-length unpublished and unproduced plays free of royalty and copyright restrictions. Scripts with smaller casts and simpler sets are preferred. Send an SASE for additional details.

>   Available to: No restrictions
>   Deadline: September 1
>   Apply to: New Playwrights Contest, above address

Mrs. Giles Whiting Foundation
1133 Avenue of the Americas, 22nd Floor
New York, NY 10036-6710

[IN] Ten *Whiting Writers' Awards*, of $30,000 each, are given in recognition of the quality of current and past writing as well as the likelihood of outstanding future work. The program places special emphasis on exceptionally promising emerging talent. *By Internal Nomination Only.*

The Elie Wiesel Foundation for Humanity
1177 Avenue of the Americas, 36th Floor
New York, NY 10036

Ⓝ The *Elie Wiesel Prize in Ethics Essay Contest* awards a first prize of $5,000, a second prize of $2,500, and a third prize of $1,500 for an essay of 3,000 to 4,000 words on "Personal Responsibility and the Common Good: An Ethical Perspective." Applicants must be full-time junior or senior undergraduate students at an accredited four-year college or university in the United States. Write for additional information and guidelines.

Available to: See above
Deadline: January; inquire for exact date
Apply to: The Elie Wiesel Prize in Ethics, above address

Wilkes University
Department of English
Wilkes-Barre, PA 18766

Ⓕ The *James Jones First Novel Fellowship* offers $2,500 for a novel-in-progress or a collection of related short stories. Unpublished American novelists may submit an outline, of up to three pages, and the first fifty to seventy-five pages of the novel. There is a $10 entry fee. Send an SASE for rules.

Available to: Unpublished American novelists
Deadline: March 1, 1996; inquire for 1997
Apply to: James Jones First Novel Fellowship, above address

Tennessee Williams/New Orleans Literary Festival
University of New Orleans
Metro College Conference Services
ED 122
New Orleans, LA 70148

Ⓓ The *Tennessee Williams/New Orleans Literary Festival One-Act Play Competition* offers a cash prize of $1,000, a reading of the winning play at the festival, and a full production of the play during the following year's festival. Only professionally unproduced, unpublished, one-act plays on an American subject are eligible. There is a $15 entry fee. Send an SASE for complete information.

Available to: No restrictions
Deadline: December; inquire for exact date
Apply to: Above address

Woodrow Wilson International Center for Scholars
Fellowship Office
1000 Jefferson Drive, SW
Washington, DC 20560
SI MRC 022

Approximately thirty-five residential fellowships are offered each year for advanced research in the humanities and social sciences. Applicants must hold a doctorate or have equivalent professional accomplishments. Fellows are provided offices, access to the Library of Congress, computers or manuscript typing services, and research assistants. The center publishes selected works written at the center through the Woodrow Wilson Center Press. The center also helps fellows locate appropriate housing. Fellowships are normally for an academic year, although a few fellowships are available for shorter periods, with a minimum of four months. In determining stipends, the center seeks to follow the principle of no gain/no loss in terms of a fellow's previous year's salary. However, limited funds make it desirable for most applicants to seek supplementary sources of funding such as sabbatical support or grants from other sources: in no case can the center's stipend exceed $61,000. The average yearly stipend is approximately $47,500. Travel expenses for fellows, spouses, and dependent children are provided.

Available to: No restrictions
Deadline: October 1
Apply to: Above address

Wind Publications
PO Box 24548
Lexington, KY 40524

(P) The *Allen Tate Memorial Award* offers $500 and publication in *Wind Magazine* for a single poem previously unpublished, of any length. There is an entry fee of $2 per poem submitted.

Available to: No restrictions
Deadline: June 30
Apply to: Allen Tate Memorial Award, above address

Wisconsin Arts Board
101 East Wilson Street, 1st Floor
Madison, WI 53702

(M) The Wisconsin Arts Board offers five nonmatching fellowships, of $8,000 each, in fiction, poetry, essay/criticism, and drama. Write for an application form.

Available to: Wisconsin residents, except full-time degree-credit students
Deadline: September 15 (contact Arts Board as deadline is subject to change)
Apply to: Above address

Wisconsin Institute for Creative Writing
University of Wisconsin
Department of English
600 North Park Street
Madison, WI 53706

(F)

(P) The *Jay C. and Ruth Halls Fellowships* offer an academic year in Madison as artists-in-residence at the University of Wisconsin to new writers working on a first book of poetry or fiction. Fellows will teach one introductory creative writing workshop per semester and will give one public reading from work in progress. The fellowship pays $20,000 for the academic year. Write for application guidelines.

Available to: Poets and fiction writers who have completed an M.A., M.F.A., or equivalent degree in creative writing and have not yet published a book
Deadline: Applications accepted throughout the month of February
Apply to: Director, above address

The Woodstock Guild
34 Tinker Street
Woodstock, NY 12498

(R) The Woodstock Guild offers residences of one to four months (from June to October) to writers and playwrights in its historic Byrdcliffe Arts Colony. The residence, which costs $400 to $500 for each one-month session, includes a private room in the Villetta Inn and appropriate studio space. Fee reductions will be offered to residents staying more than one session; limited scholarships are available to applicants fulfilling requirements. Send an SASE for brochure and application.

Available to: No restrictions

Deadline: April 15
Apply to: Above address

Word Works
Box 42164
Washington, DC 20015

(P) The *Washington Prize* awards $1,000 and publication by Word Works for a volume of original poetry of outstanding literary merit by a living American poet. Send an SASE for complete guidelines.

Available to: U.S. citizens or residents
Deadline: Submissions accepted between February 1 and March 1
Apply to: Washington Prize, above address

World Literature Today
University of Oklahoma
110 Monnet Hall
Norman, OK 73019-0375

[IN] The *Neustadt International Prize for Literature,* is given to honor a life's work, or to direct attention to an outstanding writer whose literary career is still in progress. Political and geographic considerations do not enter into the selection by the international jury. One prize of $40,000 is given biennially; the next in 1996. *By Internal Nomination Only.*

The Writers Community
The National Writer's Voice Project
of the YMCA of the USA
5 West 63rd Street
New York, NY 10023

(F)
(P) The Writers Community of the National Writer's Voice Project offers semester-long residences at Writer's Voice centers nationwide to established poets and fiction writers. Residents teach a master-level workshop and give a public reading. As of 1995, writers received $6,000 to $7,500 each.

Available to: Accomplished writers with teaching experience/interest
Deadline: Inquire for exact date at each Writer's Voice center
Apply to: Director, The Writers Community, at the following addresses:
West Side YMCA, 5 West 63rd Street, New York, NY 10023
Billings Family YMCA, 402 North 32nd Street, Billings, MT 59101
Duncan YMCA, 1001 West Roosevelt Road, Chicago, IL 60608
The Carnegie Center, 251 West Second Street, Lexington, KY 40507
West County YMCA, PO Box 4038, Chesterfield, MO 63006
Scottsdale/Paradise Valley YMCA, 6869 East Shea Boulevard, Scottsdale, AZ 85254
Silver Bay Association, Silver Bay, NY 12874
Tampa Metro Area YMCA, 110 East Oak Avenue, Tampa, FL 33602
Central Connecticut Coast YMCA, Fairfield, CT 06430
East Bay YMCA, 2330 Broadway, Oakland, CA 94612
Metropolitan YMCA, 1901 University Avenue, Minneapolis, MN 55414
Downtown YMCA, 2020 Witherell Street, Detroit, MI 48226
Great South Bay YMCA, 200 West Main Street, Bay Shore, NY 11706

Writers' Conferences & Festivals
PO Box 102396
Denver, CO 80250

The Writers' Conferences & Festivals' *National Scholarship Program* awards five scholarships of $500 each (four *WC&F/Eric Mathieu King Scholarships* and one *WC&F/ShawGuides Directors' Scholarship*) to be applied towards attendance at WC&F member programs—

literary conferences and festivals in thirty-three states and in several countries. The King Scholarships are offered in four categories: poetry, fiction, nonfiction, and minority (an open-genre category). The ShawGuides Directors' Scholarship is given to a writer of either poetry or prose who is nominated by a director of a WC&F member program. There is a $10 reading fee for each manuscript submitted for the King Scholarships; no fee for nominations for the ShawGuides Directors' scholarships. Send an SASE for entry form and complete guidelines.

Available to: No restrictions
Deadline: Submissions and nominations accepted from August 1 to October 15
Apply to: National Scholarship Program, above address

Writer's Digest
1507 Dana Avenue
Cincinnati, OH 45207

(M) The *National Self-Publishing Awards* offer a first place prize of $1,000 and promotion in *Publishers Weekly* and *Writer's Digest* for a book that was self-published in the current calendar year. The first-prize winner is chosen from among six categories: poetry, fiction (novel or short story collection), nonfiction, children's books, biography and memoir, and cookbooks. Winners in the other five categories each receive $250. Eligible books are those for which the author paid the full cost of publication in an edition of at least 500 copies. There is a $95 reading fee per book. Send an SASE for an application and complete guidelines.

Available to: No restrictions
Deadline: December 15
Apply to: National Self-Publishing Awards, above address

(M) The *Writer's Digest Article, Poetry, Script, and Short Story Contest Awards* are given for an original article of 2,000 words, an original poem of thirty-two lines or fewer, an original story of 2,000 words, and the first fifteen-page segment of an unproduced script (play, screenplay, teleplay, or radio-drama) plus synopsis. Prizes given annually include cash, trips, reference books, and awards. Entry fee is $7.

Available to: No restrictions
Deadline: Inquire
Apply to: For required entry form, send an SASE after January 1 to: Writer's Digest Writing Competition, above address

The Writer's Voice of the West Side YMCA
5 West 63rd Street
New York, NY 10023

(F)
(P) The *Capricorn Fiction Award* and the *Capricorn Poetry Award* each offer a $1,000 honorarium and a reading at The Writer's Voice to a poet and fiction writer of excellence over the age of forty. There is a $15 entry fee. Send an SASE for complete guidelines and entry form.

(F)
(P) The *Open Voice Awards* are given to published and unpublished poets and fiction-writers who have not previously read at The Writer's Voice. Each award consists of a $500 honorarium and a reading at The Writer's Voice. There is a $10 application fee. Send an SASE for complete guidelines and entry form.

Available to: See above
Deadline: December 31
Apply to: The Capricorn Award or the Open Voice Awards, above address

Writers at Work
PO Box 1146
Centerville, UT 84104-5146

(F)
(P)
Writers at Work sponsors a fellowship competition in fiction (short stories or novel excerpts) and poetry. The first prize in each category consists of a $1,500 cash prize, publication in *Quarterly West*, a featured reading, and tuition to the afternoon session at the Writers at Work summer conference in Park City, Utah. Second-place winners each receive a cash prize of $500 and tuition to the afternoon session at the conference. Eligible writers are those who have not yet published a book-length volume of original work. Fiction submissions should not exceed twenty pages, poetry, ten pages. Only unpublished work will be considered. A $12 reading fee and two SASEs are also requested. Send two copies of the manuscript with cover letter, including name, address, telephone number, and title; title only should appear on manuscripts. Manuscripts cannot be returned.

Available to: No restrictions
Deadline: March 15
Apply to: Above address

The Writers' Workshop
PO Box 696
Asheville, NC 28802

(F)
The *Writers' Workshop International Fiction Contest* awards a first prize of $600 for an unpublished story of up to twenty pages. The story's title must appear on each page; the author's name, address and phone must appear on a cover letter only. There is an entry fee per submission of $18 ($15 for Writers' Workshop members). Send an SASE for guidelines.

Available to: No restrictions
Deadline: February 1
Apply to: Fiction Contest, above address

The Helene Wurlitzer Foundation of New Mexico
Box 545
Taos, NM 87571

(R)
Residences in Taos, with free housing and utilities, from April 1 through September 30, are available annually. Residents must provide their own food. No families are accepted.

Available to: No restrictions
Deadline: None
Apply to: Henry Sauerwein, Jr., Executive Director, above address

Wyoming Council on the Arts
2320 Capitol Avenue
Cheyenne, WY 82002

Up to four *Literary Fellowships*, of $2,500 each, are offered annually to writers who are legal residents of Wyoming, at least eighteen years old, and not full-time students.

Available to: Wyoming residents
Deadline: August 1
Apply to: Above address

The *Neltje Blanchan Award*, given to a Wyoming writer whose work, in any genre, is inspired by nature, and the *Frank Nelson Doubleday Memorial Award*, given to a Wyoming woman writer in any creative genre, each carry a cash prize of $1,000. Applicants must submit up to twenty-five pages of a manuscript, either published or unpublished. Write for guidelines.

Available to: Wyoming residents

Deadline: May 15
Apply to: Blanchan Award or Doubleday Award, above address

Xeric Foundation
351 Pleasant Street, Suite 214
Northampton, MA 01060

Grants of up to $5,000 are offered to self-publishing comic book creators in the United States. Grants are designed to assist with the physical production and distribution of books: printing, color separation, solicitation, and shipping. They cannot be used to obtain professional services from existing publishers, nor can they be used for creative or living expenses. Write for additional information and application.

Available to: U.S. residents
Deadline: January 31 and July 31
Apply to: Above address

Yaddo
Box 395
Saratoga Springs, NY 12866

® Invitations are extended to writers who have already published work of high artistic merit and are currently engaged in another project, and unpublished writers working at professional levels in their fields to spend one to two months at Yaddo (a working community for writers, visual artists, composers, choreographers, performance artists, and film and video artists). Samples of work must be submitted, together with application forms and letters of recommendation and an application fee of $20. Applications are judged on their artistic merit and professional promise. Awards include room, board, and studio, primarily during May to September but open year-round. Voluntary contributions of $20 per day of stay are encouraged to help defray the cost of the residence. However, no artist who is deemed qualified for a residence at Yaddo will be denied admission because of an inability to contribute.

Available to: Nationals of all countries
Deadlines: January 15 for visits in the period of mid-May to February 1 of the following year; August 1 for visits to begin in October up to May
Apply to: President, above address

Yale University Library
The Beinecke Rare Book and Manuscript Library
1603A Yale Station
New Haven, CT 06520

[IN] The *Bollingen Prize,* of $25,000, is awarded biennially to the American poet whose work represents the highest achievement in the field of American poetry, based on a review of publications during the previous two years. The next award will be given in January 1997. *By Internal Nomination Only.*

Yale University Press
PO Box 209040
New Haven, CT 06520-9040

℗ Yale University Press publishes one new book of poetry annually as part of the *Yale Series of Younger Poets.* Selection is made through a competition that is open to any American citizen under the age of forty who has not previously published a volume of poetry. The author receives the standard royalties. An application fee of $15 is required. Send an SASE for complete submission guidelines.

Available to: American citizens under forty

Deadline: Submissions accepted during the month of February only
Apply to: Editor, Yale Series of Younger Poets, above address

Young Adult Library Services Association
American Library Association
50 East Huron Street
Chicago, IL 60611

Ⓒ The *Margaret A. Edwards Award,* cosponsored by *School Library Journal,* honors an author's lifetime achievement for writing books that have been popular with teenagers over a period of time. The award consists of a $1,000 cash prize and a citation at the American Library Association Annual Conference. Nominations may be submitted by young adult librarians and teenagers. Write for nomination forms.

Available to: No restrictions
Deadline: June 1
Apply to: Margaret A. Edwards Award, above address

Young Playwrights
321 West 44th Street, Suite 906
New York, NY 10036

Ⓓ The *Young Playwrights Festival* is an annual contest open to young writers age eighteen or under. Winning plays receive a professional production in New York City and royalties. There are no restrictions on the subject, style, form, and length of plays submitted. Adaptations of the works of others, screenplays, and musicals are not accepted.

Available to: Applicants age eighteen and under during the calendar year under consideration
Deadline: October 15
Apply to: Young Playwrights Festival, above address

Zone 3
Susan Wallace, Managing Editor
Austin Peay State University
PO Box 4565
Clarksville, TN 37044

Ⓟ The *Rainmaker Awards in Poetry* offer a first-prize of $500 and publication in *Zone 3* for an original, unpublished poem. A second-prize of $300 and a third-prize of $100 are also awarded. Poets may submit up to three poems. The entry fee of $8 includes a year's subscription to *Zone 3.*

Available to: No restrictions
Deadline: January 1
Apply to: Rainmaker Awards in Poetry, above address

APPENDIX: STATE ARTS COUNCILS

Below are listed, alphabetized by state, the addresses and telephone numbers of the various state arts councils throughout the United States (including the District of Columbia, Puerto Rico, and the U. S. Virgin Islands). Also included are listings for Canadian arts councils. When contacting them, inquire about their literature program, the components of which vary from state to state. Please note that, to be eligible for funding, a writer must be a resident of the state (or district) to which he or she is applying.

Alabama State Council on the Arts
Becky Mullen, Literature Program Manager
1 Dexter Avenue
Montgomery, AL 36130
334/242-4076

Alaska State Council on the Arts
Timothy Wilson, Executive Director
411 West 4th Avenue, Suite 1E
Anchorage, AK 99501-2343
907/269-6610

Arizona Commission on the Arts
Shelley Cohn, Executive Director
417 West Roosevelt
Phoenix, AZ 85003
602/255-5882

Arkansas Arts Council
James E. Mitchell, Executive Director
1500 Tower Building
323 Center Street
Little Rock, AR 72201
501/324-9766

California Arts Council
Ray Tatar, Literature Specialist
1300 I Street, Suite 930
Sacramento, CA 95814
916/322-6555

Colorado Council on the Arts and Humanities
Fran Holden, Executive Director
750 Pennsylvania Street
Denver, CO 80203
303/894-2617

Connecticut Commission on the Arts
Linda Dente, Senior Program Associate
227 Lawrence Street
Hartford, CT 06106
860/566-7076

Delaware Division of the Arts
Barbara King, Fellowship Coordinator
Carvel State Office Building
820 North French Street
Wilmington, DE 19801
302/577-3540

District of Columbia Commission on the Arts and Humanities
Pamela Holt, Executive Director
Stables Art Center
410 Eighth Street, NW, Fifth Floor
Washington, DC 20004
202/724-5613

Florida Division of Cultural Affairs
Valerie Ohlsson, Arts Consultant
Department of State
The Capitol
Tallahassee, FL 32399-0250
904/487-2980

Georgia Council for the Arts
Anne Davis, Literary Arts Program Coordinator
530 Means Street, NW, Suite 115
Atlanta, GA 30318
404/651-7920

Hawaii State Foundation on Culture and the Arts
Wendell P. K. Silva, Executive Director
44 Merchant Street
Honolulu, HI 96813
808/586-0300

Idaho Commission on the Arts
Margot Knight, Executive Director
Box 83720
Boise, ID 83720-0008
208/334-2119

Illinois Arts Council
Richard Gage, Director of Communication
    Arts Program
James R. Thompson Center
100 West Randolph, Suite 10-500
Chicago, IL 60601
312/814-6750

Indiana Arts Commission
Dorothy Ilgen, Executive Director
402 West Washington, Room 072
Indianapolis, IN 46204-2741
317/232-1268

Iowa Arts Council
Bruce Williams, Director Creative Artists/Vi-
    sual Arts
Capitol Complex
600 East Locust
Des Moines, IA 50319
515/281-4451

Kansas Arts Commission
Thomas Klocke, Arts Program Coordinator
Jay Hawk Tower
700 Jackson, Suite 1004
Topeka, KS 66603
913/296-3335

Kentucky Arts Council
Irwin Pickett, Program Director
31 Fountain Place
Frankfort, KY 40601
502/564-3757

Louisiana Division of the Arts
Dee Waller, Program Director
PO Box 44247
Baton Rouge, LA 70804
504/342-8180

Maine State Arts Commission
Alden C. Wilson, Executive Director
55 Capitol Street
State House, Station 25
Augusta, ME 04333
207/287-2724

Maryland State Arts Council
Linda Vlasick, Literature Coordinator
601 North Howard Street
Baltimore, MD 21201
410/333-8232

Massachusetts Cultural Council
Robert Ayres, Literature Program Director
120 Boylston Street, Second Floor
Boston, MA 02116
617/727-3668

Michigan Council for the Arts
Betty Boone, Executive Director
1200 Sixth Street, Suite 1180
Detroit, MI 48226
313/256-3731
Also: Arts Foundation of Michigan
Mark Packer, Program Director
645 Griswold Street, Suite 2164
Detroit, MI 48226
313/964-2244

Minnesota State Arts Board
Karen Mueller, Program Associate
400 Sibley Street, Suite 200
Saint Paul, MN 55101-1928
612/215-1600

Mississippi Arts Commission
Kathleen Stept, Program Administrator
239 North Lamar Street, Suite 207
Jackson, MS 39201
601/359-6030

Missouri Arts Council
Michael Hunt, Literature Program Admin-
    istrator
Wainwright State Office Complex
111 North 7th Street, Suite 105
Saint Louis, MO 63101-2188
314/340-6845

Montana Arts Council
Frann Morrow, Director of Artists Services
316 North Park Avenue, Suite 252
Helena, MT 59620
406/444-6430

Nebraska Arts Council
Jennifer Severin, Executive Director
3838 Davenport
Omaha, NE 68131-2329
402/595-2122

Nevada State Council on the Arts
Susan Boskoff, Executive Director
602 North Curry Street
Capitol Complex
Carson City, NV 89710
702/687-6680

New Hampshire State Council on the Arts
Susan Bonaiuto, Director
40 North Main Street
Concord, NH 03301-4974
603/271-2789

New Jersey State Council on the Arts
Barbara Russo, Executive Director
CN 306
Trenton, NJ 08625
609/292-6130

New Mexico Arts Division
Lara Morrow, Executive Director
228 East Palace Avenue
Santa Fe, NM 87501
505/827-6490

New York State Council on the Arts
Kathleen Masterson, Literature Program
915 Broadway
New York, NY 10010
212/387-7000

North Carolina Arts Council
Debbie McGill, Literature Director
Department of Cultural Resources
Raleigh, NC 27601-2807
919/733-2111

North Dakota Council on the Arts
Patsy Thompson, Executive Director
418 East Broadway, Suite 70
Bismarck, ND 58501-4086
701/328-3954

Ohio Arts Council
Ken Emerick, Individual Artist Fellowship
   Coordinator
727 East Main Street
Columbus, OH 43205-1796
614/466-2613

State Arts Council of Oklahoma
Betty Price, Executive Director
PO Box 52001-2001
Oklahoma City, OK 73152-2001
405/521-2931

Oregon Arts Commission
Vincent Dunn, Assistant Director
775 Summer Street, NE
Salem, OR 97310
503/986-0082

Pennsylvania Council on the Arts
Philip Horn, Executive Director
216 Finance Building
Harrisburg, PA 17120
717/787-6883

Rhode Island State Council on the Arts
Randall Rosenbaum, Executive Director
95 Cedar Street, Suite 103
Providence, RI 02903-1034
401/277-3880

South Carolina Arts Commission
Steve Lewis, Literary Arts Program
1800 Gervais Street
Columbia, SC 29201
803/734-8696

South Dakota Arts Council
Dennis Holub, Executive Director
800 Governors Drive
Pierre, SD 57501-2294
605/773-3131

Tennessee Arts Commission
Alice Swanson, Director Literary Arts
404 James Robertson Parkway, Suite 160
Nashville, TN 37243-0780
615/741-1701

Texas Commission on the Arts
John Paul Batiste, Executive Director
PO Box 13406
Austin, TX 78711-3406
512/463-5535

Utah Arts Council
G. Barnes, Literary Coordinator
617 East South Temple Street
Salt Lake City, UT 84102
801/533-5895

Vermont Council on the Arts
Cornelia Carey, Grants Officer
136 State Street, Drawer 33
Montpelier, VT 05633-6001
802/828-3291

Virginia Commission for the Arts
Peggy J. Baggett, Executive Director
223 Governor Street
Richmond, VA 23219
804/225-3132

Washington State Arts Commission
Mary Frye, Program Manager for Awards
234 East 8th Avenue
PO Box 42675
Olympia, WA 98504-2675
360/753-3860

West Virginia Commission on the Arts
Karen Jenskow, Development Coordinator
The Cultural Center
1900 Kanawha Boulevard East
Charleston, WV 25305-0300
304/558-0240

Wisconsin Arts Board
Kate LaRocque, Literary Arts Coordinator
101 East Wilson Street, 1st Floor
Madison, WI 53702
608/266-0190

Wyoming Council on the Arts
Guy Lebeda, Literature Coordinator
2320 Capitol Avenue
Cheyenne, WY 82002
307/777-7742

PUERTO RICO

Institute of Puerto Rican Culture
Awilda Palau Suarez, Executive Director
PO Box 4184
San Juan, PR 00902-4184
809/723-2115

U. S. VIRGIN ISLANDS

Virgin Islands Council on the Arts
John Jowers, Executive Director
41-42 Norre Gade
Box 103
St. Thomas, VI 00804
809/774-5984

CANADA

Alberta Community Development
Arts and Cultural Industries
Arts Branch
Catrina Edwards, Arts Development Officer
Beaver House, 3rd Floor
10158 103rd Street
Edmonton, Alberta T5J 0X6
403/427-6315

The Assembly of British Columbia Arts Councils
Deborah Meyers, Executive Director
201-3737 Oak Street
Vancouver, British Columbia V6H 2M4
604/738-0749

Manitoba Arts Council
Pat Sanders, Literary Arts Consultant
93 Lombard Avenue, Room 525
Winnipeg, Manitoba R3B 3B1
204/945-2237

New Brunswick Department of Municipalities, Culture and Housing
Arts Branch, Desmond Maillet
PO Box 6000
Fredericton, New Brunswick E3B 5H1
506/453-2555

Newfoundland Department of Tourism and Culture
Elizabeth Batsone, Assistant Deputy Minister for Cultural Affairs
PO Box 8700
St. John's, Newfoundland A1B 4J6
709/729-3650

Nova Scotia Department of Education and Culture
Allison Bishop, Director Cultural Affairs
PO Box 578
Halifax, Nova Scotia B3J 2S9
902/424-5929

The Canada Council
Lise Rochon, Information Office
PO Box 1047
350 Albert Street
Ottawa, Ontario K1P 5V8
613/566-4365

Ontario Arts Council
Lorraine Filyer, Literature Officer
151 Bloor Street West, Suite 6
Toronto, Ontario M5S 1T6
416/961-1660

Prince Edward Island Council of the Arts
Judy McDonald, Executive Director
PO Box 2234
Charlottetown, Prince Edward Island C1A 8B9
902/368-4410

Organization of Saskatchewan Arts Councils
Dennis Garreck, Executive Director
1102 8th Avenue
Regina, Saskatchewan S4R 1C9
306/586-1250

Yukon Arts Council
Glen Wadsworth, Executive Director
PO Box 5120
Whitehorse, Yukon Y1A 4S3
403/668-6284

INDEX OF AWARDS

INDEX OF ORGANIZATIONS

Tulsa Library Trust, 169

Ucross Foundation, 169
Ukiah Players Theatre, 169
Unicorn Theatre, 170
Unitarian Universalist Association, 170
United Daughters of the Confederacy, 170
UNITED KINGDOM: British Comparative Literature Association, 170
UNITED KINGDOM: Forward Publishing, 171
UNITED KINGDOM: The International Retreat for Writers at Hawthornden Castle, 171
UNITED KINGDOM: Royal Society of Literature of the United Kingdom, 171
UNITED KINGDOM: The Scottish Arts Council, 172
UNITED KINGDOM: Stand Magazine, 172
UNITED KINGDOM: The Translators Association, 172
UNITED KINGDOM: University of Cambridge, 173
UNITED KINGDOM: University of Edinburgh, 173
UNITED KINGDOM: University of London, 174
United Methodist Communications, 174
United States Institute of Peace, 174
United States Naval Institute, 175
United States Trotting Association, 176
University of Akron Press, 176
University of Alabama in Huntsville, 176
University of Alaska, Anchorage, 176
University of Arizona, 176
University of Arkansas Press, 177
University of California at Irvine, 177
University of California, Los Angeles, 177
University of Chicago, 177
University of Georgia Press, 178
University of Hawaii at Manoa, 178
University of Iowa Press, 178
University of Massachusetts Press, 178
University of Miami, 179
University of Michigan, 179
University of Michigan Press, 179
University of Minnesota, 180
University of Mississippi, 180
University of Missouri, 180
University of Nebraska—Kearney Theatre, 181
University of Nevada, 181
University of New Hampshhire, 181
University of North Texas Press, 181
University of Notre Dame Press, 181
University of Pittsburgh Press, 182
University of Rochester, 182
University of Southern California, 182

University of Texas. *See* Dobie-Paisano Project
University of Toledo, 183
University of Virginia, 183
University of Wisconsin Press, 183
The Unterberg Poetry Center of the 92nd Street Y, 183
Utah Arts Council, 184

Vermont Council on the Arts, 184
Vermont Studio Center, 184
Very Special Arts, 184
Veterans of Foreign Wars and Its Ladies Auxiliary National Headquarters, 185
Villa Montalvo Artist Residency Program, 185
The Vineyard Playhouse Company, 185
Virginia Center for the Creative Arts, 185
Virginia Commonwealth University, 186
Virginia Quarterly Review, 186
Visiting Writers Program, 186
Ludwig Vogelstein Foundation, 186

Wagner College, 187
Lila Wallace-Reader's Digest Fund, 187
Edward Lewis Wallant Book Award, 187
Washington Independent Writers (WIW), 187
The Washington Prize for Fiction, 187
Washington State Arts Commission. *See* Artist Trust
The Frank Waters Foundation, 188
Wesleyan Writers Conference, 188
The West Coast Ensemble, 188
West Virginia Commission on the Arts, 189
Western History Association, 189
Western States Arts Federation, 190
Whetstone, 190
White Pine Press, 190
White-Willis Theatre, 190
Mrs. Giles Whiting Foundation, 190
The Elie Wiesel Foundation for Humanity, 191
Wilkes University, 191
Tennessee Williams/New Orleans Literary Festival, 191
Woodrow Wilson International Center for Scholars, 191
Wind Publications, 192
Wisconsin Arts Board, 192
Wisconsin Institute for Creative Writing, 192
The Woodstock Guild, 192
Word Works, 193
World Literature Today, 193
The Writers Community, 193
Writers' Conferences & Festivals, 193
Writer's Digest, 194

INDEX OF CATEGORIES

POETRY/Ⓟ

JOURNALISM/Ⓙ

NONFICTION/Ⓝ

WRITERS' RESIDENCES/Ⓡ